The Reagan Rhetoric

The Reagan Rhetoric

History and
Memory
in 1980s
America

Toby Glenn Bates

NORTHERN

ILLINOIS

UNIVERSITY

PRESS

DeKalb

© 2011 by Northern Illinois University Press

Published by the Northern Illinois University Press, DeKalb, Illinois 60115

Manufactured in the United States using postconsumer-recycled, acid-free paper.

All Rights Reserved

Design by Julia Fauci

Frontispiece courtesy of the National Archives

Library of Congress Cataloging-in-Publication Data

Bates, Toby Glenn.

The Reagan rhetoric: history and memory in 1980s America / Toby Glenn Bates.

  p.   cm.

Includes bibliographical references and index.

ISBN 978-0-87580-654-9 (pbk.: acid-free paper)

1. Reagan, Ronald—Oratory. 2. Political oratory—United States—History—20th century.

3. United States—Politics and government—1981–1989. 4. United States—Politics and

government—1945–1989. 5. Collective memory—United States. 6. Vietnam War, 1961–1975—

Political aspects United States. 7. Iran-Contra Affair, 1985-1990. I. Title.

E877.2.B38 2011

973.927092—dc22

2011000921

For Cathy, Joseph, and Kelly

Contents

List of Illustrations

Acknowledgments

The origins of this work go back to the 1980s, when I first detected many of the phenomena I describe here. Since then I have been fortunate to find great support so I could make my scholarly contribution to Ronald Reagan historiography. I owe sincere thanks to many. Special mention goes to Jim Watkins and Frances Williams who, many years ago, opened my eyes to the wonders of history. I owe tremendous gratitude to the staff at Northern Illinois University Press, especially Sara Hoerdeman and Susan Bean. Their enthusiasm and support for this project were both personal and professional. I also thank my anonymous readers for taking a serious look at my work and for their comments, which only strengthened this book. At Mississippi State University–Meridian, Michael Dawkins, Jarrod Fogarty, Renee Gough, James Kelley, Dennis Mitchell, Melanie Thomas, and Jack Tucci all provided friendship and support. The staff at the Ronald Reagan Presidential Library could not have been more helpful, especially Michael Duggan and Steve Branch. I thank my many conference commentators who, in places like Minneapolis, San Diego, Newcastle, Australia, and Oxford, England, offered valuable encouragement and comments. I certainly must thank Shauna Rynn Waters, who read an early version of the manuscript and proved invaluable in her edits and comments.

Gratitude is owed my longtime friends Dennis Bradford, Henry "Duke" Eidt, L.T. Gathing, Andy Harper, Matt Johnson, Tommy King, Jesse Kirkegaard, Emily Machen, Brian C. Miller, Amanda Myers, Tim Overton, Greg Taylor, Michael Upton, and Jeff Walker. At my alma mater, the University of Mississippi, I must first thank Jeffrey R. Watt, who as graduate advisor took a chance on an older nontraditional student. Also at Ole Miss, I thank Charles Eagles, Chiarella Esposito, Robert Haws, Royce Kurtz, Ted Ownby, Sheila Skemp, Douglass Sullivan-González, and Stan Whitehorn. A particular nod goes to the late Winthrop Jordan, who took a special interest in my work. I must also thank John R. Neff, who first introduced me to the relationship between history and memory. In every conceivable way, John is the personification of a true friend. Last only because I want him to stand out, I thank Michael V. Namorato. For over thirty years, professionally and personally, he has influenced so many at the University of Mississippi. I am honored and humbled to have been one of his students. In so many ways, he teaches me still.

I thank my grandfather Joseph A. Montgomery, ninety years old at the time of this writing. A World War II submariner and a forty-year veteran of America's railroads, he teaches in just a few quiet words what it takes others hours to say. He is, beyond doubt, one of the last true southern gentlemen. I am today who I am, in large part, because of who he is, because of what he did, and because of what he continues to do. Much gratitude is owed my parents, Jerry and Judy, as well as my brothers, Wayne, Terry, and Todd. Wayne was not with us long. I hope I have honored his memory by approaching each day with the wide-eyed excitement, cheerfulness, and courage he displayed during his short time with us. My father also did not live to see the completion of this project. I can only hope that I brought to this book the tireless work ethic and honesty of purpose that he displayed his entire life. Finally, I want to thank my students, past, present, and future. Every single one of you makes me a better teacher and scholar.

The Reagan Rhetoric

Introduction

"Reagan possesses a sort of genius for the styles of American memory,
for the layerings of the American past."
—Lance Morrow, *Time*, July 7, 1986

"Reagan's mellifluous rhetoric lingers like a melody that evokes fond memories."
—George Will, *Jewish World Review*, June 7, 2004

"The lifeguard would grow up to seduce and shape America."
—Jon Meacham, *Newsweek*, June 14, 2004

On July 7, 1986, newsstands across the United States received the latest issue of *Time* magazine, the cover displaying a picture of a beaming President Ronald Reagan. He had good reason to smile. In the second year of his second term, Reagan enjoyed an approval rating of 68%. Domestically, most Americans felt good about their country. In 1986, the nation was in the middle of an economic boom, a ninety-two-month period of financial growth that would stretch until 1990. Internationally, America stood tall. Tensions with the Soviet Union had eased somewhat, and Libya continued silent after Reagan had ordered retaliatory bombings four months earlier after a terrorist attack in West Berlin.

Reagan's first *Time* cover article—in 1966—had examined the former actor's unlikely campaign for the California governorship. Now, two decades later *Time* asked, "Why is this man so popular?" Under the title "Yankee Doodle Magic," reporter Lance Morrow investigated Reagan's presidential success story. He tallied the recent Oval Office victories: the preparation of the Senate to move on tax reform and the House of Representatives on aid to the Nicaraguan Contras, the nomination of Supreme Court Justice William Rehnquist to be chief justice, the elevation of Antonin Scalia to fill Rehnquist's seat, and finally the continuation of negotiations with Soviet premier Mikhail Gorbachev.[1]

Beyond political success, however, Morrow also detected something else. He described a mysterious connection that existed between Reagan and the American people, saying simply, "Ronald Reagan has found the American sweet spot." Morrow recognized an intangible but very real connection between this president, trained as an actor, and a nation now serving as his eager audience. "The actor enters into the minds of others and leads them through the drama, making them laugh or cry, making them feel exactly what he wants them to feel. It is a powerful and primitive transaction, a manipulation, but at its deepest level a form of tribal communion." Morrow did not attribute all of Reagan's achievements to his abilities as an actor. He also suggested that the president's consistency of message helped to form a connection to voters, helping them to believe that Reagan "does exactly what he says he will do." As a result, Americans responded to "the *predictability* of his resolve." Morrow continued that, in this ability to reach the nation through his use of language, Reagan is "a Prospero of American memories" who "possesses a sort of genius for the styles of American memory," but he "does not delve cynically into the layers of American memory." Morrow's words turned nostalgic as he likened Reagan's presidency to "the illusion of a long summer celebration of the past."[2]

In the summer of 1986, without the benefit of historical hindsight, Morrow correctly recognized a key element of Reagan's presidential success, describing a consistency of message and imagery that allowed Reagan to play upon what the American people wanted to believe and remember about their nation, and that enabled him to connect with them successfully. However, like so many subsequent attempts to explain Reagan's command of the spoken word, the *Time* story did not go far enough.

Through his unique use of words, Reagan offered the nation new interpretations of a myriad of subjects. Millions of Americans accepted his versions. Throughout his two presidential terms and beyond, American memories of the past and attitudes toward the present were heavily influenced by his rhetoric. Reagan's words always spoke to what was best about America, and many in the country listened to him. He told his audience that America would continue to be great in the future, because of her greatness in the present and past. Millions of Americans remembered—or, more important, thought they remembered—the nation he talked about. Reagan played a pleasing melody on the chords of memory. Many Americans instinctively knew the tune (or thought they did), longed to hear it, and wanted to believe him, and therefore chose to believe him.

In 1992 Reagan himself talked of his rhetorical influence. While speaking at the Republican National Convention to promote a second presidential term for George H. W. Bush, Reagan shared a personal hope with the audience. He said, "And whatever else history may say about me when I'm gone, I hope it will record that I appealed to your best hopes, not your worst fears, to your confidence rather than your doubts."[3] In this moment too, as was the case throughout his presidency, Reagan knew precisely what he was saying and was, even then, guiding the listening audience to perceive things as he desired. If ever there was a presidency of the spoken word, it was Reagan's.

The power of Reagan's oratory has been the subject of numerous studies from a wide array of perspectives. Journalists, presidential historians, and political scientists have all found the body of speech Reagan delivered a rewarding field of inquiry.[4] Most notably, scholars of rhetoric have made important contributions to the study of Reagan's presidency. Less than eight books focus solely on the subject of his language, however, and only five have been published since his presidency.[5] I acknowledge that my use of rhetoric is not as sophisticated as the studies found in the rhetoric and communication disciplines, fields in which a great deal of important work has been published regarding the Reagan presidency. While each work well represented the particular fields of English, psychology, political science, and communication, not a single scholar who focused exclusively on Reagan's rhetoric approached the subject as a historian. In this work I will not seek to duplicate their efforts nor emulate their methods. My perspective is that of a cultural and social historian of the period, and my interest lies in drawing connections between the style and manner of Reagan's oratory and the social and cultural setting in which it played so vital a role. Others have focused on his speech as thoroughly as I will, but none has done so with the specific purpose of seeking to understand the extraordinary connections between a president's conversation with the American people and the profound changes that swept the nation under its influence. Again, at this point I make clear that the following work is not a rhetorical or communication study of the Reagan presidency. Rhetoric is often defined as using language effectively as a means of communication or persuasion. For the purposes of this book, the exact same definition applies. When I use the word *rhetoric*, I use it in the context of the aforementioned definition, and only that definition; and continuing with that meaning, Reagan was a master rhetorician. For him, rhetoric meant a style of language and particulars, the importance of mannerisms when communicating, and just as essential, not only what to say but where and when to say it. Although approaching the same topic, I offer this work as something of a bridge between the various perspectives that have so far dominated the scholarship into Reagan's presidency.

Part of the power of Reagan's conversation resulted in many Americans reacting to his words as he touched a personal belief system regarding themselves and their country. While not always in tune with reality, his language nonetheless possessed real power to generate change in the present—and, through such alterations, similar changes in how millions of Americans remembered the past. Such a phenomenon is a powerful tool, and Reagan used it masterfully.

History, however, is not memory. The former is made up of scholarship, researched and reconstructed, presented for and to an interested audience. The latter is made up of individual recollections, which combine to generate communal remembrances and thus become part of a broader collective. Because memory is such a fundamental part of the human state, individuals often are not consciously aware of the vital role it plays.

Memory studies are in a relatively new field that spans many disciplines. Recently, historians have adopted a broad scholarship in relation to the question of memory and its impact on the study of history.[6] For this purpose, it is vital that I explain my methodological approach to such a complex subject. The two models utilized for this work are Pierre Nora's theory of *lieux de mémoire*, or sites of memory, and Maurice Halbwachs's description of collective memory. Both works help explain the effect of Reagan's rhetoric on American history and memory.

Pierre Nora, a historian, continues to produce extensive work regarding the relationship between French history and memory. His theory of *lieux de mémoire* argues that sites of memory, whether they be material, symbolic, or functional, are both literal and metaphoric locations infused with significance. Individuals or groups project their recollections to these sites and draw meaning from them. In other words, sites serve as tools that aid in recalling the past and the focal points where interpretations of the past may shape the present. These sites survive as long as the individual or group remembering continues to invest importance in them. Thus, *lieux de mémoire* represent our tangible and intangible communal relationships to history and may take the form of historical documentation, archival repositories, monuments, physical locations, celebrations, rituals, and anniversaries. These sites of memory transmit particular recollections to future generations and simultaneously attempt to define the subject's particular place in history.[7]

Maurice Halbwachs was an early twentieth-century French sociologist who later died in the Buchenwald concentration camp. He asserted that individuals use diverse and discriminating mental images to reconstruct their past, normally in a pleasing and nostalgic-tinged fashion. Each individual recollection exists within a larger and more dominant collective. Individual memories, those running counter to the group, are not supported. Often these divergent recollections tend to be reshaped to fit the broader understanding. If they resist such change, they possess little power to change the more dominant collective. Halbwachs added that reconstructing one's past always constitutes altering memories or perceptions, and that remembering any earlier period always occurs under the influence of the present. These alterations can lead to different ideas and actions that are not completely accurate. The altered memories would then be carried through succeeding generations as part of the accepted collective.[8]

Both Nora's and Halbwachs's theories are essential to my argument. An unabashed optimist, Reagan incessantly spoke with nostalgia about what was right with the traditions and history of the United States. For many Americans, the acceptance of Reagan's terminology often blurred the boundary between history and memory. Most Americans celebrated Reagan for his creation of a more palatable version of events. Others protested, fearing a loss of reality in a sea of people-pleasing but unrealistic presidential prose.

For millions of Americans, once Reagan established a connection through the power of his public persona, his influence held sway. Certainly, he was not the first American president to persuade through language. Reagan's words, however, did much more than serve as a call to arms during war or garner support for a piece of domestic legislation. His speeches touched upon and affected existing national perspectives regarding numerous subjects. In other words, for millions of Americans he forged new interpretations that superseded preexisting recollections. His vision seemed to become reality.

Scholars from a variety of fields have explained Reagan's reputation as the Great Orator, some seeking to demonstrate the flaws in such a characterization, some seeking to confirm it in our interpretation of his presidency. But these works do not go far enough. Often, in Reagan historiography, the characterization of his rhetorical ability serves only as a piece of a larger narrative or a brief broad-brush historical summation. In other words, George Washington is the father of the country, Abraham Lincoln freed the slaves, Franklin Roosevelt won World War II, and Ronald Reagan made the country feel good again. Such simplistic depictions are not enough. What remains to be done in the study of this president and his influence on the nation is to understand better the connection between Reagan's communication style and consistency of message and the American people's reception of that rhetoric. This is the critical point of omission in so much of Reagan historiography. This work seeks to satisfy that need. What requires additional investigation is not only the reason his speech pattern and fluency had and continue to have appeal but, also, the reason he convinced so many to change the ways they perceived him as a politician and president so dramatically, the reason these rhetorical skills enabled him to shift the public view of the crises within his administration and even allowed him to shape his own legacy in the minds of the American people. The understanding of the Reagan presidency will continue to be incomplete until scholars examine Reagan through the lens of rhetoric and memory.

As the nation enters the second decade of the twenty-first century, Reagan remains a prominent and occasionally controversial personality in the lives of millions of Americans. He did not quietly disappear into the history books. He is not a forgotten president. Reagan endures because of the lasting effect of his policies, but more important, he continues to have a place in the American consciousness because of his personality. The nation still hears the echoes of his words. In many ways, the country still lives under his influence. That fact in itself provides testimony to the enduring power of his language.

Unlike other recent chief executives, he did not enjoy a long time to build a post-presidential legacy. Only five years after he left office, Alzheimer's disease forced his removal from the public stage. His wife, Nancy, along with the presidential library and Reagan partisans, labored hard to build and maintain his presidential heritage. Those efforts have been countered by individuals just as determined to provide alternative versions of events. Scholars preparing to work on Reagan must ready themselves to wade through a historical minefield. A quick review of a few book titles regarding Reagan historiography reveals the polarizing nature of the research.[9]

The media has not forgotten him. One example of his legacy can be found with a quick review of *Time* magazine. Reagan has appeared on the cover of *Time* magazine six times since he left office, beating in post-presidency covers John F. Kennedy by one, Abraham Lincoln by two, and Franklin Roosevelt by three. The latter three suddenly died in office. While Kennedy does not, presidents Lincoln and Roosevelt consistently rank higher than Reagan on presidential surveys. A reasonable expectation would be for the three men to garner more coverage, yet Reagan beats them all.[10]

Reagan left office twenty years ago, yet he remains the political measuring stick for contemporary politicians. He made headlines in the most recent presidential election when, in a January 2008 interview with the *Reno Gazette-Journal* editorial board, Democratic hopeful Barack Obama committed what many Democrats considered a political sin and complimented Reagan. The senator merely described Reagan as a transformative president. For many Democrats, Obama went too far with this remark and hence endured attacks from his own party. Reagan would return after Election Day as Obama went on to claim victory by 10 million votes and won more than 50% of the popular vote, the latter not achieved by a Democrat in forty-four years. The battered Republican Party, by sheer instinct, turned to the Reagan legacy for guidance. "What would Reagan do?" became the immediate catchphrase. Later, in the months after the election, many journalists and writers from both sides of the political aisle suggested that Obama seek to learn from Reagan and in many ways follow his example.[11]

In 1980 Reagan arrived at a unique time for the national media. His administration became the first twenty-four-hour-news-cycle presidency, winning the election the same year as the premier of Ted Turner's Cable News Network (CNN). Daily he encountered an aggressive news media, changed forever by the Vietnam credibility gap of President Lyndon Johnson and the Watergate illegalities of President Richard Nixon. Led by earnest reporters such as Sam Donaldson, the press hovered and hounded, looking for a story and reporting every sound bite. For the most part, Reagan did not flinch. For a man attuned to the power of communication, the incessant news cycle became a skillfully wielded tool, a continuous loop that repeated his messages and increased his exposure.

Reagan's arrival in the Oval Office demonstrated an actor's sense of timing. For almost twenty years preceding 1980, Americans had lacked presidential consistency. Certainly, this does not mean that those recent White House occupants had been devoid of leadership or vision. With presidential assassination, unpopular wars, scandal, resignation, and two consecutive failed presidencies, what had resulted was a lack of strong rhetorical consistency from the White House. This separation set the stage for someone with the polished skills of an actor delivering a consistent message.

It is not my argument that Reagan's rhetoric was so powerful that he alone remained the sole architect of change in 1980s America. Instead I argue that with his words, he plowed fertile ground and found a willing audience in this time of transition. Many Americans stood ready to put unpleasant memories of the recent decades behind them. The decade offered several reasons to feel good about the present and hopeful for the future. Political stability returned as the country had the first complete two-term president since the 1950s. Beginning in late 1982 and lasting into 1990, the economy began the longest peacetime growth in the nation's history until that time. Exciting new technologies hinted at the next decades' dot com explosion. The painful memories of Vietnam were fading, as the 1980s were the first decade since the 1930s that the nation did not engage in any full-scale wars. Even Cold War tensions, red-hot at the beginning of the decade, had cooled considerably by the end. Through the shuttle program, the United States reclaimed the lead in space exploration. In 1980 and 1984, Americans enjoyed Olympic glory on New York ice and in Los Angeles. The stage stood ready for Reagan. Many in Reagan's America were open to revisionist interpretations and more positive perspectives regarding some of the nation's past pains. Reagan is not the originator of all the national changes that occurred during the 1980s. Instead, he is such an important component of collective memory that when many Americans think of this period they cannot do so without understanding it from the point of view of Reagan's influence.

I readily acknowledge that it is hard to measure memory, public receptivity, or perception. It is difficult to draw a direct line between cause and effect. Make no mistake, during this work, I will at times ask the reader to take a leap of faith. Each time, however, the leap will originate from and end upon solid scholarship. Other historians have encountered similar difficulties when dealing with Reagan. Gary Gallagher's examination of a 1980s resurgence of interest in the American Civil War cites the influence of the Reagan presidency in regards to "changing public attitudes toward the use of military strength as a tool of national policy." With a nod to the difficult task of connecting the dots, Gallagher wrote that Reagan's influence, while certainly present, remained "hard to pin down."[12] Clearly, Reagan is but one strand in many affecting Americans' opinions in the 1980s, but he is an important strand, and maybe the most important. He did affect change, and this change in itself is an indication, a rough measure, of Reagan's influence.

In order to evaluate the media dissemination of Reagan's words, I quote extensively from various 1980s press sources. Specifically, I concentrate on the big three newsmagazines of the 1980s: *Time*, *Newsweek*, and *U.S. News and World Report*. It is important to note that each magazine made decisions with an eye on circulation and based on what would sell to consumers. Each magazine also had a serious obligation to report accurately the news of the day. *Time* was established in 1923 and during the 1980s averaged a circulation of 4.7 million. Launched ten years later, *Newsweek* enjoyed a circulation of 3.2 million. *U.S. News and World Report*—created in 1948 from the merger of two magazines, *U.S. News* and *World Report*—during the decade averaged sales of 2.6 million.[13] These three magazines do not necessarily offer a definitive look at media coverage of the Reagan years, but long before the arrival of the World Wide Web and multiple competing twenty-four-hour news channels, these periodicals remained the major source of detailed information for millions of Americans. We are unable to ascertain exactly what Americans were thinking while reading the Reagan coverage, of course, but it seems reasonable to assume that, taken together, the reporting of these periodicals is a clear measure of the volume and style the national press utilized in reporting Reagan's words.

Reagan knew how to hit his mark during three different golden ages of emerging media in American popular culture. He had garnered a large following in the Midwest during the heady radio days of the 1930s. By the 1940s, Hollywood was beckoning, and he enjoyed reasonable success in film. As television emerged in the 1950s, Reagan moved to the small screen and won a devoted following. His role as corporate spokesman for General Electric offered additional opportunities to hone his skills. Of course, the political experience he gained as governor of California certainly sharpened his delivery. Entrance, timing, cadence, and inflection all serve as vital tools of any performer. Reagan possessed a gift for each, and he trained in these fields of communication.

Acting carries a performer only so far, however. For Reagan, consistency became the key for his political success. There was continuity in his remarks for the very simple reason that he believed what he spoke. Considering the political atmosphere of the early twenty-first century, such a declaration certainly seems naive. It is important to remember, however, that Reagan came from a different era. His convictions, shaped as they were by life experience, remained remarkably consistent throughout his life, both in public communications and in private correspondence. Reagan's mind held simple truths, but these principles did not signify simple thinking. For him, his life was the American dream personified and served as testimony to the power of the individual's operating in a free society. He opposed anything that appeared to interfere with that freedom, be it an overreaching federal government or the ideology of communism. By the time he entered politics in the early 1960s, his mind-set was absolute. Elected as California's governor at the age of fifty-five, Reagan knew what he believed, and more important, he knew why he believed it. He created simple, memorable lines to push forward his ideas and constantly used the former to reinforce the latter. Once decided on an idea or position, he focused, and regardless of audience or location his words repeated the same phrases delivered at the same cadence. Because of the confidence in his beliefs and the uniformity expressed through his language, a speech in 1986 sounds very much like a speech delivered in 1976, or in 1966. A detail or two might change over time, but since Reagan's words often concentrated on the broad ideas or themes, it often seems the minutiae did not matter. Like other orators, he knew that presentation remained all important. Fine print was often lost on the audience. First one had to win the crowd—and negotiating the details came later. Because Reagan repeated the same convictions for decades, often in defiance of popular opinion, many in the nation perceived that Reagan believed his own words. As a result, such stalwart stances helped millions of Americans to believe him. Historian Douglas Brinkley cited such a connection between conviction and connectivity in the success of Reagan's celebrated D-Day address. "As a member of the Greatest Generation, Reagan truly believed his Normandy addresses to the bottom of his heart. And listeners intuited this authenticity of purpose."[14] As recently as spring 2010, journalists have acknowledged that Reagan's consistency was a key element of his political personality. In a piece comparing Reagan with possible 2012 presidential hopeful Mitt Romney, *Boston Globe* columnist Alex Beam pointed to Reagan's enduring reputation of "constancy" among some regarding opposition to communism, loyalty to tax cuts, and his unwavering support of the Nicaraguan Contras.[15]

I argue that his consistency was a remarkably useful tool that was important because it transmitted easily through the media. This is not a cynical observation on my part nor do I believe it to be an example of Reagan manipulating others. For him, consistency was a virtue. It was not a case of methodical or calculated political exploitation, but simply repetitive statements, his arguments, over and over again, learned and solidified over almost sixty years in the public eye, repeated again and again, often even when confronted with harsh realities that ran counter to his own beliefs. I am stressing the sincerity in his words, his own belief in what he was saying, regardless of political trends or polls. The vast amount of Reagan's private writing recently released conveys his genuine belief in what he said. In numerous instances, his political stance and rigid consistency cost him both personally and politically, and yet he would not change his message.

As with any politician, Reagan recognized the importance of political polls. He listened to pollsters, but it took more than snapshot surveys to change his mind. When journalists questioned Reagan, it invited a quick response supported by information gathered from numerous sources. Early in his career some opponents warned of programmed answers, because Reagan wrote information on index cards for reference during a speech, but the depth of his knowledge on a subject did not begin and end on a slip of paper. Reagan's political wake remained full of opponents who underestimated his intelligence, from Pat Brown to Jimmy Carter.

Reagan's lack of attention to detail in his remarks caused many observers to portray the president incorrectly in a role not unlike that of a carnival barker, selling a product created by others. Critics admitted that Reagan could give a speech, but many claimed that the words and ideas were often not his own. In December 1986, as the Iran-Contra issue swirled around the White House, *Time* wrote that Reagan's writers were supplying substance to his speeches while "he adds the homespun parables. His attention to speeches reflects his own perception of the job: on many issues he sees himself less an originator of policy than as a chief marketer of it."[16] The release of new evidence has proved these critics wrong. Reagan was not a mere marionette. The archives of the Ronald Reagan Presidential Library in Simi Valley, California, reveal the former president's vast files of handwritten speeches and letters.[17]

Indeed, no one recognized the importance of Reagan's repetition of message more than his speechwriters. Many had grown up watching their boss on film and television. They knew he could communicate. His staff just as quickly realized, however, that he had been writing his own material for years. Until his presidency, Reagan wrote his own speeches. Once he was in office the personal drafts dropped, but he still penned particular addresses and offered detailed corrections on submitted scripts. Former Reagan speechwriter Peter Robinson suggested that during his eight years in office, Reagan may have "composed about a half million words" and thus "done more writing than any chief executive since Woodrow Wilson."[18] Whether he wrote every single word or not, Reagan demanded that his prepared speeches echo his earlier language.

Reagan's speechwriting worked fairly simply. After an event had been added to the president's schedule, the speechwriting staff would assign a writer, along with a researcher for historical background. After the speechwriter turned in a rough draft a few days before the event, copies—at times as many as twenty-four—would be sent to the director of speechwriting and senior members of the administration familiar or otherwise involved with the event for revisions. Corrected copies would then circulate through the offices with different times in the upper right-hand corner signifying the various rewritings. One or two days prior to the event Reagan would receive a final copy, make changes if necessary, and add his final comments in the upper left-hand corner of the first page. "RR No Changes" meant just that; the president controlled final approval.[19]

Reagan's consistency of message greatly aided his speechwriters. When he arrived at the White House in 1981, he quickly hand-delivered a large collection of old speeches to the speechwriting office with instructions that the staff members "learn to imitate his style and substance."[20] Former speechwriters and close aides asserted that it remained easy to write for Reagan because of the steadiness of his language. Pollsters cited Reagan's consistency of message as the foundation of much of his popularity.[21] A speechwriter who worked with Reagan for six years, Peter Robinson recalled: "As a speechwriter, I became an expert on Reagan. We had to. We mastered every position he had ever taken, poring over his old speeches, radio talks, and newspaper columns." Reagan's writers identified with their subject to such a degree that, after the completion of a work, many would "mimic" the president's voice to test the speeches' viability. "We speechwriters were never attempting to fabricate an image," Robinson wrote. "We were only attempting to produce work that met the standard Reagan himself had long ago established."[22] In other words, consistency remained the key to success. If the remarks did not sound like Reagan from years past, the speech would not work for the president or anyone else and would be rejected.

Similarly, speechwriter Peggy Noonan recalled that, upon her arrival to the Reagan staff, aides told her to research "what he's said in the past." She penned Reagan speeches from 1984 to 1987, including two of his most memorable: the 1984 Pointe Du Hoc speech at the fortieth anniversary of D-Day and the 1986 *Challenger* space shuttle memorial. Noonan recognized the power of rhetoric in the Reagan White House and later wrote, "Speechwriting was where the administration got invented every day. And so speechwriting was, for some, the center of gravity in that administration, the point where ideas and principles still counted." She echoed Robinson's assertion that knowing Reagan's consistent style aided in the creation of his remarks. Commenting on the *Challenger* speech, she recalled adding a poem to the text because she knew he recognized the work and would appreciate the gesture.[23] Speechwriter Landon Parvin, author of the important remarks that helped Reagan survive the Iran-Contra scandal, stated that it remained very easy to write for Reagan because he possessed "a definite consistent philosophy, a consistent personality, and a consistent view of the world." His consistency made him easy to work with. Reagan had a depth of conviction and a consistency that he earned, and the fact remained, you "can't pick it up and put it on." He added of the president, "He was consistent; we [the speechwriters] could capture him." Parvin called Reagan's voice a "great instrument" that resonated with *"sincerity, likeability, reassurance"* for the listener. The audience trusted Reagan's message because they trusted Reagan. The president as a speaker "knew how to make a human connection."[24]

Richard Wirthlin, who served as Reagan's pollster and chief political strategist from 1968 to 1988, argued that "consistency" is what transformed Reagan from being merely a great communicator into one of the greatest. He added that Reagan's delivery style possessed uniformity, as each public speech always contained three elements: "a rational component" to appeal to a voter's sense of logic, a "benefit" or "consequence" to narrow the audience's choices, and an "emotional" element that would "link to a person's most deeply held beliefs."

Wirthlin's three elements echo Aristotle's three sources of linguistic persuasion: "ethos (the character of the speaker), logos (the apparent reasonableness and rationality of the speaker's arguments), and pathos (the speaker's ability to evoke emotions that will make the audience wish to act on the speaker's request)." As Wirthlin described it, Reagan's rhetoric could persuade through reason by motivating through emotion.[25]

Noonan recalled that Reagan's speeches, like the man himself, always had to sound confident and optimistic. "It always has to be positive with him. Never 'I'll never forget,' always 'I'll always remember.'" Some of her earlier work for Reagan before she reviewed his past speeches and mastered his style centered on the use of the word *worried*. A more seasoned Reagan aide advised that in speeches "The president is never worried. The president is concerned."[26] Due to Reagan's consistency and optimism, Noonan and other speechwriters had to change their writing to fit his style. His repetitive messages demanded no less.

In Chapter 1 we consider an early crucial example of the strength and influence of the Reagan rhetoric. Three months prior to the 1980 presidential election, Governor Reagan visited the Neshoba County Fair near Philadelphia, Mississippi. Many advisors including his wife, Nancy, pleaded with him not to attend the fair—in a region still steeped in the pain and memories of the 1964 murders of three civil rights workers, James Chaney, Michael Schwerner, and Andrew Goodman. Those closest to Reagan knew his standard political speech and believed the location and the event to be the wrong place at the wrong time with the wrong words. Once at the fair, Reagan's use of the term *states' rights* caused immediate problems. The controversial phrase was laden with civil rights history. His two decades of consistently using the words returned to haunt him. Reagan claimed innocence, but his own repetitiveness doomed him. His national campaign seemed over before it officially began.

In the next three chapters we examine over twenty years of Reagan's consistent pre-presidential and presidential language concerning the Vietnam War along with the subsequent impact and influence of such language upon the nation. His words swam against the national current in describing that era in the American experience. In speeches, radio broadcasts, newspaper commentaries, and both public and private letters, Reagan always included five consistent rhetorical elements in defense of the war in Southeast Asia. During the 1980s Reagan's unfailing pattern greatly influenced the portrayal of the Vietnam veteran in American popular culture.

Popular culture is hard to measure. For example, we may know how many tickets were sold for a film but we do not know who bought them and for what reason. In this book I present demonstrations of Reagan's impact on numerous examples of 1980s popular culture. The rapid changes in such projects serve as a rough proxy, a measurement, of collective perception and endorsement of Reagan's power to persuade and influence.

While the nation did not accept all five elements of the Vietnam language, Reagan's rhetoric concerning the American soldier in Vietnam helped to promote a reevaluation of the vet. As I discuss in Chapter 2, such a reevaluation actually predated Reagan but remained in its infancy. His consistent words, presentation, and actions provided key momentum for a second look at the Vietnam veteran. An entire generation of Americans too young to experience the war firsthand or vividly remember the pain of the twenty-year struggle heard and then accepted Reagan's new interpretation of the soldiers who fought in the war and the veteran's experience. Some Americans protested the new Reagan-inspired descriptions and offered a counter argument, but many unknowingly chose the very tools that only strengthened Reagan's position. Under his influence, the Vietnam War and veterans of the conflict soon underwent a marked transformation from military defeat to cultural touchstones of victory.

How repetitive language aided Reagan politically in surviving the Iran-Contra scandal is the focus of Chapters 5 and 6. With Iran-Contra, Reagan's uniformity of message first damaged his presidency and then later aided in recovery and his successfully surviving the scandal. The November 1986 announcement of arms to Iran and then an illegal diversion of funds to the Nicaraguan Contras immediately reminded the American people of Reagan's six-year crusade for rebel support. Like the Mississippi visit six years earlier, his own words returned to haunt him.

In Chapter 7 we look at the enduring memories of Neshoba, Vietnam, and Iran-Contra in regards to media coverage after Reagan's June 2004 death. His passing revealed that by 2004 certain interpretations rhetorically offered by Reagan during his presidency had become an accepted part of the collective memory for millions of Americans. By the second decade of the twenty-first century, the nation remembers Reagan because of how he laid the groundwork in the past. In death, as in life, Reagan had the last word.

On January 11, 1989, as he prepared to leave office, Reagan addressed the American people one last time as president. An old tradition, exiting chief executives take one last audience with the electorate. One-termers often want to put a brave face on a lackluster administration or a failed reelection bid. Two-termers such as Reagan simply wish to crow a little.

He had every reason. Reagan was leaving office with a popularity rating in the 65% range. He was the first president in thirty years to serve a full two terms. Finally, his own vice president won election to the presidency, something that had not happened since 1836 and Martin Van Buren. Certainly other vice presidents since 1836 have succeeded to the presidency but, during that long span, only through the death or resignation of the presidents they served.

Reagan's words clearly reveal that he recognized the power of memory. Reagan looked into the camera and shared his pride in what he described as the "new patriotism" of the 1980s. He said, "Our spirit is back, but we haven't reinstitutionalized it." He recalled that, prior to the 1960s, Americans had received lessons in patriotism from family, neighborhood, school, and popular culture. Reagan called for a return of such teachings, for the new nationalism to be thoughtful, knowledgeable, and constantly reinforced, beginning with parents teaching their children at the dinner table. He stated, "If we forget what we did, we won't know who we are. I'm warning of an eradication of the American memory that could result, ultimately, in an erosion of the American spirit."[27]

Reagan, indeed, defines the 1980s. Any retrospective on that decade clearly details how those were the Reagan years. No other president, since Kennedy and his Camelot, has a time period that carries his name. The 1980s will be, forever, the Reagan Era.[28] For eight years, Reagan presented the nation with his version of reality surrounding matters such as past racial violence, unpopular wars, and contemporary presidential scandal through rhetorically driven persuasions. He challenged the present thinking of millions by offering new perspectives and interpretations. Through the consistency of his message and his content, Reagan convinced many Americans to subscribe to the new narratives. By the time of his death in 2004, it was just as clear that he changed the way the vast majority of Americans remember.

1 / States' Rights

Reagan and the 1964 Neshoba County Murders in American Memory

"Memory and history, far from being synonymous, appear to now be in fundamental opposition."
—**Pierre Nora, "Between Memory and History:** *Les Lieux de Mémoire"*

"In Neshoba County, Mississippi, the basement of the past is not very deep. All mysteries of the present seem to be entangled in the total history of the county."
—**Florence Mars,** *Witness in Philadelphia*

Since the summer of 1899, the Neshoba County Fair in Philadelphia, Mississippi, has served as an annual gathering place for thousands of people from across the nation.[1] The week-long summer event, labeled by many as the state's largest house party, welcomes fairgoers from as far west as Utah and as far north as Michigan. The site also provides a window into time-honored southern social, cultural, and political events. Courtesy and covered dishes remain the norm. People mingle in large crowds worthy of Times Square but without the pushing or profanity. Strangers meet, shaking hands like old friends who have not seen one another in a long while. Laughing children swarm the grounds with oversized sweet treats of popsicles and cotton candy, and playful dogs follow the children, hoping gravity allows for a quick snatch. Scattered conversation lifts above the crowds, reporting the success or failures of crops, recent summer movies, planned family weddings, ongoing baseball pennant races, upcoming college football, and always, local and national politics.

Longer than most Mississippians can remember, campaign oratory has been a stalwart part of the Neshoba County Fair. Local and state office seekers receive only two days of the week, Wednesday and Thursday, and are limited to a short ten minutes each on those days to sway the minds of the gathered audiences. The normal location of the speeches remains Founders' Square, a central setting on the fairgrounds. Crowds gather, and politicians of varying notoriety apply their trade. At past fairs, orators have included former governors Ross Barnett, Theodore Bilbo, William Winter, and Cliff Finch, as well as state and later national politicians Trent Lott and Thad Cochran, as well as conservative Democrat Charles Evers, brother of slain civil rights leader Medgar Evers. In a nod to the importance of the location, a local paper reported, "No candidate for a state office would dare fail to stump at the Neshoba fair during an election year."[2] In other words, to win in Mississippi, a candidate first has to succeed in Neshoba.

On August 3, 1980, strong thunderstorms were moving quickly through Philadelphia, Mississippi, and sunshine, heat, and humidity greeted the thousands of visitors who arrived in anticipation at the fairgrounds. The schedule listed the next day, Monday, as the official beginning of festivities, but locals altered the calendar to accommodate the day's guest as an immense Sunday crowd gathered in welcome. A local band played "Dixie" and the crowd roared as Republican presidential candidate Ronald Reagan, accompanied by his wife, Nancy, arrived on the decorated bandstand. His tie and coat long discarded, Reagan rolled up his shirtsleeves and waved to crowds estimated at anywhere from fifteen to thirty thousand people.

Reagan knew the South. Beginning with an initial trip in 1952, he had soon become a familiar face. Throughout the 1950s and early 1960s he crisscrossed the region. He first visited as part of a Hollywood public relations campaign, then later as a corporate spokesman for General Electric.[3] During these years, Reagan laid down trails to be followed in future political campaigns: Texas, Louisiana, Arkansas, Kentucky, Tennessee, Georgia, North Carolina, and Virginia.

Reagan's speaking tours through the South occurred simultaneously with his ideological conversion from liberal Democrat to conservative Republican. His words reflected such a shift. At many southern locations, Reagan took his first rhetorical baby steps with words and phrases that would become familiar in later decades. Reagan seemed to say what many in the region needed to hear. Business owners and working crowds who were worried about the encroachment of federal regulation responded positively as Reagan railed against big government. People who were anxious over rising crime embraced his messages of law and order. Audiences who were concerned about civil rights liked his talk of returning the powers guaranteed by the Constitution to the states. As one scholar noted, "he cast the conservative argument as a defense of the common man."[4]

Reagan dominates the August 7, 1980, front page of the *Neshoba Democrat*. Courtesy the *Neshoba Democrat*.

Reagan also knew Mississippi. He had visited the state many times before. On November 16, 1973, he had served as keynote speaker for the state's Republican Party annual fund-raiser in Jackson. Three years later, on August 4, 1976, Reagan returned to Mississippi during his unsuccessful bid to wrest the Republican nomination from the incumbent Gerald Ford. In 1978 Reagan again returned to the Magnolia State, to test the political waters for a 1980 run for the presidency.[5]

Although it was not yet evident in 1980, Reagan and Mississippi also shared a political symmetry. Each closely mirrored the political transformation of the other. At one time, both had stood as a bastion of Democratic support. Many often forget that Reagan was once a stalwart Democrat. Early in his acting career, he had been a union man, serving seven terms as president of the Screen Actors Guild. During those years, Reagan openly campaigned for Franklin D. Roosevelt and Harry S. Truman. By the 1950s, Cold War and economic concerns began to change his mind, for he was feeling that Democrats remained too soft against communism. During his time as corporate spokesman for the

General Electric Corporation, Reagan soon railed against what he perceived to be unfair tax rates and federal regulations. By the end of the 1950s, he openly disagreed with many positions of the Democratic Party. He resigned the Screen Actors Guild presidency in 1960 and joined the Republican Party two years later. Reagan completed his transformation with his 1964 remarks in support for Barry Goldwater, known forever in Reagan historiography as "The Speech."

Mississippi was moving toward the Grand Ole Party at the same time. Between 1876 and 1960, not a single Republican candidate for the presidency ever won Mississippi. The Democrats captured the state twenty out of twenty-one contests. The lone exception—J. Strom Thurmond's States' Rights Party—won in 1948, with Mississippi governor Fielding Wright on the ticket as vice president. By the 1960s, however, the state had become fertile ground for Republicans. The issue of civil rights caused many Mississippians to abandon long-held political traditions. Unpledged electors claimed Mississippi in 1960, Barry Goldwater carried the state in 1964, and George Wallace and his American Independent Party won in 1968. After that, the rout was on. Republican presidential candidates won nine of the next ten contests for Mississippi. Jimmy Carter would stand out as the lone exception, winning the state with 49% in 1976. By 2008, the Republican candidate had carried the state in eight straight national elections.

In 1980, despite the trend from the polls, people still considered Mississippi to be Democratic country. As a result, the Neshoba scene appeared surreal. The Republican nominee stood in what was historically enemy territory. It appeared that on this hot August day, however, someone forgot to tell the crowd. With a speech that ran just under thirty minutes, Reagan won over Neshoba. As the first presidential hopeful ever to visit the fair, he received glowing introductions from local politicians, gifts from regional craftsmen, and constant cheers, laughter, and applause from a predominately white audience.

At Neshoba, Reagan offered his standard 1980 campaign speech. He joked about Carter. He dropped in political phrases he had been using since the 1950s. He echoed language that remained common enough among Republicans. Criticizing the expansiveness of federal authority, he promised to "restore to state and local governments the powers that belonged properly to them." The line had served as a Republican mantra for years. The phrase is lifted almost word for word from Goldwater's 1960 work *The Conscience of a Conservative*. The assembled masses easily accepted his campaign message. Local ears remained open to such words. A local newspaper harked back to recent civil rights struggles and described the listeners as still retaining bitterness toward the federal government.[6]

At one point in the speech, Reagan repeated a twenty-year-old mainstay of his political ideology and assured the Mississippi crowd that he "believed in states' rights." He did not accompany his assertion with a pumped fist reminiscent of Mississippian Ross Barnett or Alabamian George Wallace. In fact, he did not even raise his voice. A review of the audio of the speech reveals that his declaration produced absolutely no response from the audience. Nevertheless, the words were spoken, and they echoed far beyond the Mississippi fairground.[7]

With a pronouncement strongly laden with civil rights' meaning, Reagan snagged a rhetorical tripwire. Although accepted without a murmur locally, his words created a national political firestorm. Neshoba County, Mississippi, remained a location saturated with bloodstained memory, both locally and nationally. Reagan's speech took place sixteen years after—and physically only a few miles removed from the location of—the murders of three Freedom Summer volunteers in 1964: James Chaney, Michael Schwerner, and Andrew Goodman. On a national level, Reagan's words brought him immediate criticism. Locally, the entire speech played well. Reagan may have just won Mississippi, but he stood in real danger of losing the country. Many of his staff and supporters believed the Neshoba visit "almost blew the election before the campaign formally began."[8] This incident, so early in his first national campaign as a presidential nominee, demonstrated not only Reagan's ability to survive a potentially fatal rhetorical gaffe but also his linguistic skill to satisfy both the national and the local memories swirling around the rural Mississippi location.

His choice of words, and the resulting national uproar, revealed how many Americans remembered the events of 1964. Two differing perceptions—a national and a local collective memory—existed simultaneously concerning the murders. The memory of the country as a whole, while including other components, focused primarily on issues of race. When America bent its eye to look on Neshoba, it perceived the region, and thus the civil rights murders, through a racial prism. Quite often, due to geographic separation and the passage of time, the national recollection did not dwell on the details of the crime, instead concentrating on the racial variables of the murders.

The local memory, in contrast, emanated from Neshoba County outward. The recollections contained not only issues related to the color divide—but additional matters of community, state versus federal power, local crime and murder, as well as the complicity of the indigenous power structure in the deaths of the civil rights workers. Mississippians' memory, due to geographic proximity, remained infused with a greater degree of detail concerning the 1964 events. Unlike the memory of America as a whole, the memory of the murders in Neshoba had not been diluted by the passage of time. The killings and the subsequent national reaction still produced raw emotions in the region. The locals, for better or worse, considered the events part of their personal heritage, although with differing levels of importance. Beliefs fell along racial lines. Some whites bitterly possessed memories of federal government interference, loss of local political power, and the death of Jim Crow. Other whites experienced shame and a real desire to move away from a racist past. Neshoba County blacks recalled not-so-distant years of legal segregation, an atmosphere of hopelessness, and an acute awareness of the severe consequences of challenging regional societal tradition.

Reagan was able to survive the political consequences of his "states' rights" speech in Mississippi for three reasons. First, he could honestly point to his lengthy records of speeches and argue that states' rights had long been a part of his language. As a result, he could smile and shrug and admit he meant no harm or offense with his Mississippi words, given the painful local context. Second, he used a political trip to New York and Chicago within days of the Neshoba speech to reach out to black voters and simultaneously placate the racially centered national uproar over his words. Finally, the presidential campaign of 1980 centered on economic issues and not on issues of race.[9] As a result, the episode exposed the contemporary place of racial issues in the United States during the 1980 general presidential campaign. The nation at that time suffered from severe economic woes and a general crisis of confidence. Issues of race often did not receive a great deal of attention. Public interest remained riveted to what seemed the more pressing and immediate issue: the continuing national economic crisis. Reagan's success at quickly defusing the "states' rights" Neshoba County Fair speech reveals an old common trait of the nation's attention span: in times of national stress and uncertainty, painful memories and hard-won social victories are sometimes easily forgotten or pushed aside. In other words, it is not unfair to question just how far the United States has progressed if, in times of great stress, the nation forgets or presses to the periphery civil rights or the sacrifices paid to gain them.

Tensions between the national and local perceptions regarding Neshoba appeared long before Reagan's fair appearance. The various invitations for Reagan to appear at the Neshoba County Fair revealed how Mississippians and those outside the state remembered the murders and thus perceived the region. Requests arrived early as private citizens and public officials alike asked for an appearance. Natives, recognizing the political importance of the festival, initiated the requests. Others, on the outside looking in, sensed real danger in the choice of location. A May

30, 1980, invitation from Sandra Denson of the Mississippi Division of Reagan for President, exclaimed in part, "If Governor Reagan could only make one stop in Mississippi, this would be the best stop he could make." Other letter writers suggesting a fair visit included Charles Pickering, the 1980 co-chairman of the Reagan campaign in Mississippi; Michael Retzer, the 1980 chairman of the Mississippi Republican Party; Kenneth Klinge, who served as Reagan's regional political director for Mississippi, Arkansas, Louisiana, and Missouri; and Mississippi representative Trent Lott and senator Thad Cochran.[10]

Great debate existed around the campaign planning of the Mississippi trip. Lott recalled how resistant the governor's advisors were to the fair visit and how his efforts to bring Reagan to Neshoba were a "stirring battle," not "an easy victory." Lott added that among Reagan staffers' many concerns were "not least the fact that three civil rights workers had been murdered near there in the early summer of 1964."[11] Reagan's aides also argued that the timing of the Mississippi speech could not have been worse. The Neshoba County Fair had occupied essentially the same dates on the calendar for almost one hundred years. As a result, any Reagan visit would occur just days prior to, or just after, an important long-scheduled New York City address to the racially mixed National Urban League. The stakes for the New York address were high. Reagan did not enjoy strong support among blacks. His speech to the seventieth annual convention of the National Urban League would be his first—and, as it turned out, his only—address to an African American majority audience after his nomination. In New York, he hoped to gain some measure of black acceptance. Reagan also sought to calm some tension among African Americans angered by his failure to respond, the previous month, to an invitation to speak with the National Association for the Advancement of Colored People (NAACP).[12]

Within the campaign camp, Reagan's regional political director for Mississippi and three other southern states, Kenneth Klinge, remained fully aware of the potential national fallout attached to the bloody memory of the Neshoba area. On the other hand, he was able to see a local political opportunity. Klinge knew the area and the people. He argued that a trip to the Neshoba County Fair would send a message to the South that Reagan remained serious about winning the region in the upcoming election. Along with Lott, he forcibly conveyed his thoughts to the campaign.[13]

Reagan himself realized the potential political gain. A traditional county fair seemed the perfect locale. He had been speaking to these types of audiences since the late 1940s and his campaign speeches for Harry Truman. These were his kind of people. For him, rural folk remained genuine people with real problems who traditionally responded well to his messages. As a result, he accepted the Mississippi invitation over the objections of his aides. Nancy asked him to reconsider, but in a rare moment for their marriage, he refused her advice. With the decision made, aides scrambled to limit the damage. The main question the staff faced was *when* exactly to place the Mississippi trip. In the back of every staffer's mind remained the knowledge that a predominantly black audience of critical importance for the campaign awaited in New York, some of whom might not receive with equanimity the news of Reagan's trip to this notorious southern town.

Newspapers wrote of the unease in the Reagan camp. Press reports at the time suggested that Reagan originally planned to speak to the National Urban League *before* the Neshoba County Fair.[14] The Reagan campaign originally scheduled the Neshoba visit for August 6, one day after New York. At some point, someone moved the Mississippi trip up. A 1980 campaign schedule, printed on July 29, 1980, detailed the governor's events for August. Circled in blue magic marker was the change of date for the "Neshoba County Fair (Mississippi)" trip from August 6 to August 3.[15] Fully aware of the national sensitivity surrounding Neshoba, aides to the former governor admitted to the change in schedule and confessed to the national media that a trip in the original order "would have been like we were coming to Mississippi and winking at the folks here, saying we didn't really mean to be talking to them Urban League folk. It would have been the wrong signal."[16] Another staff member stated that people in New York would have similar concerns.[17]

Klinge remembered two decades later that the final decision even to go to Mississippi was not made until three days before Reagan's visit. Klinge maintained that the Neshoba County State Fair campaign stop was a late addition to the schedule, so Reagan's handlers could not have originally placed it behind the speech at the National Urban League. The evidence does not support his assertions. Perhaps because he was based in the South and busy campaigning in the region, Klinge was unaware of the original schedule.[18]

Busy campaigning in the South, Klinge did sense that the date could cause problems nationally. He offered four possible solutions to the problem in a pre-trip undated inter-campaign memo. He wrote that the first choice remained to "cancel Neshoba—not acceptable politically–when we need help in mid-October, we will look South for help." Option two included substituting Reagan with Nancy or with the vice-presidential nominee and his wife. Klinge added, "this makes the problem worse, in my opinion." The third option was to "go on another date—acceptable, if R.R. will buy this," and the fourth was to "cancel urban affairs theme—acceptable, and the only viable option if #3 doesn't go."[19] Klinge recognized that to go on another date remained the only option not to hurt Reagan politically. However, the governor remained boxed-in by the date limitations of the fair. To ignore the speech or send a substitute could damage Reagan in Mississippi and possibly the South as a whole. A late cancellation of a major speech in New York to attend a Mississippi state fair would similarly affect the candidate in the North.

Neshoba remained on the schedule, but one member of the Reagan team tried one last time to change the candidate's mind. Richard Wirthlin, who had served as chief pollster to Reagan since the early days in California, urged the presidential nominee to reconsider the Mississippi visit altogether. His almost twenty years of service had earned him Reagan's affection and, just as important, proximity to Reagan's ear. As a pollster for a politician who did not govern by opinion surveys, Wirthlin knew just how stubborn Reagan could be. Nevertheless, in the case of Neshoba and New York, he sensed only trouble. Reagan, in a nod to his acting and speaking circuit days, reminded his friend that he had already accepted the invitation and spoke of the importance of keeping a scheduled booking. Wirthlin did not let go. He reminded Reagan that a visit to Neshoba just two days prior to a speech to the National Urban League might send an undesirable signal. Wirthlin cited data that revealed how many moderate Republicans and independents possessed skepticism that the Republican candidate felt sympathy for the problems of minorities and the poor. He worried that, although the speech to the National Urban League could diminish these concerns, a visit to the Neshoba County Fair could instead solidify the anxieties of minorities. Wirthlin also expressed concerns that, while Reagan sought the black vote in New York City, the national media would almost certainly simultaneously report stories and commentaries concerning his Mississippi visit. The debate went back and forth. Wirthlin pushed too hard, and Reagan actually grew angry. In a rare case of overt temper, he threw his briefing papers at Wirthlin, and the discussion ended.[20]

As Wirthlin attempted to change Reagan's mind, one Mississippian began to echo the pollster's concerns. Initially supportive of the Neshoba trip, Mississippi Republican senator Thad Cochran, with only two years in the Senate at that time, had changed his mind. He thought a visit to the state remained a good idea but that the fair no longer was the proper venue. He knew the visit to Philadelphia, Mississippi, would generate state gains but also remained fully aware of the possible national fallout. Cochran shared his concerns with others and experienced only frustration. He remembered that Representative Lott "pushed hard" for Reagan's appearance. Cochran remarked that he believed the trip "was over the top," "not smart," "a blunder," and "not a good idea."[21]

In the end, the local Reagan supporters, Lott, Klinge, and others won the day. Those who promised the candidate a regional gain defeated those who feared a national backlash. The Mississippi engagement remained on the schedule and firmly in its place before New York City, and Reagan remained on a direct collision course with the national memory surrounding the 1964 Neshoba County murders. Animosity, however, lingered in the Reagan camp. Klinge received advice from an aide to avoid Nancy Reagan on the way to the Neshoba County Fair. Mrs. Reagan, like Wirthlin, continued to express concerns about the Mississippi appearance.[22] As debate within the Reagan camp finally ended, local newspapers heralded his upcoming appearance. In what would have certainly added deep concern for Wirthlin, Cochran, and others, pictures in a local paper showed that Confederate battle flags flew in full view from many of the cabins on the Neshoba fairgrounds.[23]

Reagan appeared at the Neshoba County Fair. He won over the thousands of locals in attendance. With cheers and applause ringing in his ears, he left the stage satisfied with the successful trip and flew to New York. Meanwhile, reporters scribbled on pads and feverishly typed about the Mississippi trip. The stories spoke of large crowds, roaring ovations, and five words: "I believe in states' rights."

The moment the words came from Reagan's mouth, the sound of a collective forehead slap echoed throughout his campaign. Aides could not believe he had actually said those words, not now, not at this sensitive location. The boss had seemingly forgotten the debate surrounding the visit. They knew Reagan was no fool, and even if "states' rights" had been a part of his speeches in the past, they believed it must not be a tool to be wielded in Neshoba County, Mississippi. True, the regional gain may be positive, but the national backlash could be devastating.

An undated handwritten piece of yellow legal pad paper, discovered at the Ronald Reagan Presidential Library, contains an interesting reference to Reagan's use of "states' rights." Because of their content, it is clear that the words were written after Reagan's August 3 Neshoba appearance. The paper suggests that Reagan received a nudge to use the phrase. The document's author is unclear, although the name Mike Retzer, the chairman of the Mississippi Republican Party, is prominently written at top left.[24] The paper details, point by point, state tensions within the efforts of the 1980 Mississippi Republican Party in electing Reagan. Lott does not fare well as the paper complains of favoritism. The handwritten note suggests intra-Mississippi competition between "Lott vs. Cochran at State Convention" and then lists "Reed, Retzer (Cochran Side)." The writer complains that 1980 scheduling for Reagan supporters remained "too heavy into 5th District (Lott's) and surrogates." On Neshoba, the document is brief, but it blames the entire episode on Lott by stating "states rights flap (Lott wanted language in speech)."[25] As a Mississippi native, Lott had pushed hard for a Reagan visit to the fair. As a local, he certainly recognized the benefit of rhetorically playing to the crowd. If the author of the document is Retzer, the paper itself suggests an intra-Mississippi tension and a possible bias versus Lott.[26]

A nudge from Lott, whether or not it happened, really did not matter. Reagan did not possess the same concerns as his staff. Again, he could simply point back to what he had said in years past. A cursory examination of his past speeches finds numerous examples of direct spoken support for "states' rights." In an October 1966 interview in *Time*, he recalled casting his first presidential vote for Franklin Roosevelt, saying, "Remember his platform? It was all for states' rights. . . . Well, I'm still in favor of that." As governor of California, he consistently repeated the belief. In a 1967 address to the National Sand and Gravel Association, he remarked, "Well, states' rights, I believe, are a built-in guarantee of freedom." At the same time while giving speeches in South Carolina and Kentucky, he complained that the Democratic Party had "repudiated the constitution, concepts of individual freedom, local autonomy, and states' rights." Before the National Conference of State Legislative Leaders in San Francisco he declared, "Those who sneeringly reject the term 'states' rights' ignore the great part the state plays in providing a built-in guaranty against tyranny." In Reagan's earlier visit to Mississippi, in 1978, the Jackson newspaper reported that the visiting politician spoke on the importance of states' rights and a strong military. Reagan also used the phrase in private correspondence, using the argument for states' rights against nationally electing state senators.[27]

Regardless of any previous declarations for states' rights, Reagan's campaign team believed that he knew better than to use the phrase in Neshoba, and they were absolutely right. Reagan perfectly played the entire episode. He utilized a consistent tool from past speeches to win over a regional audience and, as a result, could correctly claim that he meant no harm with his words. Additionally, Reagan's skills as an actor served him well. When the time came for the declaration, he dropped his voice and quietly delivered, "I believe in states' rights." Thus Reagan could again claim, regardless of location, that the words possessed no special meaning beyond what he had said so many times in the past.

Locally, the Reagan campaign got what they wanted from the visit. Southerners left the speech well satisfied. Regional newspapers boasted of great applause and support for the California politician. Michael Deaver, assistant to the governor who would later go on to direct much of President Reagan's public appearances, received from the campaign deputy director

William Timmons a copy of a pro-Reagan Neshoba County Fair picture from the August 4, 1980, *Jackson (MS) Clarion-Ledger.* An included note read, "To Mike Deaver—Good Stuff! BT."[28] The local Reagan campaign workers felt vindicated.

As feared by many of his staffers, however, Reagan's visit stirred national memory of the civil rights murders and attracted criticism from the nation's press. The larger newspapers confirmed Wirthlin's worst fears. The Jackson, Mississippi, papers the *Clarion-Ledger* and the *Jackson (MS) Daily News*, in addition to the *Washington Post* and the *Atlanta (GA) Journal-Constitution*, all quoted the portion of Reagan's speech that included the "states' rights" assertion.[29] Going even further, the *New York Times* and the *Memphis (TN) Commercial Appeal* not only included the "states' rights" quote but used the phrase in headlines. The *New York Times* columnist Anthony Lewis stated that, in Neshoba, Reagan either at worst openly courted the racist vote or at best remained unaware of the symbolism.[30] In New Orleans, the *Times-Picayune* wrote of the irony of the Neshoba appearance in relation to Reagan's upcoming National Urban League speech.[31] The *New York Times*, *Commercial Appeal*, and *Atlanta Journal-Constitution* also included brief mentions that the Republican nominee spoke to a crowd consisting mostly of whites.[32] Reagan left Mississippi having accomplished locally exactly what he had hoped and nationally what many feared.

As newspapers reported his Mississippi words, Reagan arrived as planned in New York City. For forty minutes, he visited the recuperating Urban League president Vernon Jordan, wounded on June 5 by a sniper's bullet in Fort Wayne, Indiana.[33] The following day, Reagan spoke to the National Urban League. As video clips of the governor's trip to Neshoba played across the country and newspapers detailed the "states' rights" speech, the Republican presidential candidate openly sought the African American vote.

In a carefully worded speech, Reagan asked the predominantly black Urban League audience not to see him as a caricature conservative but, instead, to be aware of the broad areas of agreement between black America and the Republican Party. In an effort at historical linkage, he referred to Catholic Democratic nominee John F. Kennedy's 1960 speech to Protestant ministers; he, similarly, was asking his 1980 audience to discount preconceived labels. Realizing the paramount issue on most Americans' minds, the former governor received some applause as he talked about jobs and economic opportunity for black Americans. Mississippi, however, had followed Reagan to New York. No doubt in a nod to the national attention generated by his Neshoba speech, Reagan inserted a statement late into his previously prepared text. He added, "I am committed to the protection of the civil rights of black Americans. This commitment is interwoven into every phase of the programs that I will propose."[34]

While the press disagreed on the reaction of the New York crowd and the overall success of his speech, Reagan received polite applause for his talk of expanding the "economic pie." [35] The *Atlanta Journal-Constitution* reported that applause interrupted Reagan fourteen times and that he received a customary standing ovation at the conclusion of his speech.[36] The *Clarion-Ledger* and the *New York Times* reported that the former governor received restrained applause at the beginning and the end of his remarks with scattered "hand-clapping" eleven times.[37] Other papers disagreed. The *Chicago Tribune* called the Republican's reception by the audience "less than enthusiastic," and another story in the paper labeled his treatment as "polite but cool."[38] Two days after Reagan's Urban League speech, the *New York Times* suggested that Reagan's cautious reception by the National Urban League resulted from his earlier words in Mississippi.[39] The Urban League speech could not be called an outright failure, but Reagan's remarks did not generate the press his campaign had hoped for. Newspapers continued to report on Neshoba. As Wirthlin, Nancy Reagan, Cochran, and others had feared, the Mississippi visit seemed to be heading the campaign toward a serious disaster.

Reagan's aides should not have worried. Reagan's efforts of outreach during the National Urban League speech and his actions in subsequent days stopped any possible long-term political damage. His speech in Mississippi had satisfied the local assembly surrounding the murders. Now his subsequent actions in New York City and during an unscheduled Chicago visit placated the national audience. While in New York and in response to a suggestion of a black staff member, Ron McDuffie, Reagan agreed to travel to the South Bronx for a game of political showmanship. The Republican nominee planned to stand on the exact spot where President Carter had proclaimed four years earlier to make a commitment to urban renewal. The Carter programs had never arrived and the Republican nominee sensed a photo opportunity. Reagan wished to hold a press conference at the same location and portray Carter as a person who could not be trusted. Reagan arrived and began his remarks surrounded by a small crowd and the press. Soon, however, others locals approached, listened for a short period of time, and then began to heckle the Republican candidate. Calling itself the People's Coalition, the locally based, largely black self-help group did express disgust with Carter but also skepticism about the former California governor. At first Reagan attempted to talk with the group, then grew angry at their constant taunts, and finally cried out in frustration, "I can't do a damn thing for you if I don't get elected." The taunts eased as the crowd began to listen.[40]

The raw emotion worked well not only with the crowd but also with the assembled press. The CBS and NBC Evening News included only a few lines from the Urban League Speech but broadcast much of the South Bronx confrontation. Newspapers reported that after his emotional outburst the former governor held the ear of most of the crowd, drew applause, and earned serious attention. The media turned the event into a campaign plus.[41] Reagan's words and actions shifted the focus of the media. The press reported the Urban League speech and the South Bronx confrontation as two somewhat successful Reagan interactions with black Americans. Neshoba slowly began to edge toward the periphery of national attention.

The Reagan camp moved quickly now, with momentum restored. The campaign scrapped the direct return flight to California for a quick stop in Chicago.[42] Aides sensed another opportunity to continue the favorable press generated in New York. After touchdown, Reagan traveled to Reverend Jesse Jackson's Operation PUSH headquarters for a one-hour meeting with the civil rights leader. Minutes of the meeting, kept by the Reagan campaign, detailed eleven items specifically raised by Jackson. Topics ranged from economic issues to the resurgence of the Ku Klux Klan. Seven of the eleven points raised by Jackson dealt specifically with economics, in a nod to the importance of the economy in the 1980 presidential election. In that conversation, Jackson did not let Reagan off the hook. He mentioned the candidate's Neshoba speech. According to notes taken by Reagan staffers, Jackson communicated that "'states rights' seen by blacks as localized oppression; are fearful that a return to states rights means that federal standards for civil rights, etc. would be eliminated. Governor should dispel this idea." Reagan assured Jackson that his commitment to equality remained strong.[43] After the meeting, Reagan and Jackson posed together for the assembled press. Wire stories quoted Jackson as saying that "he and Reagan agreed on some issues and disagreed on others." The *Chicago Tribune* did not mention Neshoba but instead quoted Jackson as praising the Republican presidential nominee for opening a dialogue with black America.[44] The unannounced trip seemed a success. Headlines at the end of the week read far differently than they had just a few days earlier. Reagan and his entourage headed west. As the plane left the ground, many in Reagan's camp hoped that successful trips to New York and Chicago had left Neshoba even further in the distance.

The importance of Reagan's visit to Neshoba continued to fade from national press coverage. Two days after Reagan's visit with Jackson, the *Chicago Tribune* quoted nationally syndicated black columnist and Mississippi native William Raspberry: "more and more blacks are shifting away from the Democrats and toward the *devil* who has not yet proved his incompetence, Gov. Reagan." In an editorial titled, "'Nice words' and black votes" the Chicago newspaper described Reagan's visit to Vernon Jordan and his speech to the National Urban League. The article stated that current black voters were disillusioned with the Democratic Party and were increasingly willing to take the candidacy of Reagan seriously.[45] Raspberry, a black Mississippi-born writer, most certainly understood the local perceptions and memory surrounding Neshoba. His words, however, clearly denote Reagan's success in replacing newspaper headlines about Neshoba with other issues. The August 16, 1980, *Chicago Defender* also included a piece by Marianne Means entitled "Reagan Woos Black Vote." The author reviewed Reagan's efforts to reach out to the black vote during the New York trip and sympathetically concluded, "He shouldn't be faulted for trying to explore the unknown. He might even learn something."[46] The Neshoba trip did not merit a single mention. Again, Means's column exposed the success enjoyed by the Republican nominee in removing the "states' rights" speech in Mississippi from the national media stage—in less than a week. Reagan's aides began to breathe a little easier. Richard Wirthlin, who had expressed such anxiety over the Mississippi trip, sent Reagan memos on August 9 and 11. In an unspecified but obvious reference to Neshoba, the first memo recognized the "difficulty we experienced last week in effectively coordinating and implementing the focused impact theme of urban affairs." The second memo sent two days later more specifically lamented the "mixed message" that the Mississippi trip produced when in "close proximity" to the New York speech. As the national controversy over Reagan's Mississippi words continued to fade, however, Wirthlin seemed pleased with the end result and praised the South Bronx "confrontation," and favorable coverage in the black press.[47] Mississippi Senator Cochran reflected on Reagan's ability to head off a crisis, and Cochran admitted that in the end he "was wrong on the Neshoba County Fair decision" and ultimately called the visit "a great success."[48]

August 1980 ended with both local and national audiences satisfied. An examination of newspapers and magazines in the following days and weeks revealed no additional mention of the Mississippi visit. A letter from the National Urban League dated August 29, 1980, thanked the governor for his speech and included the following: "I think you could tell from the response of the audience that your remarks were very well received."[49]

While Reagan won on all accounts in regards to Neshoba, two additional actions in 1980 briefly brought the "states' rights" speech back to national attention. These were President Jimmy Carter's repeated comments and

Reagan's October return to Mississippi. Each of these events again reveals the difference in the national and local experiences surrounding the 1964 Neshoba murders. They also highlight Reagan's ability to satisfy both understandings of the event.

As a native southerner but also a national politician, Carter stood in a unique position. He easily recognized the local civil rights attitudes surrounding Philadelphia, Mississippi. He perceived the complicated regional emotions existing in such a location. Carter also understood the initial national reaction. As a president seeking reelection, he knew that in this complex situation lay a political opportunity. He personally did not know what was worse, that Reagan had said "states' rights'" or that he had paid no lasting political penalty. After the furor over Neshoba faded, Carter hoped to bring it back. He planned to remind the country of Reagan's words, of how the phrase revealed his opponent's thinking regarding civil rights, and thus he would reawaken the debate over Neshoba. The tactic was not new. Carter's campaign had attempted earlier to link Reagan and racial divisiveness. Carter's secretary of health and human services, a black woman named Patricia Harris, correctly pointed out to reporters that the Ku Klux Klan endorsed the Republican nominee, a backing subsequently rejected by Reagan.

Carter wanted Neshoba back in the national headlines, and in his own state he made his move. On September 16, 1980, in Atlanta before a mostly African American audience of over four hundred people gathered at the Ebenezer Baptist Church, the president talked of Neshoba directly. Even the site was perfect for Carter's purpose. Here at the former church home of Martin Luther King, Jr., Carter argued that the Republican nominee introduced racial hatred into the presidential campaign. The Democratic incumbent stated that the campaign had seen "the stirrings of hate and the rebirth of code words like 'states' rights' in a speech in Mississippi."[50] He continued, saying that "if my opponent should be elected you're going to have a hard time getting a telephone answered at the White House."[51]

A few days later in an Oval Office talk with reporters, Carter mentioned the Klan endorsement three times and Reagan's Neshoba speech twice.[52] At a Chicago fund-raiser a few weeks later, Carter remarked that voters would decide by the ballot box whether the United States would remain united or "if I lose the election, whether Americans might be separated, black from white, Jew from Christian, North from South, rural from urban."[53]

For obvious reasons, Reagan was not eager to revisit these issues publicly and initially offered no response to the accusations. He let others address the charges. Vice-presidential nominee George H. W. Bush labeled the statements "mean and ugly."[54] Former president Gerald Ford stated that Carter's comments "demean the office of the presidency itself" and added that the statements stood as "one of the lowest, most intemperate assaults ever made by a United States president."[55]

Such responses were to be expected from Reagan supporters, but the national media, to the surprise of Carter, echoed the Reagan partisan defense and did not join the president in a national review of the Neshoba visit. Instead, reporters concluded that Reagan had successfully closed the Neshoba issue after his effective New York and Chicago trips. As a result, the press painted Carter's claims as a desperate candidate resorting to "mean" politics.

The unexpected reaction of the media forced Carter to backpedal. During a press conference the president, under increasing pressure from the national media to clarify his Ebenezer Church comments, stated, "I do not think my opponent is racist in any degree." He tried again to remind the country of the words of his Republican opponent. "I did not raise the issue of states' rights and I believe it is better to leave these words, which are code words to many people in our country who suffered from discrimination in the past, out of the election this year."[56] Of the press conference questions, 25% revolved around the president's racially charged comments.[57]

Presidential aides worried that Carter's perceived "meanness" might prove a lasting political issue.[58] Carter supporter and former U.N. ambassador Andrew Young further complicated the president's position when he declared that, if Reagan won the White House, "it's going to be all right to kill niggers."[59] The White House immediately responded and declared that Young's views certainly did not reflect the opinions of Carter. The president, however, received some blame for helping to create an atmosphere where that type of comment found expression. The *New York Times* columnist Anthony Lewis wrote, "There is a mean streak in Carter the campaigner and there always has been."[60] *Newsweek* magazine stated, "The campaign style was vintage Carter, but it did not go down well around the country."[61] Internal Reagan campaign memos declared, "His vitriolic personal attack on us clearly backfired."[62] For a second time in as many months, Reagan's words at Neshoba faded from the national consciousness.

Nevertheless, as Election Day approached for the nation, many Americans began to rethink their support for Reagan. The national media reported that, for the first time in weeks, the Republican nominee's poll numbers slipped below that of the incumbent president.[63] In Mississippi, Reagan campaign internal polling revealed that "we breathe down his [Carter] neck."[64] For this reason Reagan considered making another visit, this time to a children's ranch in Columbus. While gaining ground in

Mississippi was good news, for the candidate even to consider another trip to the region as his national poll numbers dropped reveals that any "states' rights" political fallout from his remarks of August did not concern Reagan. Any return to the state would naturally generate reminders of the August speech. Yet already Reagan had twice survived national attention regarding his Neshoba speech. As a result, the October trip provided scant mention of the August Neshoba County Fair comments.

The nation may have moved on, but painful memories of August still remained in the Reagan campaign. The staffers took more of a notice of their candidate's relationship with the local black community. In preparation for Reagan's visit, the Policy Coordinator Office put out a "Mississippi Political Brief." The directives mentioned that the governor believed he could win Mississippi because "Governor Reagan appears to be doing better than Ford among Mississippi blacks." The Reagan-Bush team believed they could triple Ford's 5% in the state. A more succinct "Columbus Political Brief" suggested that Reagan reach out to people of all parties by ignoring the local Republican organization and welcoming everyone. However, the brief continued that one local Republican official the campaign could not ignore was Sam Coley, the vice chairman of the county party. "Coley is a retired government worker who has been working hard for Governor Reagan. He often answers the phone at the Lowndes [County] Reagan-Bush headquarters. Coley is black." For the October trip the Reagan campaign hedged their bets. With the nation seemingly no longer concerned about Neshoba, and the August trip satisfying Mississippi whites, the campaign concluded that gains remained possible among the state's black population. Additionally, calling attention to a prominent black Reagan supporter would perhaps aid in quelling any local anger that might remain among the Mississippi black population.

The campaign had to be sure not to go too far. A memo dated October 22, 1980, titled "Points for Columbus, Miss. Barbecue," offered the following advice. "2. States Rights: Last time in Mississippi RR's use of 'states rights' drew attack from black leaders. Avoid use of states rights." The note went on to suggest the term "equal justice under law for all Americans" might be a good replacement for the more problematic phrase but then added, "(NOTE: whole issue very sensitive—discuss with local people before making any statements even remotely suggestive of race relations.)"[65] The wording of the memo is important. With the Neshoba fairground speech fading from national memory, the Reagan campaign obviously did not want a repeat of August. For the letter to defer to the "local people" in matters of race, however, reveals a consciousness from the Reagan camp of just who in Mississippi controls the narrative of racial matters.

With Reagan movies playing at nearby theaters, the Republican nominee arrived on October 20 to visit the Mississippi Sheriffs' Association
Boys and Girls Ranch near Columbus.[66] At the home for approximately
twenty-five troubled or abused youths, Reagan visited with the residents
and then ate a barbecue dinner planned for over eight thousand, although
later estimates put the crowd at just over five thousand.[67] The Republican
nominee also picked up an important endorsement from a prominent
black American, Charles Evers, the mayor of Fayette, Mississippi. The
political maverick and brother of slain civil rights leader Medgar Evers
declared support for Reagan's planned economic package, although
again in a nod to the white locals he did not accompany the Republican
nominee to the stage.[68]

Evers's support of Reagan's economic agenda followed recent backings
from Reverend Ralph Abernathy and Hosea Williams, two individuals of
considerable power in the civil rights movement. Both supported the Republican nominee for his proposed economic plans, again revealing that
economics was the overall key factor in the 1980 election, and what each
believed would be possible potential gains for the black community with a
Republican victory. While Reagan ate barbeque in Mississippi and gained
the Evers endorsement, the issue of *Newsweek* on newsstands contained a
picture of Reagan and Abernathy holding hands. Under the picture a caption read, "Was anybody watching?"[69] The endorsements by Abernathy,
Williams, and Evers revealed that Reagan's economic promises eclipsed,
at least temporarily, any national concerns of race brought on by the Republican nominee's August Mississippi speech. Therefore, the Republican
candidate could return to Mississippi and fear virtually no Neshoba reprisal, as the Reagan Neshoba states' rights speech no longer posed any real
political danger for the candidate. Politically comfortable, Reagan stayed
at the Mississippi Sheriff's Ranch almost four hours, a much greater time
than he spent in August at the Neshoba County Fair.[70]

In yet another example of the diminishment of the importance of the
Neshoba Fair story, the *Chicago Tribune*, *Times-Picayune*, *Washington
Post*, and *New York Times* did not mention the August visit or the "states'
rights" speech in their coverage of Reagan's return to Mississippi.[71] Despite the lack of discussion of that previously all-important topic, some
issues of race did arise, however. The coverage differed depending on
whether the newspaper was local or national. During a discussion with
the media concerning the Evers endorsement, one reporter asked the
presidential nominee about his usage of the term "states' rights" during
the earlier Mississippi visit. Reagan answered, "As I told Mayor Evers,
I recognize that the phrase is a buzzword—it creates some unpleasant

images in some people's minds, but what I had in mind is that some functions are better managed at the state level." Local media then reported that few blacks appeared to hear Reagan speak at the Sheriff's Ranch, but those who did attend left the speech impressed.[72] The *Washington Post* reported that John Bell Williams, an outspoken segregationist, endorsed Reagan during the event.[73] The paper did not report if Reagan made any reaction to the declaration. The *New York Times* classified the Sheriff's Ranch as an "all-white" institution and quoted one ranch official who stated that the institution had plans to build a separate residence for black youths. Another ranch official, however, while not denying the "all-white" accusation, stated that no plans existed for construction of a separate residence.[74] Newspapers of the time reveal no follow-up to the *New York Times* "all-white" sheriff's camp report.

The campaign proceeded without further mention of Neshoba and states' rights. The Carter campaign certainly did not want to revisit the issue. The September spanking from the national media still hurt. An intra-campaign memo, written one day after Reagan's visit, offered talking points for the upcoming debate between the two men. His aides warned Carter to select his words carefully. His team wanted the president to remind the nation that Reagan was "not a racist but insensitive on states' rights."[75] The week before the election the president and his wife, Rosalyn, separately visited Mississippi; she spoke in Columbus, Mississippi, while the next day her husband campaigned in Jackson. It was not enough. The press added Mississippi to the Reagan column just after 7 p.m. Central Standard Time. Statewide, he edged President Jimmy Carter by just 1.33%, or 11,808 votes. Reagan easily carried Neshoba County with 57% of the vote.[76]

In the years to come, however, political opponents could not let go of his visit. The target proved too tempting. By 1988, a two-term presidential civil rights record now existed for assessment, providing a toll for appraisal that had not been possible in 1980. For some, the memory of the "states' rights'" episode served as a preview of the subsequent indifferent attitude of the Reagan-Bush administration regarding civil rights. Revisiting Reagan's Neshoba speech, however, did entail some danger. Any reexamination of his words involved engaging the local and national memories of the region. For politicians who did not possess the linguistic skills of Reagan, the tactic could boomerang as it had for President Carter.

In 1988 Democratic presidential candidate and three-term Massachusetts governor Michael Dukakis could think of no better place to campaign in Mississippi than the Neshoba County Fair. While still trailing vice president and Republican nominee George Bush in the state, Dukakis nevertheless possessed high hopes. The Democratic candidate had gained four percentage points in Mississippi in six weeks in the summer of 1988 and by the beginning of August stood at 43% of likely voters.[77] Some believed that Mississippi could possibly return to the state's more traditional place as a Democratic mainstay. The positive gain in Mississippi also excited the Dukakis camp since the governor's campaign scored a distant third in the Mississippi Democratic primaries to Jesse Jackson and Albert Gore, Jr.[78]

Dukakis purposely arranged his schedule so that his Neshoba appearance would fall on August 4, the twenty-fourth anniversary of the 1964 discovery of the bodies of the three murdered civil rights workers. A strong speech at a site in Mississippi that possessed such historical political significance would aid him not only in separating his Neshoba visit from Reagan's but also by clearly distinguishing his civil rights record and the record of the Reagan-Bush administration. To Dukakis, the entire situation looked like a win-win.

Before the speech, Dukakis openly declared to his campaign staff that his visit would be significantly different from that of Reagan. He planned to confront directly the words of the president from eight years earlier and simultaneously use the opportunity to express a new direction for race relations in the nation. He hoped that media coverage of his speech would remind the country of Reagan's 1980 words and as a result place Bush in an uncomfortable crossfire.

Not everyone in the Dukakis camp possessed the same level of excitement as the nominee. Similar to the frustrations of the Reagan campaign, the story of the intra-camp struggle concerning what should be actually written within the Neshoba speech revealed strong conflict. Some in the Democratic nominee's campaign possessed an understanding of the racially charged national atmosphere concerning the 1964 murders and argued strongly that any visit to Neshoba must include a mention of the events of Freedom Summer. Dukakis speechwriters Victoria Rideout and James Steinberg campaigned for a direct reference to the 1964 anniversary. They realized that to appear at the Neshoba County Fair and not mention the civil rights murders would certainly become a focus of negative national attention. Donna Brazile, a black political operative in the Dukakis campaign, agreed and supported a direct reference to Schwerner, Chaney, and Goodman. Others also warned Dukakis not to ignore the murders. Susan Estrich, co-chairman of the Dukakis campaign, wanted the men mentioned, as did Arkansas governor Bill Clinton.[79]

Others just as strongly disagreed. Late in the evening before the Neshoba visit, Dukakis communications director Kirk O'Donnell told Rideout, Steinberg, and Brazile that the 1964 subject remained off-limits. The three did not give up. The next morning on the airplane to Mississippi, the censored trio took their case to and received support from Paul Brountas, the co-chairman of the 1988 Dukakis campaign. He told the Massachusetts governor he did not see how he could avoid the issue, in either good conscience or skillful political judgment. Dukakis agreed. Therefore, a late addition to the Neshoba speech included a linkage from the dark Mississippi past of 1964 with the mid-1970s Boston struggle over school desegregation. Dukakis planned to mention only the similarities, then emphasize each area's progress since the respective events, and finally state that constant advancement remained imperative. All seemed settled, and the plane landed in Mississippi.

The demands of placating local white expectations soon changed the speech once again. After landing in Meridian, Mississippi, and perhaps as an omen of potential problems, Dukakis's limousine suffered a flat tire on the way to Neshoba.[80] In a different vehicle, Dukakis sat next to Mississippi secretary of state Dick Molpus for the forty-five-minute drive. The Mississippi politician stressed that the Democratic nominee should steer clear of any mention of the 1964 murders. Other locals soon chimed in as well. Estrich recalled, "honestly I think it was a van driver or a local volunteer, said to him 'don't say that' no one wants to be reminded of that."[81]

At the last minute, literally a few miles from the gates to the Neshoba County Fair, Dukakis discarded the prepared—and thrice-altered text— and therefore any mention of the slain civil rights workers. Whereas Reagan eight years earlier had added words to please a local audience, Dukakis edited his remarks for the same reason. To a crowd estimated at between three and twelve thousand, he gave a twenty-minute speech in which he outlined his plan for the presidency.[82] Dukakis attacked Reagan's fiscal irresponsibility, attorney general Ed Meese's legal problems, foreign policy troubles with Manual Noriega and Iran, and promised a "real" war on drugs.[83]

The story of Dukakis at Neshoba is not about what he did say, but instead about what he did not. He relegated the issue of civil rights and the anniversary of the discovery of the three slain Freedom Summer volunteers to a mere two sentences. The Massachusetts governor declared his support of civil rights and concerning the anniversary Dukakis stated, "Here in Mississippi, you know the importance of equal rights and civil rights. Especially today I say to all Americans, not just here in Neshoba County, but all over America, we've got to work together to bring down the barriers to opportunity for all our people."[84] Dukakis did not mention the events of 1964. Estrich regretfully recalled, "He [Dukakis] ignored us, the team that was trying to help him, in favor for what a local said about the sensitivity to the subject."[85]

As many staffers had feared, the only national news gained from the trip to Neshoba was Dukakis's failure to mention the 1964 murders on the very anniversary of the events. National newspapers—working within a racially charged national recollection of the murders and only too aware of the significance of the date—quickly reported Dukakis's blatant anniversary-day omission of any mention of the slain Schwerner, Chaney, and Goodman.[86] The *Los Angeles Times* wrote that Dukakis's "mention of civil rights was but one brief line in the middle of a 20-minute speech." The paper continued, "His only reference to the anniversary was an oblique one, telling the crowd that 'especially today I say to all Americans . . . let us work together.'" An article in the *LA Times*, which also reported the internal campaign debates, reported that Dukakis's black Mississippi state chairman, Mike Marshall, who had been announced to the media that day, was not introduced during the appearance. "Instead," the *Times* article observed, "Dukakis was accompanied by his state coordinator, who is white."[87] One author concluded that Dukakis remained silent at Neshoba because the Democratic presidential nominee feared a racial political backlash, similar to what occurred to Carter eight years earlier.[88]

Other newspapers cited Dukakis's lack of attention to the 1964 murders. The *New York Times*, *Chicago Tribune*, *Washington Post*, and *Clarion-Ledger* remarked on the omission and stated, "Dukakis defended the decision not to talk about racial politics. He said he preferred to address economic issues, the 'fundamental issues' in the South today."[89] The *New York Times* headline read, "At a Fair in Mississippi, Dukakis Plays Politics in Black and White" as underneath a picture of the candidate a caption declared, "Mr. Dukakis, speaking to an almost entirely white audience 24 years to the day after three slain civil rights workers were found under a nearby earthen dam, made only a passing reference to the problems of minorities."[90] Andrew Rosenthal of the *New York Times* stated that Dukakis toned down his speech from a more liberal message he had given recently to the National Urban League in Detroit.[91] One local newspaper, again with a nod to the local white audience, did not report the omission of the 1964 murdered civil rights workers.[92]

One Dukakis aide lamented that the national media provided only negative coverage of the Massachusetts governor's trip to Mississippi.[93] Similar to Reagan's experience, however, the attention paid to the subject did not linger. As the general campaign continued, Dukakis's numbers in Mississippi began to slide. The racially charged Willie Horton commercials and subsequent accusations and subsequent debates with Vice President Bush quickly filled the newspapers. The Massachusetts governor did not have to defuse the Neshoba issue as Reagan did, but he also did not reap any Mississippi reward. Bush carried the state with 60% of the vote and Neshoba County with 68%.[94]

Reagan left office the same year as the twenty-fifth anniversary of the 1964 murders. New scholarship and a successful Hollywood film, *Mississippi Burning*, focused renewed national attention on the killings.[95] Simultaneously, early evaluations of Reagan's presidency arrived on bookshelves. Some writers began to characterize but not necessarily reexamine the 1980 Reagan visit. The Neshoba speech became a rallying point for criticizing Reagan's presidential civil rights policies. In other words, his "states' rights" remarks became an indicator of his perceived indifference regarding racial equality. So important was this new criticism that an entirely new story concerning the origin of Reagan's campaign emerged in the national media, asserting that Reagan began his official race for the White House in Mississippi. Reagan's formal campaign actually began on Labor Day, 1980, in Liberty Park, New Jersey.[96] To be fair, Neshoba was his first stop after the Republican convention, not the official kickoff of his campaign. No paper, however, described the Mississippi visit as the official campaign kickoff in 1980. Other cities attempted to claim that honor. For example, one story to report the campaign kickoff incorrectly that year was the *Chicago Tribune* of August 19, which detailed Reagan's Chicago visit to present a speech to the Veterans of Foreign Wars and claimed the honor of being the official starting place to the 1980 presidential campaign.[97]

Ironically, one of the first incorrect attributions of Neshoba as Reagan's launch came from Jesse Jackson in 1987. While speaking at Harvard University in 1987, Jackson declared that Reagan began his 1984 presidential reelection campaign in Neshoba County, Mississippi. Jackson continued with this assertion in 1988 while campaigning for Dukakis. The August 5, 1988, *Chicago Tribune* quoted segments of Jackson's speech to the National Urban League in Detroit: "Throughout the campaign, Mr. Dukakis resisted the temptation to appeal to our baser instincts." Jackson continued, "He didn't launch his campaign in Philadelphia, Miss., with the KKK standing in the background endorsing him, as Reagan did."[98]

Jackson's angry accusations in 1987 and 1988 do not match his words during and after his meeting with Reagan in 1980.[99] The *Chicago Tribune* at the time did not mention any discussion of the Neshoba trip of three days earlier or any overt Jackson anger about Reagan's use of the term *states' rights*. Reagan again returned to Chicago in late August 1980 to address the Veterans of Foreign Wars. An undated internal campaign briefing paper read in part, "Reagan last visit here into the black community generally produced favorable press. The veterans should be very receptive."[100] If Jackson or the media possessed any great anger over the Mississippi trip, it is unlikely that a Reagan campaign memo, sensitive after Neshoba, would say otherwise. Jackson's late change in narrative is not hard to understand, however. By the end of Reagan's presidency, his opponents had almost eight years of civil rights policies to examine. The speech in Philadelphia. Mississippi, thus became an easy example to exploit for the president's seeming lack of interest in black America.

Besides Jackson's contributions, the 1988 campaign contained other incorrect accusations concerning campaign origin. While covering the Dukakis Mississippi trip that year, the August 4 *Clarion-Ledger*—followed the next day by the *New York Times*, *LA Times*, *Chicago Tribune*, and *Washington Post*—either stated that Reagan had begun his 1980 campaign in Philadelphia, Mississippi, or quoted declarations by Jackson stating that Reagan had begun his campaign for president at the Neshoba County Fair.[101] The 1980 editions of the same newspapers did not report such a claim.

The false story soon moved from newspapers to published scholarship. Carl T. Rowan's *Breaking Barriers: A Memoir* in 1991 contains an interesting exchange that occurred late during the Reagan administration between the author and President Reagan. Rowan states that he asked the president why he would begin the 1980 general election campaign from Neshoba considering the history and memory associated with the location. According to the author, Reagan replied, "I don't even remember that I did that." His confusion is understandable; the president could not remember what never happened. Over the years, numerous scholars have uncritically accepted the story, including Kenneth O'Reilly in *Nixon's Piano: President's and Racial Politics from Washington to Clinton* (1995), Jeremy Mayer in *Running on Race: Racial Politics in Presidential Campaigns, 1960–2000* (2002), Jere Nash and Andy Taggart in *Mississippi Politics: The Struggle for Power, 1976–2006* (2006), and Joseph Crespino in his *In Search of Another Country: Mississippi and the Conservative Counterrevolution* (2007). Craig Shirley's 2009 *Rendezvous with Destiny: Ronald Reagan and the Campaign that Changed America* defends Reagan against charges of racism but in doing so includes the "nasty insinuation" from liberal columnist Paul Krugman that Reagan began his campaign in Neshoba.[102] Not all newer works subscribe to the false origin story. Andrew Busch's 2005 work, *Reagan's Victory: The Presidential Election of 1980 and the Rise of the Right*, states that the 1980 general election campaign possessed no "clear" starting point. Historical works examining the 1980 presidential campaign that were published prior to 1989 do not include the false origin story.[103] By the time Reagan died in 2004, the incorrect campaign-origin narrative had gained a firm hold on Reagan historiography. Many newspapers and newsmagazines printed the fabrication as fact in remembering Reagan. In the months and years that followed, newspapers, editorials, and magazines have continued the trend.[104]

On a hot 1980 Mississippi afternoon, a Reagan speech converted a crowd of thousands. His choice of words, however, worried millions. In the days that followed, he survived by using the same language skills to answer national concerns. Therefore, Reagan rhetorically satisfied entrenched local and national audiences that contained far different perceptions and memories of the 1964 murders. Subsequent attempts by others to revisit the issue succeeded only in creating a false narrative regarding the origin of his campaign. The episode demonstrates the importance of memory as well as Reagan's ability to make his audience serve his needs.

While campaigning for reelection in October 1984, Reagan stopped in Gulfport, Mississippi, where a crowd of forty thousand greeted him. In response to a question regarding the possibility that the state might possibly become a future site for the dumping of nuclear wastes, Reagan responded that he would never do anything against the will of a state, "having been a governor myself of a state, I believe in states' rights."[105] Although just four years and less than two hundred miles from Neshoba and all its potent memories, no one printed a word of criticism.

2 / "A Noble Cause"

Twenty-Five Years of Consistency in Reagan's Vietnam Rhetoric

> "Those who in the 1960s and early 70s saw no virtue in anything America did and nobility of purpose on the part of North Vietnam cannot of course accept any story about that war which doesn't follow that theme. Indeed they can't accept the truth let alone a fictional version of it."
> —**Ronald Reagan, 1979**

> "He was, as you know, a famously optimistic man. Sometimes such optimism leads you to see the world as you wish it were as opposed to how it really is."
> —**Ronald Prescott Reagan, 2004**

On August 18, 1980, Republican presidential candidate Ronald Reagan spoke to the Veterans of Foreign Wars national conference in Chicago, Illinois. The speech came amid "Defense Week," a self-proclaimed campaign strategy organized by the Reagan political team. The VFW gathering offered another opportunity for the candidate to point out what he perceived to be weaknesses within the foreign policy and domestic veteran programs of incumbent president Jimmy Carter. Additionally, the Reagan team hoped to maintain momentum from a well-received earlier address to the American Legion. He stood on solid political ground with veterans; ever important for an orator, Reagan knew and liked this audience. Throughout the years, his conservative messages had traditionally played well to military crowds. He could almost predict which lines would earn polite clapping and which would receive triumphant applause.

Reagan felt comfortable on the subject of foreign policy. Unlike economic and social issues, it seemed, foreign policy did not contain so many complex levels. The Cold War offered a simple story line. His lifelong and well-documented hatred for communism easily identified allies and enemies.

For Reagan, foreign policy could be summed up in basic black or white elements, right or wrong, good guys or bad guys, us versus them. With the official campaign launch not happening until Labor Day, the VFW remarks offered an opportunity to reach the nation early. Chief pollster Wirthlin realized the importance of the Chicago speech. He reminded Reagan in a campaign memo that the assembled VFW crowd was not the only audience listening. Millions of Americans would hear pieces of the speech.[1]

In Chicago, Reagan took the stage and basked in the glow of a VFW presidential endorsement, the first given in eighty years by the organization. He stood at the podium and smiled and nodded to the assembled crowd of over five thousand as they greeted him with cheers and applause. He had first addressed a VFW national conference in 1975. Now, five years later, his words and ease of delivery mirrored his comfort level, and the assembled veterans interrupted the speech many times with cheers of approval. The message was vintage Reagan. In full campaign mode, Reagan talked of the value of military preparedness, the need for an increase of conventional forces, the danger of Soviet expansion, and the necessity of a strong stance against world terrorism. He shared his core beliefs with a time-tested rhetorical rhythm repeated for decades from earlier speeches, newspaper commentaries, and radio addresses.

In his comments, Reagan expressed his discontent with the current state of military affairs and soon turned his remarks to the Vietnam War, specifically describing the veterans of that conflict. Given that only five years had passed since the end of US involvement, for millions of Americans the subject remained a raw nerve. Additionally, for public office seekers, the war could best be described as a political liability. In 1980, many in the nation could only too easily replay the mental image of the past twenty years: death and protest, followed by defeat, with the shameful recollection of helicopters fleeing from a roof superimposed over it all.

Reagan knew the pain associated with the war, but as at so many times in his life, he rhetorically moved forward. The direction did not surprise his aides and longtime supporters. Since the early 1960s, even prior to the March 1965 introduction of American combat troops, Reagan often shared with anyone within earshot his personal beliefs on the subject of Vietnam. His convictions did not follow any contemporary polls or national trends; quite often, they ran against them. Instead, in both public speeches and private correspondence, regardless of national feelings of patriotism or protests, he consistently echoed the same message. He was a devoted hawk on the war, dismissed any talk of a Vietnamese civil war, and portrayed the conflict as but one part of a broader struggle against world communism. He stressed that the twenty-year conflict was when it happened and remained at the time of his address a noble cause. Reagan frequently described the veteran as an innocent warrior betrayed by a government that would not allow victory, going on to say that lack of vital federal support further denied those same soldiers the deserved title of hero. He consistently compared Vietnam with other less divisive and more gloriously remembered wars in US history. Finally, Reagan did not encourage debate over American involvement and asserted that many of the protestors served as dupes of America's enemies.

An examination of almost twenty years of pre-presidential speeches, press conferences, interviews, radio broadcasts, newspaper columns, and both public and personal letters reveals that Reagan seldom deviated from his stance concerning American military involvement in Southeast Asia.[2] He constantly visited the subject both as a private citizen and as a politician. In his long political engagement prior to 1980, Reagan had articulated these same core themes concerning Vietnam in hundreds, if not thousands, of talks to various individuals and groups, having been the primary speechwriter for those events himself.

Reagan did much more than write and speak during those early years. Not yet in the California governor's mansion a year, he pushed the Governors' Association to pull the organization's support for how Johnson managed the war. He openly called for a more serious application of American military power. To Reagan it remained simple; if a situation was serious enough for a nation to commit troops to resolve it, the application of war should be total. In the 1960s Reagan continually called for the closing of Haiphong Harbor, an amphibious invasion of North Vietnam. He also defended the bombing of Cambodia and wanted to keep the possible threat of nuclear weapons viable. His support was personal as well as political. For years he wore a POW/MIA bracelet bearing the name of the missing Marine Captain Stephen Hanson, only finally taking it off in 1973 when officials declared Hanson dead. He hosted prayer breakfasts and receptions for returning soldiers. The veterans appreciated his support and often rewarded Reagan with battlefield trinkets. He even went as far as personally delivering flowers to the wife of a soldier serving in Vietnam. The husband knew of Reagan's support and asked the governor to express a gesture to his wife of how much he loved and missed her. Of course, California in the 1960s did not serve as a bastion of Vietnam War supporters. Many citizens strongly disagreed with his words. At the swearing-in ceremony for his second term, protestors defiantly waved Viet Cong flags.[3]

In October 1971, Reagan traveled to Southeast Asia on behalf of President Richard Nixon. He visited Taiwan, Singapore, Thailand, South Vietnam, South Korea, and Japan. While in South Vietnam, he held a working lunch with President Nguyen Van Thieu and reiterated America's pledge not to abandon the country. In a personal show of support, Reagan changed the Vietnam security protocols that insisted he travel everywhere by helicopter. Instead, despite a bombing campaign recently initiated by the Viet Cong, he traveled by motorcade. His words and actions made such an impression with the South Vietnamese president that later when Thieu traveled to the United States, he visited with Reagan in Los Angeles.[4]

Thus through both actions and words, Reagan's association with and support for Vietnam remained consistent. He repeated a simple Vietnam narrative over and over again, regardless of national attitude or audience. The 1980 VFW speech served as just another opportunity in a long line of venues. In Chicago, Reagan may not have suffered any uncertainty about his words, but the same could not be said of his support staff. Similar to feelings generated in the days prior to the Neshoba visit, assistants worried about the speech. The initially prepared Chicago remarks, penned mostly by Reagan, contained his customary references to Vietnam. A nervous aide, aware that the words could generate controversy within a presidential race, removed the passages. Reagan reviewed the speech and found the deletions. As he had done so many times in the past he reached in his pocket, produced a pencil, and in the margins added to, and in his mind no doubt improved upon, the prepared words. Once again, the themes he reiterated that August evening echoed many of his previous comments dating back to the mid-1960s.

In the August 1980 Chicago remarks, Reagan shifted any blame for the loss of the Vietnam conflict away from the veterans and instead pointed a finger at elements within American society that had been duped by the enemy. "They had a battle plan," he said. "It was to win on the city streets of America and in our news media what they could not win on the field of battle. As the years dragged on, we were told that peace would come if we would simply stop interfering." He continued with another oft-repeated theme: "There is a lesson for all of us in Vietnam; if war does come, we must have the means and the determination to prevail or we will not have what it takes to preserve the peace. And while we are at it, let us tell those who fought in that war that we will never again ask young men to fight and possibly die in a war our government is afraid to let them win." Reagan then shifted his attention to the Vietnam veteran's place in American society and history: "It is time that we recognize that ours was, in truth, a noble cause. We dishonor the memory of fifty thousand young Americans who died in that cause when we give way to feelings of guilt as if we were doing something shameful, and we have been shabby in our treatment of those who returned." Reagan linked these soldiers to a proud American military tradition: "They fought as well and as bravely as any Americans have ever fought in any war. They deserve our gratitude and respect." The assembled crowd of veterans enthusiastically cheered his Vietnam words. Reagan left the stage to a standing ovation.[5]

As they had earlier in Mississippi, Reagan's comments echoed far beyond a conference in Chicago. Afterward, many Americans leapt to their feet as well as to their typewriters, some to cheer and some to complain. That night, his Vietnam remarks led the NBC nightly news broadcast.[6] The following day the *Chicago Tribune* reported incorrectly that Reagan opened his campaign in Chicago "with a resounding defense of the Vietnam War" and stated that when the candidate asserted that never again should the American government lack the commitment to win a war, "he earned his loudest and longest accolades for a standard speech line."[7] With the description "a standard speech line," the national newspaper recognized Reagan's habitual repetition of an oft-quoted stance concerning the Vietnam War. The *New York Times* reported the former governor's words that feeling shame toward American actions in Vietnam brought dishonor to the men who died in the conflict. The paper described the former governor's remarks as "a strong tribute to Vietnam veterans who took part in what Mr. Reagan called 'a noble cause.'" Reagan's future biographer Lou Cannon, who at the time wrote for the *Washington Post*, reported that Reagan's line concerning lasting commitment to future wars "brought most of the 5,000 to their feet."[8] Coverage spanned the nation, as the *LA Times* detailed the speech and subsequent reaction. Reagan's words echoed for days, and as late as August 25, the *LA Times* published letters, both positive and negative, regarding the candidate's Vietnam defense.[9]

Not everyone in the nation, however, wanted to hear a new version of the Vietnam War. Many citizens remained reluctant to entertain a new interpretation of the conflict, especially from a right-wing politician. Reagan remained the very type of person, many argued, who had pushed for the war to continue. As a result, anger festered and grew in equal measure with those who approved of his message. White House press secretary Jody Powell provided a glimpse of the coming battle. When pressed for a response to Reagan's line describing Vietnam as "a noble cause," he replied tersely, "I will leave his statement without comment to the judgment of the American people."[10] Powell believed the comment a gaffe and also believed the nation would see the phrase the same way.

Rowland Evans and Robert Novak detailed in the *Washington Post* how Reagan rewrote the "noble cause" portion back into his remarks after an aide had removed the words. Both men provided a nod to Reagan's consistent rhetorical pattern when they wrote, "the great majority of those

voters need no reminder of where he stands. They know. For many others, however, the reversion to Vietnam reopens old wounds beginning to
heal." Evans and Novak added that Reagan aides were "appalled" and that
the candidate's habit of "telling it like he feels" demonstrates his "inability
to understand the automatic and highly emotional reactions" of voters.[11]
The reaction reveals that for many, including some Reagan supporters, his
stance regarding Vietnam was not yet reflected by a great deal of the nation's consciousness.

The fallout from the Chicago remarks continued for over a week. The
August 22, 1980, *LA Times* included a political cartoon of a uniformed
skeleton standing in a hard rain with the caption, "'Vietnam War a noble
cause.'—Reagan." Syndicated columnist Jimmy Breslin wrote a story concerning death in Vietnam underneath the Reagan quote, "America's mistake
in Vietnam was not entering the war, but failing to win it."[12] On August 24,
the future Reagan chronicler Haynes Johnson argued in the *Washington
Post* that Reagan's recent language did little to change the opinion of many
in the public who possessed concerns surrounding his candidacy. Of the
Chicago remarks, he wrote: "It wasn't just his references to Vietnam; it
was the defiant way he courted controversy over one of the most painful
episodes in the American experience." He concluded by repeating Reagan's
convictions that the North Vietnamese successfully utilized propaganda
inside the United States and that a fearful federal government betrayed
the American soldier by denying a real commitment to victory. "Reagan
couldn't let it lie there undisturbed. He deliberately stirred the fires with
the old trigger words."[13]

Anger at Reagan's remarks was not just limited to the national press
or nervous Reagan supporters. Irate citizens wrote letters to newspaper
editors. One Vietnam veteran called Reagan a "war-monger" and stated
that, "the Republican candidate thinks he can woo Vietnam veterans
to his cause with a few platitudes and obvious rhetoric." Another letter
stated that if Reagan truly believed Vietnam a noble effort then "what a
comment on his intelligence." The *LA Times* printed an editorial from
former Marine Captain Frank McAdams. The Vietnam veteran stated,
"A noble cause, Mr. Reagan? I would call it a horrible experience."[14] The
criticism stung. Considering the other events of August 1980, Wirthlin
offered a sober warning. He discovered that the "noble cause" comment
inflicted more damage to Reagan's campaign than anything else that entire
month.[15] Even the most casual political observers easily recognize that
statements and promises announced on the campaign trail often contain
the political shelf life of a mayfly. Candidates-turned-winners quickly
encounter reality and temper their language and thus their expectations

of fulfilling those promises made during the intense battle to gain their office. Reagan observers knew better. Others quickly realized that regarding Vietnam, he meant exactly what he said. Unlike Neshoba, however, the campaign did not need to engage in damage control. Economics and other campaign topics soon pushed the Vietnam remarks to the periphery. The words generated an intense but brief fire, not unlike political flash paper. Supporters and opponents alike acknowledged the comments as standard Reagan fare. Reagan's long-standing consistency on Vietnam indicated to all that his version of the war would continue to be an issue if he gained the White House. As a result, each accordingly praised or protested in unison.

Reagan's VFW speech and the subsequent reactions to it provide a window into how millions of Americans responded to his Vietnam rhetoric. His Chicago speech offered desired vindication for many veterans of the conflict who shared his sentiments and wished for a new narrative concerning the war. Reagan's words, however, simultaneously caused anger in millions of others who feared the loss of the reality of Vietnam in a sea of pleasing but unrealistic presidential prose.

After the war, Americans heard from the commander in chief regarding Vietnam. Other presidents did not completely ignore the subject. For example, President Richard Nixon in March 1974 declared a "Vietnam Veterans Day." That same year, President Gerald Ford focused an entire Veterans Day speech on the Vietnam vet and described the soldier as the "forgotten hero." President Jimmy Carter declared a Vietnam Veterans Week to coincide with Memorial Day in 1979 and dedicated Veterans Day of that year to Vietnam veterans.[16] None of these men, however, could come close to Reagan as champion for the Vietnam veteran. Not content with just the occasional moment, and regardless of location, he provided a constant cadence of Vietnam rhetoric. Reagan's long commitment virtually ensured that he would make similar but more substantial gestures once in the White House.

With his 1980 election to the presidency, Reagan achieved the vast power of the bully pulpit and an attentive national audience. Never before in his life had he possessed the size and scrutiny of such a congregation. He had a new opportunity to make a difference. Electorally he had defeated Carter with a landslide, 489 to 49. By sheer percentages, however, he only achieved 51% of the popular vote. Some politicians might have exercised caution with such results, but not Reagan. He continued frequently to repeat his personal Vietnam convictions. To him, winning the presidency did not mean a lowering of the volume. The job simply presented another setting in which to broadcast his version of events and individuals. No longer limited to radio or newspaper syndication, he now possessed a national stage. Presidential proclamations and presiding over memorials now joined the familiar arsenal of speeches and letters. Speechwriters worked hard to mirror what had been said before. The power of the Oval Office combined with absolute media attention allowed the new president to reach a broader audience and to offer his version of the conflict and his image of the veteran consistently. Reagan's timing, as was so often the case, remained impeccable.

By the beginning of the 1980s, most Americans agreed that the Vietnam War remained a colossal blunder. But as the years passed and the nation moved away from the actual heat of conflict, millions stood ready to embrace a new interpretation of the men and women who served in Southeast Asia. The passage of time softened the sharp edges of anger. New images generated concerns and replaced old prejudices. A change in the national mood had begun, but progress remained painfully slow. Many believed it unfair to continue to let the Vietnam veteran flounder in the backwash generated by anger at the war itself.[17]

World events, news coverage, commemorations, and academic research also played a role and offered new information to consider. The 1975 fall of Saigon and the subsequent displacement and deaths of millions in Vietnam caused many to reflect on the sacrifices of the veteran. The 1978 Vietnamese invasion of Cambodia and subsequent 1979 fighting with China offered credibility to those who subscribed to the domino theory arguing that the Vietnam War was but one part of a larger struggle against communist expansion.

Domestically, during the late 1970s and early 1980s, newspapers, magazines, and academic presses printed sympathetic depictions of the relationship between Vietnam veterans and post-traumatic stress disorder, Agent Orange, and homelessness. Motion pictures such as *Coming Home* and *The Deer Hunter* echoed the same sentiment. The planning, construction, and completion of the Vietnam Veterans Memorial reminded millions of Americans of the soldiers' sacrifice in Vietnam. In 1983, PBS released the critically acclaimed thirteen-part documentary *Vietnam: A Television History*. Through such a prism, pity replaced anger. Americans began to separate the soldier from the conflict.[18]

As fate would have it, a master storyteller now received his mail at the White House, and some in the nation now slowly began to accept what he had been preaching for years. Reagan arrived with a handwritten Vietnam script, perfected from twenty years of conviction and repetition. And he found a receptive audience.

As with so much of what historians call the Reagan Revolution, there is much debate about how much Reagan personally directed from the White

House. The argument is not only between partisans but is a real question of how much a president actually affects the society he governs. The 1980s Vietnam veteran reevaluation is no different. To be sure, Reagan did not awaken one day and pronounce that he, alone, would change how Americans perceived the veteran. What he did do was greet each day as a new opportunity to repeat what he had said so many times before. In regards to the new image of the Vietnam veteran, Reagan stood as *the* right person at the right time. The messenger met the moment. To be sure, Presidents Nixon, Ford, and Carter had spoken of the sacrifice of the Vietnam soldier. Occasional utterances at ceremonial events, however, could not match the Reagan record. No other president could have influenced such a change because no one else possessed such consistency on the subject. In three parts, his twenty-year narrative combined with the power of the presidency and joined with a nation ready to rethink the place of the veteran in their society. Many Americans stood ready; they only lacked a leader to show them the way and provide a push. Critics could argue that as a smart politician, Reagan sensed the coming change and simply moved to the forefront with a hope of earning political credit, but such a stance ignores his personal commitment and his consistent Vietnam themes. His rhetorical pattern clearly demonstrates that Reagan would have kept repeating his Vietnam narrative regardless of the atmosphere of the country. The nation joined in lockstep with Reagan, not the other way around.

Once in Washington, Reagan did not need the recent memory of Chicago to remind him that Vietnam remained a controversial issue. He knew he could not afford to be unreserved on the subject. If he did, he knew that he could possibly pay a political price as his opponents would play upon the fears of many Americans who still harbored suspicions that Reagan stood as nothing more than a far-right cowboy. As a result, the first few months in office, he carefully picked his spots and utilized subtle language to put forth his argument. He knew a brief mention in the right place could produce a lasting effect, but when an opportunity presented itself for a bolder approach, Reagan did not hesitate to seize it. As his administration continued, the new president increased his discussion of the war and the veteran. Year by year the tempo increased, the rhythm repeated, the opportunities expanded, and the volume grew louder. The rhetorical crescendo continued so that by 1988, the cadence of Reagan praising the Vietnam veteran had become simply part of what Americans expected from him.

Easing into a subject, however, did not mean that Reagan wasted any time. He had only been president a few moments when he uttered his first presidential Vietnam comment. In the very first speech of his administration, his inaugural address, Reagan repeated an old personal conviction that Vietnam deserved equal footing with past American military glories. Carter had not dared to mention Vietnam in his inaugural address four years earlier. Reagan embraced the opportunity. He spoke of Arlington National Cemetery and the rows of headstones that marked the final resting place for those who had sacrificed for freedom. He called each marker a monument to a hero. "Their lives ended in places called Belleau Wood, the Argonne, Omaha Beach, Salerno, and halfway around the world on Guadalcanal, Tarawa, Pork Chop Hill, the Chosin Reservoir, and in a hundred rice paddies and jungles of a place called Vietnam."[19] As thousands in attendance listened in the cold, and millions more watched at home, he served notice that Vietnam was no longer a taboo subject. He let the veterans know they now had a champion in the White House.[20] He wanted the citizens of the nation to connect the war with past military victories. No more did soldiers of that conflict need to bow their heads in shame because, to Reagan, those men and women had fought just as hard and nobly as any of their predecessors.[21]

During the 1980s, in public and in private Reagan continued his pattern of placing Vietnam beyond the status of a mere proxy American war or Vietnamese civil conflict. In a 1984 letter to the Vietnam veteran Robert Eastburn, the president wrote, "It is a cause that continues. . . . You did not lose a war, the war goes on. You were engaged in a battle of that ongoing fight for freedom and the battle was lost not by you who were fighting it but by political misjudgments and strategic failures in the highest levels of government."[22] Three years later, Reagan attended the Los Angeles World Affairs Council luncheon. During a question and answer session at the Century Plaza Hotel, he argued again that Vietnam remained but one step in a communist plan for global expansion. "Cambodia is another tragic example of aggression and occupation, imposed by Vietnam and backed by the U.S.S.R." Again and again as president, he discovered numerous opportunities to reassert his belief that the conflict in Vietnam represented but one battle in a worldwide struggle versus communism.[23]

Another consistent element in the Reagan language that continued into his presidency concerned the Vietnam War protestors. Still seeing them as dupes of America's enemies, he did not change his message as president but did soften his tone. He recognized the dissension generated by the war, but his messages left no doubt as to which side he believed right. He also employed what he perceived to be the past criminal actions of protestors to serve his administration's more immediate needs. On April 15, 1981, Reagan broadly invoked the image of the Vietnam War draft evader as he granted two presidential pardons to W. Mark Felt and Edward S. Miller. Both men had worked for the Federal Bureau of Investigation and had been convicted in November 1980 by a US district court for conspiracy and unlawful wiretapping against antiwar groups during the Vietnam era. As part of his rationale for issuing the pardons, Reagan stated that each man's actions served the best interest of national security of his nation during a time of war. In absolving the men of past actions, Reagan involved the memory of the Vietnam War protestors: "Four years ago, thousands of draft evaders and others who violated the Selective Service laws were unconditionally pardoned by my predecessor. America was generous to those who refused to serve their country in the Vietnam War. We can be no less generous to two men who acted on high principle to bring an end to the terrorism that was threatening our nation."[24] Reagan no doubt enjoyed the irony of utilizing the actions of the Vietnam War protestor to absolve the crimes of two FBI men of "high principle."[25]

Three years later in an address at the dedication ceremonies for the Vietnam Veterans Memorial Statue, Reagan recognized that differing opinions still surrounded the conflict and called for healing. The president revealed, however, which side had his support. "There's been much rethinking by those who did not serve and those who did. There's been much rethinking by those who held strong views on the war and by those who did not know which view was right. There's been rethinking on all sides, and this is good. And it's time we moved on in unity and with resolve—with the resolve to always stand for freedom, as those who fought did, and to always try to protect and preserve the peace."[26] He clearly stated that both sides of the Vietnam argument needed to follow the example set by the veteran in fighting for freedom and peace. In a much different context, that in which he sought aid for Contras, Reagan asserted that the protestors of the past erred in opposing the containment of communism. "Those who've been naive about the dangers of communism in the past, those who've been wrong about the nature of Communist regimes in Vietnam, Cambodia, Grenada, and El Salvador are uneasy now with their views on the Sandinistas and the freedom fighters. So, here is my prophecy: We're going to get the freedom fighters the help they need, and we're going to get it to them soon."[27] The use of words such as *naive* and *wrong* leave no doubt of his feelings toward the Vietnam-era protestor.[28]

Reagan persistently offered the other elements of his Vietnam story line as well, without any regard for their unpopularity. He echoed his long-held assertion that the American government had betrayed the soldier in Vietnam. In his understanding, the treachery usually surrounded the noncommittal nature with which the government approached the conflict and, as a result, denied the veteran final victory. He continued to discover innovative methods to sustain this conviction. In a March 1982 letter,

Reagan responded to Reverend F. Andrew Carhartt of Boulder, Colorado, and his concern that American involvement in El Salvador would soon become another Vietnam. Reagan wrote, "We have no intention of sending American combat forces there [El Salvador]. You spoke of the lesson of Vietnam. In my view the immortality of Vietnam was asking young men to fight and die for a cause our government had no intention of winning."[29] In another letter eight months later, Vietnam veteran Mark Smith of Kenosha, Wisconsin, thanked Reagan for his efforts to return pride not only to the Vietnam veteran but to the military service as well. Reagan returned the thanks and concluded of Smith's Vietnam military service, "Yours was not a failure, the failure was in a government that asked men to die for a cause the government was afraid to let them win."[30] In February 1983, he repeated the belief while speaking to the Conservative Political Action Dinner at the Sheraton Hotel in Washington, DC. One year later, he echoed the claim almost verbatim in a May 1984 Memorial Day speech honoring an Unknown Serviceman of the Vietnam Conflict.[31] On April 12, 1985, during a question and answer session at a dinner for regional media editors and broadcasters, he called a lack of commitment to victory "the great disgrace" of Vietnam.[32] Finally in May 1987, as the Iran-Contra scandal swirled around the White House, Reagan responded to a letter from Todd Thornton of Columbus, Ohio. In defending himself, Reagan simply repeated personal principles regarding Vietnam. He asserted that Congress, by denying funding to the Nicaraguan Contras, risked repeating the same mistakes as those during the end of the Southeast Asian conflict that deprived the nation an opportunity for victory.[33]

The final element of the oft-repeated Reagan Vietnam rhetoric also happened to be the most consistent in the 1980s: the language that defended and praised the veteran and painted the war as a righteous cause. As should be expected, both aspects remained inseparable. In his optimistic mind, the veteran answered the nation's call without complaint, served on the battlefield without shame, yet had returned home without proper recognition. Reagan simply could not understand anyone who would disagree with such a claim. Again, regardless of setting, Reagan consistently portrayed the Vietnam veteran as a hero fighting a moral war for freedom.

Reagan knew that to tell a good story and influence an audience the narrator needs a hero. He required a face for his rhetoric. Master Sergeant Roy P. Benavidez became that main character and stood as the example for the new narrative for three years. Early in his first term, on February 24, 1981, Reagan visited the Pentagon to present the Congressional Medal of Honor to Benavidez for his May 1968 actions of gallantry in Vietnam. The ceremony provided the president with a blank canvas on which to illustrate several of his Vietnam beliefs. In dramatic prose Reagan told the story of Benavidez. The president described how Benavidez voluntarily boarded a helicopter and inserted himself into a search for wounded and dead Americans after a fierce battle west of Loc Ninh, South Vietnam. Wounded six times during the event and under constant enemy fire, Benavidez continued to help locate the dead and wounded Americans while simultaneously fighting North Vietnamese forces. When enemy fire brought down the helicopter that had arrived to lift them to safety, Benavidez then aided in the rescue of the crew and established a defense perimeter. He protected incoming helicopters by calling in air strikes to suppress North Vietnamese fire. Benavidez aided the extraction of the wounded and dead and returned to the battlefield to continue the struggle. Later that day, he fought in hand-to-hand combat with the enemy. In total, he received credit for saving the lives of no less than eight soldiers. To Reagan, the story contained all the best "isms": volunteerism, heroism, and patriotism. He could find no better example of what he saw as the selfless valor of the American soldier in Vietnam.

At a February 24, 1981, Pentagon ceremony, President Reagan presents the Congressional Medal of Honor to Sergeant Roy Benavidez. Courtesy Ronald Reagan Library.

Reagan also knew better than to waste an opportunity. He realized the medal presentation to Benavidez offered an occasion to repeat many of his beliefs surrounding the Vietnam War. His introduction of the award recipient contained a brief suggestion that perhaps the sergeant's heroic story intentionally had been suppressed. "Thanks to the Secretary of Defense, Cap Weinberger, I learned of his story, which had been overlooked or buried for several years." He declared that American soldiers in Vietnam "obeyed their country's call" and "had fought as bravely and as well as any Americans in our history." He lamented that the veteran returned home "without a victory not because they'd been defeated, but because they'd been denied permission to win." He continued: "They were greeted by no parades, no bands, no waving of the flag they had so nobly served. There's been no 'thank you' for their sacrifice. There's been no effort to honor and, thus, give pride to the families of more than 57,000 young men who gave their lives in that faraway war. . . . There's been little or no recognition of the gratitude we owe to the more than 300,000 men who suffered wounds in that war."[34]

Reagan spoke of the humanitarian impact of soldiers' efforts in Vietnam. He reminded the gathered audience of the medical aid and education that the troops had shared with the Vietnamese people, the help in constructing orphanages and schools for the children of the nation, and the toys distributed. Reagan added that many soldiers provided winnings from poker games to the local people in order to help better their lives. He quoted the entertainer Bob Hope's praise for the humanitarian efforts of the American servicemen. Reagan concluded with a nod toward recent popular culture: "None of the recent movies about that war have found time to show those examples of humanitarianism."[35]

In Benavidez, Reagan found his Vietnam hero. The story of the soldier's heroism played well and provided a good description in which to grab the audience's attention and talk about Vietnam. The actions of Benavidez and the delay in the awarding of the citation provided Reagan with just the right props at precisely the proper time. The president seized upon the heroism of the veteran to illustrate his argument for proper recognition of the valor for those who had served in Vietnam. He returned to the account many times during his presidency, often suggesting hidden motives in the suppression of Benavidez's story.[36] The unexplained wait in the awarding of the medal provided Reagan a sinister example for a president advocating a thesis of American government apathy toward the Vietnam soldier.

Other opportunities offered a far grander stage than a Pentagon podium to speak of the heroism of Vietnam veterans. On May 28, 1984, Reagan spoke at the Amphitheater at Arlington National Cemetery during Memorial Day ceremonies honoring the interment of an unknown serviceman of

Relate to Soldier in True today?
No bus welcome home

the Vietnam Conflict. Although an election year, Reagan saw no reason to temper his rhetoric. Any added media coverage would only help him put forth his argument. Reagan repeated many of his Vietnam assertions. He talked of an absence of welcome home "speeches and bands," veterans "who were never defeated in battle" and "were heroes as surely as any who have ever fought in a noble cause." Reagan then spoke of the recent dedication of the Vietnam Veterans Memorial. "There was a feeling that this nation—that as a nation we were coming together again and that we had, at long last, welcomed the boys home."[37] Reagan called for a full accounting of those Americans missing in action. He offered questions about the life of the unknown laid to rest. "We'll never know the answers to these questions about his life. We do know, though, why he died. He saw the horrors of war but bravely faced them, certain his own cause and his country's cause was a noble one; that he was fighting for human dignity, for free men everywhere. Today we pause to embrace him and all who served us so well in a war whose end offered no parades, no flags, and so little thanks." Reagan closed with, "A grateful nation opens her heart today in gratitude for their sacrifice, for their courage, and for their noble service. Let us, if we must, debate the lessons learned at some other time. Today, we simply say with pride, 'Thank you, dear son. May God cradle you in His loving arms.'"[38]

The remarks were quintessential Reagan. Running for reelection, many politicians in his place would understandably have shied away from a controversial issue in such a solemn setting. At the very least, many would have safely concentrated on the unassailable story of the unknown. Not Reagan. The amphitheater served as just another stage to present his narrative. The thousands of rows of tombstones, representing to Reagan the best of America, presented the perfect backdrop. In addition, by 1984 Reagan himself detected a shift in public perception of the Vietnam veteran.

Beginning in his first year in office, many Americans let Reagan know they heard his words. Many appreciated his efforts to bring a new interpretation to the Vietnam experience, especially in the case of the veteran. These acknowledgments arrived often in letters as well as in invitations to events for veterans. On February 25, 1981, one day after Reagan presented the Medal of Honor to Master Sergeant Benavidez, he received a telegram from F. Andy Messing Jr., the founder of Vietnam Veterans for Reagan. Messing reported, "I want to advise you that I was flooded with calls praising your meaningful action and words yesterday. The award ceremony was an appropriate way to honor not only this heroic Special Forces soldier, but the over 2.5 million Vietnam veterans who fought for our country."[39]

The following month Jan Scruggs, president of the Vietnam Veterans Memorial Fund and one of the driving forces behind the Vietnam Veterans Memorial in Washington, DC, commented on the Benavidez award. He invited the president to a May 1981 memorial service for Vietnam veterans. He wrote, "I believe you share my interest in doing something to recognize, at last, the men and women who served their country with honor in the Vietnam War. Your feelings toward the Vietnam veterans, as recently stated in the Medal of Honor ceremony for Master Sergeant Benavidez, are my feelings, and more importantly, the feeling of the veterans, their families, and most of the citizens of the United States."[40] Already scheduled to attend a ceremony at the Tomb of the Unknown Soldier in Arlington, Reagan declined the invitation.

On March 20, 1981, a thank-you arrived from the American Legion. Reagan had met recently with seven Vietnam veterans who then reported to their comrades that "the President was deeply concerned about veterans." In April, Reagan received an invitation to attend the "Anderson Welcome Home Vietnam Veterans Parade" in Anderson, Indiana. In December, Jan Scruggs wrote again, this time to Nancy Reagan, "I want you to know how much that everyone involved with the Vietnam Veterans Memorial Fund appreciates having you as a member of our National Sponsoring Committee."[41]

Letters and invitations continued to arrive. In March 1982, Scruggs again thanked Reagan for supporting the Vietnam Veterans Memorial Fund and invited the president to the groundbreaking for the Veterans Memorial. The letter provided only one week's notice and Reagan did not attend. In June the president received an invitation to attend the dedication of a Vietnam Veterans Memorial in Massachusetts.[42] In December 1982, Reagan responded to a letter from Master Sergeant and Vietnam veteran Michael T. Henry, stationed at Keesler Air Force Base in Mississippi. The president wrote that the Vietnam Syndrome was fast becoming a problem of the past. He added that the country finally was beginning to reveal signs of recognition of the service of the Vietnam veteran and the nobility of the war itself. "They are at last aware of your sacrifice and are beginning to realize how worthwhile the cause truly was."[43] In May 1983, the Vietnam Veterans Project of San Francisco invited Reagan to the Vietnam Veterans Fair. In October, Scruggs again wrote and thanked the president for continued support of Vietnam vets. He once again invited Reagan to speak at the memorial; Reagan declined.[44]

Vietnam veteran–related invitations continued to arrive at the White House. In February 1984, Reagan received an invitation for a Vietnam memorial dedication in Sacramento, California, then another for March in Danvers, Massachusetts. A Scruggs letter in April invited the president to attend the interment of an Unknown Soldier from the Vietnam War. In May, a Vietnam veterans group from Rhode Island sent an invitation

to the president. June had invitations from Vietnam Veterans of Strouds-
burg, Pennsylvania, and the St. Charles, Illinois, chapter of VietNow, who
thanked Reagan for his words at the May 1984 service at the Tomb of the
Unknown by saying, "a lot of us needed that." July included an invitation
to Tujunga, California, and Vietnam veterans in Kokomo, Indiana, requested a Reagan visit in September.[45] In September 1984, Reagan flew to
Salt Lake City, Utah, to address the American Legion. He pointed out the
new patriotism sweeping the nation. Reagan provided a list of possible
origins, including the heroism of the Vietnam POWs who had returned
home and "said, 'God bless America,' and then actually thanked us for
what they said we had done."[46] By including the service of the veteran in
league with the dramatic 1980 hockey victory over the Soviets and the
Iranian hostage release, he matter-of-factly placed the sacrifices of the
men and women who served in Southeast Asia with other more recent
celebratory moments in America's past.

Reagan continued to point out the shift in perception. On May 7, 1985,
he signed Proclamation 5336 for Vietnam Veterans Recognition Day for
that year. The wording of that proclamation echoed the new unity the
president continually called for in his rhetoric:

> As President and Commander in Chief, I have been pleased to witness a
> new and abiding recognition of those brave Americans who answered their
> country's call and served in the defense of freedom in the Republic of South
> Vietnam. That recognition, figured in the Memorial the Federal govern-
> ment accepted last November as a permanent sign of our determination to
> keep faith with those who served in that conflict, is both the result and the
> cause of a new unity among our people. . . . [N]o one can withhold from
> those who wore our country's uniform in Southeast Asia the homage that
> is their due. Their cause was our cause, and it is the cause that animates all
> of our experience as a Nation. Americans have never believed that freedom
> was the sole prerogative of a few, a grant of governmental power, or a title
> of wealth or nobility. We have always believed that freedom was the birth-
> right of all peoples, and our Vietnam-era veterans pledged their lives—and
> almost 60,000 lost them—in pursuit of that ideal, not for themselves, but for
> a suffering people half a world away.[47]

That same day, twenty-five thousand Vietnam veterans marched in New
York City, showered by ticker tape and cheered by over a million people.
Other cities held parades to celebrate the Vietnam vet. In June 1986, two
hundred thousand Vietnam veterans marched in Chicago, another two

hundred thousand in Houston in May 1987, joined by General William Westmorland. Towns across America from California to Vermont held smaller parades.[48] Event organizers in Indiana, Maryland, New York, California, and Tennessee all invited Reagan to attend events related to Vietnam veterans. His consistent rhetoric in support of Vietnam veterans found eager ears and many who wanted to say thank you personally.[49]

Reagan's Vietnam rhetoric came full circle on Veterans Day, November 11, 1988, at the Vietnam Veterans Memorial. After eight years in office, he was preparing to leave the White House. He believed his presidency had been a successful one, a certainty greatly reinforced by the landslide election of his own vice president three days earlier. Reagan once again chose to use the occasion to echo numerous themes from past speeches concerning the Vietnam War and veterans of that conflict. To the assembled crowd, Reagan described the Vietnam veterans as gentle heroes: "we remember the devotion and gallantry with which all of them ennobled their nation as they became champions of a noble cause." Reagan then detailed the struggle of the Vietnam veterans to gain their rightful place among other heroes of America's past. "For too long a time, they stood in a chill wind, as if on a winter's night's watch. And in that night, their deeds spoke to us, but we knew them not. And their voices called to us, and we heard them not." He continued, "The night is over. We see these men and know them once again—and know how much we owe them, how much they have given us, and how much we can never fully repay. And not just as individuals but as a nation, we say we love you."[50]

Reagan recognized his impact. A year later he described the speech: "If I had to pick out one speech in 1988 that most represented what I had accomplished over my two terms in office, the . . . speech [of 11 November 1988] might be the one." He included, "One of the best letters I ever received as president was from a Vietnam veteran in Texas who said that I'd helped him hold his head up. If I did have anything to do with that, my entire two terms in office would be worth it."[51]

Two letters in the summer of 1988 are significant in explaining the connection between Reagan and the reevaluation of the Vietnam vet. John Wheeler, a Vietnam veteran and chairman of the Vietnam Veterans Memorial Fund, in June and July sent two letters to Fred Ryan, personal assistant to the president. Wheeler wanted to organize an event in which veterans could show their appreciation to Reagan and his wife. The letters reveal how many Vietnam veterans viewed the president as instrumental in promoting a national rethinking regarding their service in Southeast Asia. The first letter, dated June 9, 1988, detailed Reagan's efforts for Vietnam vets as governor of California, including the personal visits he often held with returning soldiers. Wheeler then wrote, "As president, Ronald Reagan led the efforts to turn people around the false image of Vietnam vets as people to pity. He helped us vets show America the truth; that Vietnam vets gave much to their country and have much to give in the decades to come." Later in the letter, Wheeler reminded Ryan of the president's programs for veterans, support of the Vietnam Veterans Memorial, and the 1981 awarding of the Medal of Honor to Sergeant Benavidez. He concluded, "There would be no Vietnam Veterans Memorial on the Mall if the President and First lady had not helped us." One month later, Wheeler again wrote to Ryan but included a copy of the letter for Edmund Morris, the recently designated Reagan biographer, saying, "Fred, could you pass this on to Edmund, for his use in research on his book on the President?" and later adding, "I am available to discuss this with Edmund if he wishes." Wheeler repeated his assertions of the June letter and concluded, "Many men and women who served in Vietnam are now contributing much to our country. The President and First Lady were instrumental in giving us the boost we needed so this could happen *as early as it has.*"[52]

Wheeler's letters, arriving at the end of the Reagan presidency, reveal a great deal. As a Vietnam veteran and chairman of the Vietnam Veterans Memorial Fund he, more than most, recognized the Vietnam vets' postwar struggles to gain acceptance. He acknowledged Reagan's contributions as governor and then as president to the national reevaluation of the Vietnam veteran. Wheeler reminded Ryan and Morris that in his opinion, without Reagan in the picture, the situation of the vet in American would be much different: there would be no memorial on the Mall, and any national reevaluation would have occurred more slowly. Additionally, Wheeler believed in Reagan's contribution so adamantly that he wanted the president's official biographer to know his thoughts.

Whether as governor, former governor, or president, Reagan's Vietnam War and veterans rhetoric did not alter. From 1966 to 1988, in both public and private communication, he consistently repeated many of his long-held convictions. To Reagan, Vietnam remained a noble cause equal in effort with past military forays and a part of a larger struggle versus worldwide expansionistic communism. War protestors possessed shallow convictions and served the interests of the enemy. He believed that the American government did not fully commit the power of the nation to the war or the support of the country to the American soldiers fighting the conflict and therefore denied them the chance for victory. Finally, Reagan contended that as a result the American soldier lost the opportunity for the rightfully earned title of hero.

During the 1980s, Reagan reconstructed the Vietnam narrative to a more pleasing description. His oratory contained moral props and nostalgic images that were vital for influencing a national collective memory surrounding the Vietnam War. The power of the presidency combined with Reagan's rhetoric and soon produced a certain acceptance of particular elements of his Vietnam language. Not everyone agreed with the new direction, however, and an opposing interpretation emerged, which tried to reply to the new Reagan-inspired Vietnam narrative.

3 / "Do We Get to Win This Time?"

Reagan, Rambo *and* Platoon, *and the Vietnam Veteran*

> "Rambo is a Republican."
> —**Ronald Reagan, 1985**

Reagan's Vietnam oratory quickly entered the political and social bloodstream of the nation. Television broadcasted his words, newspapers quoted his phrases, and supporters and opponents alike took notice. His language simultaneously produced celebration and concern that reflected the initial reactions to his August 1980 Veterans of Foreign Wars address.

Americans, however, soon began to hear his language echoed from a surprising source: Hollywood. Always looking for a profitable angle, those in the entertainment industry easily detected the shifting American mood regarding the Vietnam veteran, and projects changed to fit the times as a result. Many of the popular culture products of the decade no doubt pleased Reagan. The very existence of a market echoing Reagan's Vietnam language is in itself an indication of the effectiveness of his words. Many of those working in Hollywood had known Reagan or heard his Vietnam narrative for years either as personal friends or former constituents. Many actually pointed to his influence; others found irony that Hollywood found financial success in projects that essentially brought to life characters and imagery from Reagan speeches. In a way, Reagan exercised an influence over 1980s Hollywood not unlike that previous power he enjoyed as the Screen Actors Guild (SAG) president.

Depictions portraying the Vietnam vet as a sadistic baby killer or brooding drug abuser gradually faded. In their place emerged a new image, a more positive picture that included the elements of Reagan's account. Many films from studios soon began to echo Reagan, at times by directly repeating or paraphrasing some of his key doctrines, but this willingness to follow the president's lead could also be seen through subtle imagery, plot, characters, and themes. In other words, Americans could hear a Reagan Vietnam speech broadcast from Washington, change the channel or drive to a local theater, and then indirectly hear the same message. The film industry produced numerous formulaic projects concerning the Vietnam conflict that directly reflected Reagan's words. Television in the 1980s brought a more sympathetic Vietnam veteran into the nation's homes as each of the "big three" networks broadcast programming that reflected the changing imagery of the Vietnam veteran. Comic books too, long a staple of American popular culture, first dealt directly with the Vietnam War in the Reagan era. Caped crusaders, men in tights, and evil scientists took a backseat as the American soldier moved to the forefront of the narrative.

Positive Vietnam imagery did not dominate all productions. As with Reagan's VFW speech in Chicago, not everyone approved of the new reevaluation of the Vietnam War and its veterans. Less celebratory portrayals—some argued, more realistic ones—still found expression, but in far smaller numbers. Many artists responded to the president's imagery with their own Vietnam projects. The impact of their work, however, remained limited. To be certain, some of the projects opposing Reagan's Vietnam version also enjoyed financial and critical success, but for the most part these less positive portrayals did not earn blockbuster status as would so many of the productions that echoed his words. The new Reagan-influenced account proved too strong. As a result, those who opposed Reagan's rhetoric concerning the war actually and unknowingly followed his rhetorical pattern and aided in the continuing growth of the very atmosphere that allowed the reevaluation of the Vietnam veteran. As a result, the Reagan rhetoric fed a new paradigm that swept aside a great deal of the former language and by the end of the decade had successfully created a new and more positive image of those who fought in Vietnam. In subsequent years, for millions of Americans, this version would become an accepted collective memory.

Box office receipts and high ratings encouraged those who supported and those who opposed the Reagan language. The more negative productions earned more critical acclaim and industry awards; the more positive projects, however, possessed far more lasting influence through their message, merchandising, and their hold on the collective popular memory. More accessible to the American public, the more idealistic works echoed Reagan and reached deep into the nation's society. The sanguine Vietnam story line produced popular culture heroes expressed in such diverse items as movie sequels, toys, Saturday morning cartoons, coloring books, lunch boxes, Halloween costumes, and even pajamas. By the end of the decade, the Reagan supported story line seemed everywhere. In subsequent decades, it is these Reagan-influenced projects that millions remember when recalling the 1980s.

The momentum and course of the new Vietnam story line mirrored that of a large ship, changing direction at sea. The captain orders the crew to turn the rudder and through the propellers to adjust the speed. Initially, through sheer impetus, the vessel continues to drift in the original direction. The ship's crew make corrections for numerous variables: the strength of the wind, the power of prevailing currents. Slowly though, when all pieces are in place, the ship yaws onto the new course and regains momentum. An examination of 1980s Vietnam popular culture exposes just such a change in course. America was opening to new perspectives regarding the Vietnam veterans as Reagan first used the power of the presidency to introduce the nation to his vision of the war. The new narrative reached a crescendo in 1985, with his Vietnam rhetoric deeply entrenched in the national psyche. By 1988, Reagan's version of Vietnam had achieved general acceptance as the country moved forward on a new course. An entire generation, too young to remember personally the pain and suffering of the twenty-year struggle, therefore, learned about the war and those who fought in it through popular culture entangled with the rhetoric of Reagan.

Reagan's Rhetoric, Motion Pictures, and Vietnam

Perhaps no sequence of movies in the 1980s reflected Reagan's interpretation regarding the Vietnam War more clearly than that of the highly successful *Rambo* motion picture series.[1] The success of these films displays a parallel arc that exactly displays the impact and influence of the Reagan rhetoric. The first film in the series, *First Blood*, premiered in 1982 as the new Vietnam collective memory first began to materialize. It was based on a novel published in 1972, though the creators of the motion picture made dramatic changes in the original story to fit it better to the emerging expectations of moviegoers concerning the soldiers who served in the Southeast Asian conflict. As a result, in many places, the imagery of the Vietnam veteran in the film mirrored the rhetorical pattern of the new president. Reagan's influence also permeated the highly successful sequel *Rambo: First Blood Part II*. The motion picture was released as the new Reagan narrative reached a national crescendo not only in rhetorical regularity but also in national acceptance. Finally, in 1988, the failure of *Rambo III* symbolized the changing tenor of the Reagan oratory as Reagan prepared to leave office and Cold War tensions eased. In symbolism and syntax, the *Rambo* pictures, audience comments, and critical reviews resonated with many of the Reagan themes.

The first film in the series, *First Blood*, followed the trials of Vietnam veteran and Special Forces soldier John Rambo (played by Sylvester Stallone). In the beginning of the movie, Stallone's character arrives at the home of a fellow vet only to discover that his friend has died, a victim of cancer induced by the defoliant Agent Orange, widely used by the US military in the jungles of Vietnam. He leaves, dismayed and adrift. Soon accosted for his appearance by a small town sheriff Will Teasle (played by Brian Dennehy), Rambo escapes custody, flees to the nearby Pacific Northwest woods, and utilizes his military skills in nonlethal methods to defend himself against sheriff's deputies and National Guard troops. When he is flushed from the forest, only the timely arrival of his Vietnam-era former commanding officer, Colonel Samuel Trautman, keeps Rambo from destroying the entire town. The finale of the motion picture reveals Rambo hiding in a darkened gas station, surrounded outside by American soldiers and tortured within by personal demons. Suffering a complete nervous breakdown, he shouts a speech that resonates with many of the Reagan Vietnam themes. Rambo cries to his commanding officer Trautman, "Nothing is over. Nothing. You just don't turn it off. It wasn't my war. You asked me, I didn't ask you. And I did what I had to do to win. But somebody wouldn't let us win. Then I come back to the world and I see all those maggots at the airport. Protesting me. Spitting. Calling me baby killer, all kinds of vile crap. Who are they to protest me? Huh?" The rambling montage of emotions and words in the final scene echo many of Reagan's assertions.[2]

The story of the film's tortured production reveals the difficulty of finding a place for a Vietnam project prior to the 1980s. In 1972, David Morrell, a graduate student at Pennsylvania State University and later at the University of Iowa, successfully published his story of a tormented vet's battle with a small town sheriff. He sold the rights to the story to Columbia Pictures. Success on the written page did not quickly translate onto film, however. Unable to find a place for the product, Columbia Pictures soon yielded the rights, and Warner Brothers assumed control of the story. The studio attempted numerous times to move the film forward, even considering actors as varied as Paul Newman, Steve McQueen, and Sydney Pollack to play the title role. By 1981 the rights to the film changed hands again as Carolco Production took over the project and production began.[3]

To Morrell's dismay, the 1982 motion picture differed a great deal from the novel of ten years earlier. The book portrayed a cold and psychotic Rambo, more in line with the negative stereotypes of the 1970s. Soiled by the horrors of 1960s Vietnam, he finds himself locked in combat with the local sheriff who served in the Korean War, himself a product of the conformist 1950s. The book's plot follows each man as they join in a slowly escalating game of mortal conflict that climaxes with the death of both characters. Morrell wanted the narrative of the novel to mimic the gradual escalation of American involvement in Vietnam.[4] The producers of the *First Blood* film changed many aspects of the story in the hopes of making the main character more sympathetic and thus making the film more acceptable to movie audiences. Not coincidentally, making story elements more acceptable to the audience meant moving those elements to be more in line with Reagan's consistent message on Vietnam.

The main character, Rambo, received a new characterization. The psychotic and bloodthirsty vet instead became a tormented and vulnerable soldier. In an effort to generate sympathy, the producers added scenes not in the original 1972 novel, such as the early visit to the family who had lost a loved one to Agent Orange. The executive producer of *First Blood*, Andrew Vajna, recalled that "the book had an angry vet, the movie was about a lost vet, a victim of circumstances." Another change from the original book revealed how the surrounded veteran dealt with the deputies and soldiers sent to hunt him. In the novel, Rambo killed anyone who stood in his way, including at one point a young teenager hunting with his father. By the early 1980s, the country was ready for a new image. As a result, those involved with the *First Blood* film did not wish to portray the Vietnam soldier in such a manner. The director of the film, Ted Kotcheff, recalled years later that the idea for Rambo to use nonlethal force against his enemies came from the star of the movie, Sylvester Stallone. The actor also changed the original ending wherein Colonel Trautman killed Rambo, as Stallone wanted the tortured veteran to survive. He worried that if the main character died, then other beleaguered vets would perhaps interpret the ending as their only solution for peace and stability. Kotcheff also remembered that the test audiences agreed. Those groups hated the original ending and supported the survival of Rambo.[5]

Kotcheff explained the timing of the film. His words reflected not only the two-decade-long rhetorical pattern of Reagan but also real changes in the attitudes of millions of Americans brought about by an awareness of postwar events in Southeast Asia and domestic trials of veterans. "By 1982 I think the American public realized that the Vietnam veterans had been treated very shabbily, and there was a mood of guilt about it, and the Vietnam veterans were being used as a scapegoat for all their negative feelings about the war." Stallone agreed. "The message was we shouldn't be so hard on the bearer of bad news, these people were just doing a job, and I felt that at the very end of the speech Rambo gives about wanting to come back and he is America's child, 'I was just doing a job and now I cannot even get a job parking cars. What did I do wrong? I was just being patriotic.'"[6]

Morrell asserted that, "in his opinion," he believed the atmosphere of the nation did not have much to do with the success of *First Blood*. Instead, he suggested that the creative team simply "found the right ingredients" for a successful action film that would be "acceptable" to domestic and international audiences. His use of the word "acceptable" is telling, and perhaps contradictory. He dismissed the significance of the national mood but he agreed that for the film to succeed the country had to accept the project. The national mood notwithstanding, Morrell admitted that the film arrived at the beginning of an "arc in clear terms of Reagan identification and the mood of the country."[7]

Reflecting upon the changes to his book and main character, Morrell detected the slowly changing atmosphere surrounding the Vietnam veteran. He stated that the motion picture, through the use of nonlethal force and personal torment, worked hard to make Rambo a sympathetic figure while the novel had made no such effort. He added that the book, written as the war raged, stood as an antiwar message, but that the movie "was altered in such a way that a new theme emerges." The decision to make Rambo a more sympathetic figure "picked on" by local authorities changed the film to a more black-and-white account, more in line with the uncomplicated Reagan interpretation. "This movie is a story, now remember this movie came in just as the 80s were getting underway, 81 and 82, and Ronald Reagan, the Reagan years are about to go into full bloom, this is a Reagan, a Ronald Reagan kind of movie about healing the wounds of the past and teaching pride and patriotism." Although ambivalent about some of the changes made, Morrell was enthusiastic about the Rambo speech at the end of the film. He remarked that, while the original novel did not contain such dialogue, he thought the final speech "wonderful." He added, the speech "really spoke to a lot of veterans. I remember after the movie came out many veterans and wives of veterans I ran into at book signings and what have you came up to me and said 'You know, I wanted to thank you for this character because at least the film saved my marriage. He came back from Vietnam and never talked.'" Morrell expressed happiness that both the book and the film, although reflecting two different decades and two very different examples of tone, produced a new conversation surrounding those who fought in Vietnam.[8]

The critical response to *First Blood* revealed the emerging tension between the older paradigm of the Vietnam War and vet and the new evaluation reflecting the Reagan oratory. Roger Ebert, reviewer for the *Chicago*

Tribune, called a great deal of the movie "implausible." He noticed the addition of Rambo's final speech and added, "the screenplay gives Stallone a long, impassioned speech to deliver, a speech in which he cries out against the injustices done to him and against the hippies who demonstrated at the airport when he returned from the war, etc."[9] Janet Maslin, a critic with the *New York Times*, criticized the final speech, saying, "Mr. Stallone has almost no dialogue in 'First Blood'; a final sobbing speech, in which he explains why he has lashed out against the small town, has him sounding even more incoherent than the screenplay warrants." She echoed past stereotypes of the Vietnam veteran as she wrote, "The movie tries hard to make sure that Rambo will be seen as a tormented, misunderstood, amazingly resourceful victim of the Vietnam War, rather than as a sadist or a villain."[10] The film's review in *Newsweek* stated that in the early 1980s many in the mass media detected the emerging reevaluation of these returned soldiers but did not necessarily agree with the reassessment. The weekly magazine described *First Blood* as "a slick piece of manipulation, but not an altogether honorable one." While acknowledging that the local police force "provoked" the Vietnam veteran, it still described the Rambo character as a "psychopath." *Newsweek* recognized the various political messages contained in the film "by making the hero both a maligned patriot and a counter cultural loner." As a "macho fantasy" the film worked, "but by the time it comes to its sobering, let's-put-this-all-in-a-sane-perspective conclusion, one has a right to feel powerfully misused."[11]

Stallone's comments in a 1985 interview for the *New York Times* suggest that while *First Blood* contained some elements of the Reagan rhetoric, the release of the first film arrived at the infancy of the reassessment of the war and its soldiers. His words reveal that, during production of the 1982 film, the producers possessed no knowledge of any ongoing new evaluation of the veteran. "There's been a big change in the country's mood but we didn't know that then." The artists unknowingly worked within a newly emerging interpretation surrounding Vietnam veterans over which Reagan possessed great influence.[12]

In *Rambo: First Blood Part II*, which came out in 1985, the character returned with a vengeance. Three years after the success of the first film and after far more widespread public acceptance of Reagan's vision, the time for subtle messages was over. The sequel relied on the increasing strength of the vets' reevaluation and the national crescendo of the Reagan influence. Scholars in various disciplines have detected how the second film echoed more elements of the president's Vietnam language and how it clearly suggested a more conscious decision by the film's producers to mirror Reagan's version. A few scholars have even demonstrated how the reevaluation possessed

Approximately six months after the release of *First Blood*, President Reagan visited the Vietnam Veterans Memorial on May 1, 1983. Courtesy Ronald Reagan Library.

elements not uncommon to Reagan. No work, however, has detailed his consistent twenty-five-year rhetorical pattern or detailed how Reagan's language provided momentum for a new collective interpretation surrounding the Vietnam veteran that spanned the decade of the 1980s and how such as new version became in time a new collective memory.[13] *Rambo: First Blood Part II* depicted the US government now employing the skills of the former Special Forces officer to seek out American soldiers missing in action in Southeast Asia. The prisoners of war and the missing-in-action issue had gained a great deal of attention in the early 1980s. On numerous occasions Reagan had included the subject in his discussions of Vietnam.[14] In the sequel, the government has released Rambo from prison so he may seek out POWs/MIAs still listed as missing from the Vietnam War. If successful, the convicted veteran could earn a presidential pardon for his earlier actions. Thus, the film depicts the government as an ally during the first act, taking Rambo to a remote base in Thailand and equipping the former Green Beret with state-of-the-art equipment to aid in his mission. The filmmakers even utilized an overt symbol of the new cooperative relationship between the government and the veteran. On a bulletin board at the Thai headquarters, a smiling picture of Reagan is prominently displayed, easily discernable to Rambo and cinema audiences alike.

In accepting the mission and the subsequent help from the government, Rambo asks Trautman, "Do we get to win this time?" His former superior officer replies, "This time it is up to you." The exchange, like the Reagan picture, signifies a new connection between the Vietnam veteran and the American government. Unlike during the war, this time the soldier can count on the full support of Washington, DC. A US government official, Marshall Murdock, supplies the latest technical tools and weaponry and orders Rambo to infiltrate Vietnam, look for evidence of missing American servicemen, take pictures, and then return to an extraction point for evacuation. Afterward, teams of Special Forces would rescue any prisoners of war found. Unknown to Rambo, the mission is a complete farce. All of the camps are already known to be empty. The bureaucrats hope the veteran will simply take pictures of empty camps, thereby ending the domestic debate concerning the issue of POWs/MIAs. Hence, the film echoes Reagan and reminds the audience of his language regarding the lack of commitment of the government toward the vet in supplying a mission with no hope for success. It is significant that, in subsequent scenes and after the US government's deceit is revealed, Reagan's picture has vanished from the bulletin board. It would not do for an advocate for the Vietnam veteran to be seen as a party to his betrayal. Murdock, however, did not account for Rambo's tenacity. After completing his mission, he reaches the extraction point with a live American prisoner of war. Murdock orders the mission scrubbed and as a result betrays the veteran again, this time with Rambo mere inches from rescue.

Having been abandoned by the government for a second time, Rambo is tortured by the Vietnamese and then later by their Soviet allies. The film thus portrays Reagan's assertion that Vietnam remained a war against worldwide communism. Of course, Rambo escapes, kills dozens of Vietnamese and Soviet troops, frees the remaining POWs, and returns to confront the corrupt government official. As in the first, the second film ends with an emotional speech by Rambo demanding acceptance for Vietnam veterans. Upon being asked by his mentor Trautman what he wants, Rambo offers a poignant response: "I want, what they want, and what every other guy who came over here and spilt his guts and gave everything he had wants. For our country to love us, as much as we love it. That's what I want."[15] As the credits roll, the Vietnam veteran walks back into the jungle to search for more missing Americans. The entire film reads like Reagan:

the power of a final speech, the themes of a lost cause, the denial of victory, the betrayal of the fighting man by his government, the assertions of Soviet involvement, and the demand for acceptance.

The film cost its studio approximately $44 million to produce and amassed over $70 million during the first three weeks of release, bringing in more than $150 million domestically. The film eventually made more than $300 million worldwide.[16] Many vets and contemporary military servicemen alike enjoyed the film. Stallone was happy that the film helped to generate patriotism and acceptance for Vietnam vets.[17] Newspapers carried stories that many servicemen appreciated the motion picture's message concerning the issue of the Vietnam soldier and the topic of POWs/MIAs.[18]

Reagan loved the film, and the former actor recognized the power of popular culture to influence society. The movie echoed with so much of his Vietnam language, he might even have written the script. On more than one occasion he personally praised the film. In the summer of 1985, he generated headlines by placing *Rambo* as a possible instrument of American foreign policy. On the eve of the release of the American hostages hijacked to Beirut aboard Trans World Airlines Flight 847, he remarked, "I saw *Rambo* last night, and next time I'll know what to do." According to Stephen Randall, executive vice president for marketing at TriStar Pictures, the president's comments may have added fifty million dollars to the domestic box office.[19]

While Reagan cheered with audiences, others cringed in disgust. Morrell remembered that the Reagan comments hurt him professionally. His 1972 novel *First Blood* had been taught in high schools and universities since the early 1970s. The book had been recommended for the classroom because of the work's portrayal of civil disobedience. After Reagan's comments, however, numerous schools dropped the book. Independent bookstores reacted by pulling Morrell's works off the shelves and assumed the author "was part of a right-wing conspiracy." The author recalled, "I had some foul years there when I didn't have the support of the independent booksellers." He concluded that the owners of the smaller bookstores never discovered the differences in the Rambo novels and films because, "They didn't read the damn book."[20]

Regardless of box office success and in a similar fashion to *First Blood* three years earlier, critics and the Hollywood industry offered harsh responses to *Rambo: First Blood Part II*. The reviewers often attacked the very element of the picture that echoed the oratory of Reagan. Many columnists who heard Reagan talk continually of Vietnam knowingly cited the president. *Life's* critic, Loudon Wainwright, acknowledged that the film stood as a "revenge fantasy" for Vietnam veterans who "weren't allowed to win" but concluded, "I doubt that many people believe Stallone's cockeyed, comic book version of history." Wainwright then alluded to Reagan's comments about Beirut when he added, "The truth was enough to make anyone, even a president, long for Rambo and his avenging solutions."[21]

Richard Cohen of the *Washington Post* detailed similarities between the film and Reagan's vision. He mentioned the president by name. Cohen also linked the film to contemporary foreign policy issues and commented that the film's content might allow for a more aggressive American policy in Central America. In an article entitled, "Next: Rambo goes to Nicaragua?" Cohen observed that many Americans seemed to be buying "revisionists' history of the Vietnam War, complete with a stab-in-the-back theory." He wrote of the film, "the villains come right out of a Ronald Reagan speech: communists and Washington bureaucrats." He added that, in the film, the Vietnamese held Americans POWs because "they are evil, but not as evil as the Russians, who are—as it is said—the focus of all evil." Cohen in this statement alludes to Reagan's 1983 Florida speech to evangelicals when he declared the Soviet Union was "the focus of evil in the modern world."[22] Cohen then suggested a danger of revisionist history concerning the Vietnam War was that some in the Reagan administration might utilize the nation's mood to move into Nicaragua. He wrote, "There is little in 'Rambo' with which Reagan would differ. Like Rambo, he has the same enemies both here and abroad and, like Rambo, he seems to have learned only one lesson from the Vietnam experience; if he's going to fight, he's going to fight to win." He added, "Life is no movie, but lately the two are often confused."[23] Cohen's comments illustrate that, by 1985, Reagan's Vietnam language was firmly entrenched in the national consciousness but was, as well, a source for political backlash.

The *Washington Post* columnist was not alone in his worries over the popularity and power of Reagan's language on Vietnam and the possible policy spillover it might have into Latin America. More than once, especially in the early years of his administration, the president deflected questions that connected the two issues.[24] *Time* magazine concluded that many in the nation dreaded the influence the film could generate as "it reflects a growing anti-communists fervor and could help make military conflicts in Nicaragua or elsewhere more likely at home."[25] The Latin American connection would remain a constant among columnists discussing the revisionists' images of the Vietnam conflict.

The film affected critics harshly, but some got caught up in its popular appeal despite their best efforts to the contrary. *Ms.* magazine in August 1985 offered an appraisal of the film. The reviewer, Ari Korpivaara, not only detected tangible influences of the Reagan rhetoric in the film but also admitted that such frightful sentiments remained alluring. "*Rambo: First Blood Part II* is a hard movie to like. Its politics are atrocious—pure Reaganite revisionism: America could have won the Vietnam War if only our leaders hadn't betrayed our fighting men. Even Stallone's big speech— the country should embrace its Vietnam vets—is troubling, given the context of the film." Korpivaara lamented the attraction of the violence in the film but admitted that the motion picture's desire to "get even" worked well with audiences, as he confessed, "I loved it."[26]

Morrell also had such concerns over the character he had created and Rambo's impact on the national mood. Although he did not write the story for *Rambo: First Blood Part II*, he agreed to write the novel adaptation of the sequel. Concerned with a simplistic script, he added to the film's story line and wanted to provide Rambo with additional depth. Late in the novel, as Rambo flies the rescued POWs to freedom, he informs the exhausted men of all that they have missed during their years in captivity. Learning that Reagan now sits in the White House, one POW replies, "Well, holy fuck," to which Rambo responds, "Yeah, I said that many times." Morrell's novel continues: "And Rambo couldn't bring himself to tell them that Vietnam was about to change its name to Nicaragua. Or that the sound of John Lennon's 'Give Peace a Chance' had changed to the rattle of sabers."[27] Morrell's Rambo was hardly the thoughtless testosterone killer of the film. The novel adaptation sold well and later was serialized in a national newspaper. Morrell's references to Nicaragua reflected his own political sensibilities, and he later recalled that the book possessed a great deal of his own editorializing. Of the Nicaragua reference in the adaptation, he stated, "that's me . . . that's all me." The author was concerned over the Reagan revisionism of the Vietnam history and "that the kind of emotion the motion picture was trying to develop in its audience could eventually lead to something like going into Nicaragua." Morrell admitted that one reason he accepted the task of writing the novel adaptation of the second film "was to try to make sure some of these issues were balanced and a modest warning was being given."[28]

Other critics may not have mentioned Reagan by name but they nonetheless responded to the echoes of his rhetoric resonating in the film. Vincent Canby wrote in the *New York Times* that Rambo "does nothing less than rewrite history." He continued, "Even before he starts, the mission has been sabotaged by a lily-livered, pinko, bleeding-heart-liberal Congressman, representing the same people who lost the original war."[29] A few days later Canby wrote that the film is "not about the war as it was fought and as it came to an end ten years ago, but as it has come to look to the macho mind of today." He wrote that many films of the 1980s that dealt with Vietnam "restart the war that, they say, United States Government fuddy-duddies would not allow to be won ten years ago and, this time, score decisive, totally fictitious victories over enemies that frequently look more Chinese or Japanese than Vietnamese." Other critics echoed similar comments. Almost to a person they criticized the very elements of the film that Reagan voiced with consistency.[30]

By the end of summer 1985, Rambo had secured a place in American mythology. *Time* magazine, the *New York Times*, *Advertising Age*, and *Business Week* all reported the emergence of Rambo action figures, vitamins, replica weapons, message Rambograms, and numerous other items. The US Army had begun hanging Rambo posters outside recruiting offices in an attempt to lure enlistees. *Time* quoted Stallone as saying, "People have been waiting for a chance to express their patriotism. Rambo triggered long-suppressed emotions that had been out of vogue." In regards to the Vietnam veteran, "The vets were fed by a sense of duty. They wanted to come home and be heroes on their blocks. They're saying, 'We showed you we were worthy. We just want to be appreciated.'" *Time* pointed out the portion of the film that depicted Rambo betrayed by the government and called that section of the film "potent." *Time* even picked up on the Reagan rhetorical momentum and actually used a word repeated so often by the president: "The public's receptivity to tales that lend nobility to the Vietnam War has grown."[31]

Morrell later recalled the extent of "Rambomania" through a trip to Poland where he discovered to his surprise that many in the nation believed the film aided the Solidarity Underground group. Although the Polish government banned the film, members of the movement would watch smuggled copies of the film "in order to get themselves emotionally worked up in a confident fashion and would dress up with a bandana and go out and demonstrate against the authorities." In the opinion of some Poles, *Rambo* played a role in the withdrawal of the Soviet Union from Poland. Morrell added that he possessed pictures of the 1989 fall of the Berlin Wall where someone had painted "Rambo" on the Cold War barrier.[32]

As 1985 came to a close, *Rolling Stone* printed the annual year-end issue. Eagerly awaited by readers, the edition reviews the past twelve months of American culture. David Edelstein reflected on the impact of the *Rambo* films in "Somewhere over the Rambo." Kurt Loder wrote about the new patriotism sweeping the nation in the 1980s in "Jingo Bells: The Country Overdoes on Apple Pie and Baloney." Reagan's connection to the new national patriotism was unmistakable. His relationship to Rambo was obvious. Edelstein wrote that films like *Rambo* "want to go back and win the Vietnam War" and take America's mistakes in history "and spin it [all] into a nationalistic myth." He added, "The sad truth is that a lot of people get their politics from the movies—our president, for instance, who invoked the name of Rambo in the aftermath of the TWA hostage crisis." Loder added, "In 1985 there was a new patriotism among us, a great flexing of the national pecs. You could see it everywhere, from the Oval Office down to the local concert hall." He pointed to Reagan as the embodiment of the American moment. *Rolling Stone* printed that the second *Rambo* film "appealed to the quickening jingoistic sentiments of millions of Americans, including President Reagan, who referred to the movie in a verbal attack on terrorists."[33]

Stallone commented on the timing of the second *Rambo* film and *Rocky IV.* "We just happened to come along at the right time. This country has needed to flex its muscles again. You might say America has gone back to the gym." He added, "I think the intelligentsia should understand that this country now is functioning on emotional energy more than intellectual energy." When asked about all of the patriotism "whipped up" by Reagan, Stallone responded, "President Reagan has provided this country with a lot of incentives to feel better. When you think about what it was coming off of with the last three presidents, Reagan has been a godsend. The country's esteem is on the rise."[34]

Other national periodicals bore witness to Reagan's role in the reevaluation of the Vietnam veteran and the new patriotism sweeping the nation. *Newsweek* detailed the influence of the *Rambo* series and the resurgence in national patriotism in American popular culture. The magazine asserted that the new nationalism "started in the country beginning with the Bicentennial and crested with Reagan." The article remarked on the themes that ran throughout *Rambo: First Blood Part II*—betrayals of the Vietnam veteran, denial of victory, corrupt politicians, and the love of the veteran for their nation. The article also praised Stallone's sense of timing: "He taps the same wellsprings as Bruce Springsteen, say, or Ronald Reagan; he is a filmmaker to a damn mad blue-collar America that doesn't want to take it anymore." The article compared the Rambo character to past national icons such as the Minutemen, Davy Crockett, and Daniel Boone, declaring, "They are nearly as much a part of the symbolic furniture of Reagan's America as the president himself—a can-do America re-emergent, in his vision, from a can't do past." Stallone denied creating the new patriotism and remarked that his characters of Rambo and Rocky merely rode a wave of patriotism sweeping the country. "We're back to geopolitics on an even keel. We're not coming in there quaking, 'What do I do?' We're coming in as an equal."[35] Stallone's words mirror almost exactly the sentiment of a *U.S. News and World Report* cover story of one month earlier concerning the Geneva Summit between Reagan and Gorbachev. The cover photograph revealed a stern-faced Reagan sitting at his Oval Office desk gesturing broadly underneath the headline "Going In Strong."[36]

By 1985 Rambo and Reagan were speaking, it seems, almost in rhetorical lockstep. It was not by accident. Filmmakers altered Morrell's character to fit the times and produce a successful film. In doing so, they created a protagonist that echoed twenty years' worth of Reagan Vietnam language. Because of Reagan's rhetoric, the newspapers and magazines of the mid-1980s had no problem mentioning Reagan in the same sentence with Rambo. The media clearly detected that Reagan was a key element behind much of the patriotic momentum propelling Rambo into the nation's cultural consciences. All elements of the film were imbued with the fortieth president: over-the-top flag waving that many feared would generate jingoism, exaggerated and almost cartoon communist villains, a deceptive and inept federal government, and the ability to win wars that had once been lost. Years later when reflecting on Reagan and Rambo, Morrell remarked, "Well, he [was] an actor and he knew the value of props and images, so as long as he thought it served his purpose I could see him using that character [Rambo] as a way for people to identify his policies. It was a pretty clever method."[37] Mark Helfrich worked as an editor on the motion picture. He recalled the viewers' excitement to the wanton killing of the enemy while screening the picture. "Of course this was the Reagan era so I guess it was appropriate but it was wild." Andrew Vajna, executive producer of the film, recalled with laughter a personal letter and photograph sent from the Reagan White House. "Actually I have a photograph that was sent by Reagan where he stands in his jogging outfit and is holding up a [sweatshirt] that says 'Rambo is a Republican.'"[38]

Since the first two *Rambo* projects generated enormous box office profits, it did not take too long before production began on *Rambo III* with a release scheduled for May 1988. As with the earlier films, Reagan influenced the direction and success of the picture. The year 1988, however, was neither 1982 nor 1985. Whereas his language and arguments had aided the first two films, by the release of the third changes in the geopolitical climate had altered the Reagan rhetoric and as a result affected the environment and success surrounding the new movie.

Rambo III began with Rambo living and working in a Buddhist temple deep in the jungles of Thailand, his personal and professional battles left behind him. Colonel Trautman appears and asks Rambo to join him in providing military aid to the Mujahedeen rebels fighting the Soviets. Rambo refuses and Trautman undertakes the mission alone. Upon learning of Trautman's capture and torture by a sadistic Soviet colonel, Rambo changes his mind and leads a rescue mission allied with the Mujahedeen rebels. The Vietnam veteran rescues his former commanding officer, kills hundreds of Soviet troops, and along the way learns a little about the Afghan freedom fighters locked in a desperate struggle with occupying Soviet forces. Unlike the first two films, however, *Rambo III* does not engage the memory of Vietnam and focuses instead almost exclusively on an anticommunist message.

The film opened on May 25, 1988. Critics, just as they had done with the earlier films in the *Rambo* series, quickly denounced the motion picture, and this time, the box office receipts were not going to contradict them. The film did not succeed domestically; budgeted for 63 million dollars, an enormous studio financial undertaking in the late 1980s, the motion picture generated domestic profits of only a little over $53 million. The international market recouped the cost of the film with $135 million in ticket sales.[39] Compared to the success of the earlier two *Rambo* installments, however, Hollywood viewed the movie a failure. For his third portrayal of Rambo, Stallone won the flippant Razzie award for Worst Actor.[40]

It is important to note that the failure of *Rambo III* cannot be blamed exclusively on the production of a bad film. Two central reasons fostered disappointment in the project: its timing in relation to world events and its distancing of the plot from the Vietnam elements in Reagan's rhetoric. The film presented a narrative that many in America no longer recognized. By its release in mid-1988, the US domestic stage had changed a great deal from when it had welcomed *Rambo: First Blood Part II* in 1985 and the original *First Blood* in 1982. Additionally, with bad timing for Hollywood, the Soviet Union began to pull its troops out of Afghanistan several weeks before the film's premier, so the film's plot was then historically dated in portraying the immorality of the Soviet occupation of Afghanistan. Peter MacDonald, the director of the film, pointed out years later that the Russian withdrawal obviously "hurt the picture."[41] Furthermore, a thaw in the relations between the Soviet Union and the United States took place almost as soon as Soviet premier Mikhail Gorbachev rose to power in 1985, when Reagan and the new communist leader established a personal connection almost from the moment they first met in Geneva, Switzerland. Therefore, the three years between the second and third Rambo films contained a warming of the interactions between the two nations and a subtle change in the anticommunist rhetoric of the fortieth president. Reagan had not changed his stance on Vietnam, but he had changed in regards to the Soviet Union.

Reflecting on *Rambo III* fifteen years after the film's release, Stallone cited the changing political landscape and the personal relationship between the Reagans and Gorbachev as a key element in its failure. He lamented, "*Rambo III* unfortunately had some unlucky timing in its release date. I knew we were in trouble when Gorbachev came over and kissed Nancy Reagan hello." He concluded, "everybody was just so happy that the Cold War was basically over."[42] Stallone's memory served him well. *Time*, less than two weeks after the release of *Rambo III*, on June 13, 1988, carried a cover story that detailed Reagan's recent summit visit to Moscow. Displaying a large photo of the American president standing in Red Square and smiling with his arm draped tightly around the shoulders of Gorbachev, the banner headline quoted this hard-liner—the man whom many had come to view as the world's grand champion against all things communist—as saying, "I Never Expected to Be Here." Inside the magazine were pages of accounts of the "veteran anti-Communist" responding to the warmth of the Soviet people and the new relationship between the two superpowers. The magazine reported that Reagan "finds himself breaking out of his stereotype as an unvarnished foe of what he once called the 'evil empire.'" Gorbachev seemed to agree and stated, "As we see it . . . habitual stereotypes stemming from enemy images have been shaken loose." This new atmosphere between the two superpowers that possessed no "evil empires"—and a lack of "habitual stereotypes"—remained a foe that *Rambo*, mired in less progressive politics, could not defeat.[43]

The final reason for the film's failure at the domestic box office came from its choice of venue, the deserts of Afghanistan. The echoes of Reagan rhetoric concerning Vietnam that had permeated so much of the first two chapters of the film series and made moviegoers empathize so strongly with its themes and characters were absent in the third. The move to the desert took the story from the Vietnam War and veterans and placed audiences in a war for which they had no personal connection or tortured memories. Away from the tangled rain forest and recollections of Vietnam, the film then became more about Rambo and the Soviet expansionistic menace. While the struggle against communists' assimilation had long been a part of Reagan's language, by 1988 even his words no longer completely supported that stereotype. Critic Hal Hinson in the *Washington Post* detected as much: "To some extent in the first film, but especially in the second, Rambo was the articulation of unexpressed sentiments in the culture, a projection of some of our baser national needs. And in that sense the character may have served a useful mythic function." Hinson added that the filmmakers in *First Blood* and *Rambo: First Blood Part II* possessed a desire to respond to a national need for reevaluation concerning the Vietnam War, a desire the reviewer believed was missing in *Rambo III*. He charged that *Rambo III* was only about making money.[44]

Morrell, who once again wrote the film's novelization and added character elements to his creation as he did so, stated that the expense of the film
and a bad story played a key role in the failure of *Rambo III*, but he added
that the timing "was awful as the film came out almost to the day that the
Soviets decided to leave." He again returned to the idea of a demonstrable
Reagan influence throughout the 1980s in determining the subject matter
and the success or failure of all three Rambo films. Morrell described the
fading influence of Reagan in the failure of *Rambo III*: "As the 80s grew to
a close so did that mind-set."[45]

While the 1980s witnessed numerous Vietnam War projects from Hollywood that reflected Reagan's interpretation, not all the decade's projects
fell in line. Without doubt, not everyone enjoyed the new Vietnam narrative. Cartoon heroes spouting grunts for dialogue and settling old scores
with improbable body counts hardly passed for a serious treatment of the
Vietnam War. For many in Hollywood and around the country, the release
of the *Rambo* films portrayed the worst attempts to rewrite history, and the
fiction on film only mirrored the invented stories being broadcast from
the White House. In the midst of "Rambomania," other producers and
directors took it upon themselves to oppose Stallone's films—and with
them, Reagan's language. They would use the power of Hollywood to show
what they felt to be the real story of Vietnam. If, indeed, the nation really
stood ready for a reevaluation of the war, these individuals would work to
make sure that the country would remember realistically. Ironically, these
very projects, created in part to dispute Reagan's Vietnam, included the
very elements being disseminated by the White House.

One year after *Rambo: First Blood Part II*, Hollywood released another
imposing Vietnam epic, Oliver Stone's *Platoon*.[46] *Platoon* opened to a great
deal of fanfare. Described by the national media as well as critics as a more
realistic portrayal of the veteran's experiences in the Southeast Asian conflict, the producers of *Platoon* publicly distanced the film from the more
fantasy-laden *Rambo* series. *Platoon* included the horrors of war and less
than flattering imagery of some veterans. The purposeful estrangement did
not matter, however. In an unsubtle marketing move, the studio chose the
following tagline to promote the film: "The first casualty of war is innocence."[47] The film's central theme—an innocent young recruit is caught up
in a war he did not choose, the horrors of which he cannot escape, yet he
answered his nation's call—echoed the Reagan message contained in *Rambo*.
Stone did not know it, but his project existed within and therefore reflected
the very new Reagan-influenced interpretation he hoped to correct.

The story of Stone's quest to put his image of Vietnam on the silver screen
reveals the changing mood of the nation. He had shopped the idea of *Platoon*

around Hollywood studios for ten years. Early in the 1980s, he lamented to *Fangoria* that a "truthful" depiction of Vietnam had yet to be made. The magazine itself added, "Considering the national mood in the post-hostage era, it seems unlikely that any Hollywood studio would underwrite a reminder of that national tragedy."[48] Producer Martin Bregman recalled the initial problems in the late 1970s and recalled that Vietnam projects at that time were "still a no-no." As the country began to take a second look at the Vietnam veteran and as Reagan brought his two-decade-old rhetorical pattern to the White House, Stone finally found Hollywood receptive to his Vietnam project. He gained financial backing to the amount of $6 million through the British Hemdale Film Corporation. Domestic help arrived when Orion Pictures provided an additional $2 million. Thus, produced on a relatively minuscule budget of just over $8 million and originally released in only six theaters, *Platoon* quickly exploded across the nation and garnered over $137 million in domestic profits. The film also received numerous award nominations, among them eight Academy Award nominations including Best Picture, Director, and Writing. *Platoon* received Oscars for Best Picture, Film Editing, and Sound while Stone won a Director's Guild of America Best Director Award. Stone, in his Oscar acceptance speech, stated, "I think that through this award you are really acknowledging the Vietnam veteran, and I think that what you're saying is that for the first time you really understand what happened over there."[49]

Critics and moviegoers upset with the cartoon action of Stallone's Vietnam projects and Reagan's "noble cause" language latched onto the film, praising the picture and condemning what they described as recent revisionist history surrounding the war.[50] Vincent Canby in the *New York Times* added his voice to the critics praising the realism of the film and denouncing more recent treatments. He wrote that *Platoon* "is not like any other Vietnam film that's yet been made—certainly not like those revisionist comic strips *Rambo* and *Missing in Action*." Jack Mathews in the *LA Times* hoped that the film would "neutralize some of the romanticized notions of Rambomania."[51] Activist actress Jane Fonda also praised the realism of *Platoon* and rejected recent Vietnam films like Stallone's *Rambo*, describing that product as "revisionists cinema" that "obscures the truth." In a dig to the Rambomania then sweeping the country, she recalled that, during her days of protesting the Vietnam War, Stallone taught at an all girls' school in Switzerland. Fonda's comments also revealed she believed that, thus far, Hollywood had not examined the causes of the war and subsequent debates for and against American involvement. She compared *Platoon* with her 1978 film *Coming Home*. That film fit the 1970s stereotypical portrayal of the veteran and told the story of a

Vietnam veteran's difficulty in returning to civilian life. The actress stated, "*Platoon* explains *Coming Home*." Fonda concluded, "I'm still waiting for a movie that explains why we were there at all—why it all happened." Others noticed the lack of politics in the film and suggested the absence may have aided in gaining the film broader support.[52] The observation was almost certainly correct. *Platoon* did remain politically silent regarding the causes of the conflict, and in doing so, the film echoed Reagan's avoidance of any debate regarding the war.

Hollywood icons such as Woody Allen, James Wood, Brian De Palma, and Steven Spielberg praised the film. Author David Halberstam, who covered the conflict for the *New York Times* and, in 1972, authored the highly successful *The Best and the Brightest*, stated: "*Platoon* is the first real Vietnam film and one of the great war movies of all time. The other Hollywood films have been a rape of history."[53] Even Vietnamese refugees joined in approving *Platoon* at the expense of *Rambo*. The *LA Times* interviewed several former expatriates living in California. They universally praised the "dramatic accuracy" of Stone's work, although Yen Do, editor of Orange County's *Nguoi Viet Daily News*, wished for more on the experience of the Vietnamese people. Ultimately, however, despite that shortcoming, Yen Do concluded, "Yes, it is better than *Rambo*. We can be glad for that, can't we."[54]

Other news media celebrated the realism of *Platoon*. *Newsweek* and *Time* wrote glowing descriptions of the film. *Time* declared, "Oliver Stone is a muckraker disguised as a moviemaker" and added, "*Platoon* is still the most impressive movie to deal with the fighting in Vietnam." One month later, the weekly periodical dedicated an entire cover story to the film. The front of the magazine displayed a black background and in large white letters "*Platoon*: Vietnam As It Really Was." The lengthy story praised the realism of the film and described the motion picture as a "phenomenon." Interestingly, the magazine also included an interview with Dale Dye, a retired Marine captain and decorated Vietnam veteran who had served as technical advisor on the film. While the vet aided Stone in creating a project perceived by many reviewers to be answering the Vietnam revisionist histories of the 1980s, Dye agreed more with Reagan. *Time* reported that "Dye's politics, not surprisingly, are anti-communist" and pointed out that "he edited *Soldier of Fortune* magazine and unofficially trained Nicaraguan Contras." The magazine quoted the veteran: "My hope is that it [*Platoon*] will encourage America not to waste soldiers' lives in wars that it is not willing or able to win."[55]

Interestingly, many of the creators of projects that some critics had deemed "revisionist" joined in praising *Platoon* while simultaneously defending their own work. *First Blood* director Ted Kotcheff called Stone's work "absolutely brilliant." He defended his own work in that Rambo remained a "Frankenstein monster" created in Vietnam and that, as the director, he "certainly never saw *First Blood* as any kind of celebration of jingoism." Joe Zito, director of the first two Chuck Norris *Missing in Action* films, commented of *Platoon*, "Without question, it is the best war movie ever made." Of his own projects the director remarked, "I tried to make video games out of them, and audiences had to know that we weren't playing realistically."[56]

Not everyone enjoyed the self-proclaimed realistic portrayal of the veteran contained within *Platoon*. Chuck Norris himself disliked Stone's film. He carried a personal connection to the war as his younger brother, Wieland, died in Vietnam in the summer of 1970. He stated about his brother that, "in his letters he wrote about brotherhood and camaraderie. There wasn't anything about the kind of stuff that went on in '*Platoon*.'" The actor argued that the film resulted in "a slap on the face to all medal of honor winners" and worried that Stone's project could result in more "negative movies" about Vietnam. Finally, he concluded that communist nations would use the imagery of *Platoon* for propaganda. Norris's comments, unconsciously, revealed a mind-set that surrounded his own work on the subject of Vietnam, an attitude that supported a more fantasy-tainted portrayal of the war. "The thing is, there's so damn much negativity in the world. We face it every friggin' day. I don't want to have to face that when I go to the movies." He concluded, "I mean, jeez, if you want all that realism, if you want to be depressed, you can watch the news at night."[57] Stallone greeted *Platoon* with silence. He did not comment on the film or the criticism being leveled at his approach to Vietnam. When asked about his thoughts, one of his assistants answered, "He is busy getting into his character for *Rambo III*."[58]

Many Vietnam vets balked at *Platoon's* representation of the American soldier. Stone's vision appeared over the top, and for many he had squeezed every negative image and memory of the war into a two-hour film. The 1970s stereotype, it seemed, had returned with a vengeance. The *LA Times* reported that vets seemed equally divided according to political beliefs surrounding the war. Those who saw Vietnam as a "noble cause" did not support the film while antiwar veterans either supported *Platoon* or "condemn it for not taking a more overt political stand against the war."[59] Al Santoli, Vietnam veteran and author, stated, "I was insulted by it. In my division, we didn't burn down villages, we didn't slaughter villagers." Bob Duncan who served at the same time as Oliver Stone stated, "He managed to take every cliché—the 'baby killer' and 'dope addict'—that we've lived with for the past twenty years and stick them in *the* movie about Vietnam."

Another veteran added, "I hope this doesn't bring back those old depictions. God help us, I don't want to go back into the closet again." Keith Gustin, a Detroit vet counselor, declined to see *Platoon* but added, "I can watch the *Rambo* movies because that's Hollywood. I even liked it when he killed all those Russians. It was a catharsis."[60]

A year after *Platoon*'s release, Stone responded to the ongoing Reagan-influenced Vietnam reinterpretations. In the magazine *Film Comment*, Stone stated that the portrayal of war in films like *Rambo* and *Top Gun* looked "easy." That same year in *Positif* he declared that he made *Platoon* because, "I felt the truth of this war had not been shown."[61] In 1988, in *Cineaste* magazine, Stone recognized that the atmosphere in the mid-1980s allowed the production of *Platoon*. He suggested that the film would have been accepted in 1976 and 1984, but "it was probably most acceptable in 1986." That same year in *Playboy*, he repeated the assertion and added his hope that the work would answer other recent films that echoed imagery and rhetoric of the Reagan era. Of *Platoon* Stone stated, "It became an antidote to *Top Gun* and *Rambo*. It's an antidote to Reagan's wars against Libya, Grenada, and Nicaragua." He observed a rebirth of "American militarism" in the 1980s and called *Top Gun* an "essentially fascist movie."[62]

Other Hollywood figures agreed that the mid-1980s worked to *Platoon*'s advantage. Ashley Boone, an established figure in the marketing and distribution of film with successful stints at Twentieth Century Fox and Metro Goldwyn Mayer, stated in 1987, "If *Platoon* had been released ten years ago, people would have said, 'Don't remind us of our mistakes.' No one would have watched or cared. A lot of things with historical background are too painful to address when they're fresh."[63] Ten years later, Stone continued to recognize the box office success of Stallone's films and the subsequent imagery concerning the Vietnam veteran contained within each of his works. At the 1997 annual meeting of the American Historical Association (AHA) he recalled, "*First Blood* in 1982 and *Rambo* in 1985 were very successful. We can't forget them or their impact. It was especially difficult for an idea like *Platoon* to go up against the message these films were propagating."[64]

Attacks on *Rambo* and assertions of the "realism" of *Platoon* from columnists, actors, the creators, and scholars did not matter. In *Platoon*, Stone hoped to "save" the Vietnam experience and those who fought in it from what he perceived as unhealthy revisionist history. By concentrating on the innocence of the vet, the filmmaker unknowingly reinforced a key element of the Reagan rhetoric. The film did offer a counter perspective to the Reagan-driven new narrative. The opposing imagery, however, could only exist within the parameters designed by the more dominant interpretation. Stone and others declared *Platoon* more realistic and approached the memory of the war differently than *Rambo*. Both films, however concentrated on the experiences and innocence of the veteran. As a result, both contained key elements of the president's oft-repeated oratory. In continuing to present these same vital core themes, despite their surface differences and opposing political and philosophical stances, *Rambo* and *Platoon* both aided the ongoing national reevaluation of the Vietnam veteran and in subsequent years helped to solidify an emerging collective memory.

4 / Reagan, the Vietnam Veteran, 1980s Television, and Comics

"A crime they didn't commit."
—*The A-Team*, 1983–1987

In the 1980s American audiences did not have to drive to a local theater to hear and see Reagan's Vietnam story. In millions of living rooms across the nation the same description played every week on network television. A quick turn around the dial found likeable and laudable veterans serving as main characters on successful programs such as *Miami Vice, Hunter,* and *Rip Tide* on NBC and *Airwolf* and *Magnum P.I.* on CBS. All contained major or supporting characters that had served in the war. With the exception of *Magnum P.I.*'s debut in 1980, the other series arrived in 1983 and 1984 as the Reagan narrative took hold.[1] As the decade progressed, television executives—attuned to ratings, and thus, profits—responded to the reevaluation of the Vietnam veteran. Their recognition of a shift in the national mood allowed for character portrayals that had been impossible just a few years earlier. With Reagan championing such an image from within the White House, the negative stereotyping of the Vietnam veteran prevalent during the late 1960s and 1970s no longer fit the times and a more heroic representation took its place.

Entertainment television had already somewhat dealt with the memory of the war. No series, however, dealt directly with the subject. The creators of programs used the conflict only as background material or as a means of explaining the origin of a convenient villain. With one exception, perhaps, television ignored debate over the war. The long-running weekly antiwar series *M*A*S*H*—broadcast from 1972 to 1983—utilized the Korean conflict to criticize American action in war, generally, and in Vietnam specifically. In the series' landmark last episode, the writers provided a harbinger of future conflict as the script mentioned the 1953 allocation of American aid to the French in Indochina.[2] Like the brief mention of Vietnam in *M*A*S*H*, however, the war received no lasting examination on American television.

During the 1980s, the American people could not miss the new account. Each of the "big three" networks, NBC, CBS, and ABC, broadcast its own show bringing the war and the experience of the vet to the small screen in a way never before seen. Similar to the motion pictures of the time, Reagan could have written many of the scripts. Each series chose the safe route and ignored the controversy and politics of the war by concentrating on the personal trials of the veterans. As a result, Reagan's message discovered a weekly outlet into American popular culture and helped push the new interpretation of Vietnam veterans.

NBC's *The A-Team* began in 1983 and aired for four years. Created by Stephen J. Cannell Productions, the show became an immediate success when it debuted after the Super Bowl that year. Each week millions of Americans tuned in to follow the postwar adventures of the four likeable Vietnam veterans now turned private army-for-hire. The show opened with martial style music of a singular drumroll as a narrator stated in a crisp voice, "In 1972, a crack commando unit was sent to prison by a military court for a crime they didn't commit. These men promptly escaped a maximum-security stockade to the Los Angeles underground. Today, still wanted by the government, they survive as soldiers of fortune. If you have a problem, if no one else can help, and if you can find them, maybe you can hire . . . the A-Team."[3] With the blaring sounds of machine-gun fire the name of the program flashed upon the screen in military stenciled letters. Bullet holes that contained pictures of the show's stars raced across the credits. The rest of the opening consisted of a succession of explosions and gunfire from the series.

The blueprint of the series echoed the Reagan rhetoric in numerous instances. The series consisted of four Vietnam veterans innocent of an alleged crime. In keeping with the new interpretation, however, the crime did not produce images of My Lai or other wartime atrocities. Instead, the creators of the series fell back on a tried-and-true transgression: bank robbery. The soldiers had allegedly robbed the Bank of Hanoi under orders from a superior officer. Thus, in line with the Reagan language surrounding the Vietnam veteran, the men of *The A-Team* committed no crime and instead were manipulated by superiors. The team's subsequent escape found the innocent vets relentlessly pursued by the US government, a constant Reagan rhetorical foil for the failure in Vietnam. Throughout the series, reporters aided the veterans so that the A-Team received favorable media coverage and gained important intelligence to use in various missions. Reagan consistently blamed the media for their biased portrayal of the Vietnam-era fighting man. Accordingly, the assistance the A-Team received from newspaper reporters could also be interpreted as a news media attempt to apologize for inaccurate or unfair coverage of soldiers during the war. For a program to portray the media as honoring the actions of Vietnam vets reveals the extent of the reevaluation.

Although the show dealt with the soldiers' adventures after the war, Vietnam remained on the periphery. The conflict, nonetheless, maintained a constant positive presence during the series. The lead characters expressed respect and friendship for one another that had been earned in shared combat and sacrifice. They called one another by their previous military ranks. When in trouble, each would often evoke particular situations in Vietnam that would produce a solution. The team broadcast stories that played to the innocence and victimization of the veteran. In a November 22, 1983, episode the mercenaries aided a group of disabled Vietnam veterans bullied by a greedy land developer, showing the vulnerability and humanity of those formerly shown only in negative terms by the mass media.

The A-Team even returned to Southeast Asia. In the last episode of the fourth season, General Harlan Fulbright, the government official pursuing the team, tells them that the officer who could exonerate them for their alleged Hanoi crime was indeed alive and a prisoner of the Vietnamese. As they sought to rescue the officer, each reflected on their experience of the war through flashbacks. In a plot twist reminiscent of *Rambo: First Blood II*, the men discovered that the government official had tricked them and only wanted the team in Vietnam to rescue a child that may be his. Fulbright died at the end of the episode but not before uttering the line, "I never really thought you were innocent . . . until now."[4] By the mid-1980s in living rooms across America, millions of America could agree with Fulbright's words.

The pattern of reviews and ratings for television series mirrored the release of those motion pictures that echoed a great deal of Reagan. Millions of Americans loved the program while critics lambasted the series. The subject matter touched a nerve with many in the nation while other viewers scoffed at the revisionist themes. *TV Guide* called the program the "shrewdest idea for a series" and labeled one of the stars of the program, Mr. T., the "brightest newcomer" of the 1982–1983 television season. The same magazine would quote Mr. T. one year later. Describing his recent trip to the White House, when Nancy Reagan sat on his knee, the actor proclaimed, "I love America! I even love the Reagans! I might vote for 'em again, yes, *again.*" In less than a year the program rose to number two in the nation.[5] The show gained such popularity that Marvel Comics, the national leader in the comic book industry, briefly printed *The A-Team* comic. Toys, Halloween costumes, and even a breakfast cereal celebrated the characters.[6] *TV Guide* printed an article in May 1984 that revealed some of the program's biggest fans remained kids. The magazine reprinted children's letters from Gladwyne Elementary School in Gladwyne, Pennsylvania. One third grader wrote of the actor, Mr. T., "He prevents teenagers from taking drugs with Mrs. Reagan."[7] The very idea, however, that elementary school teachers would give such an assignment demonstrates the immense popularity of the program with the American viewing public.

Critics could not have disagreed more with the program's first four years of popularity. Robert MacKenzie, the *TV Guide* critic whose own magazine had praised the program, did not like the series. He recognized the Vietnam connection, describing the team as a "former Vietnam combat ensemble" and "soldiers of fortune with formidable skills," but he concluded, "There's something obsessive about the way this show glorifies destruction."[8] Mary Harron in the *New Statesman*, an English socialist magazine founded in 1913, acknowledged the elements of black and white truths surrounding the Vietnam veteran that were consistent in the Reagan rhetoric. She also perceived revisionist history surrounding the popular program. "The gradual assimilation of Vietnam into acceptable popular mythology, which began solemnly with *The Deer Hunter*, has reached its culmination with *The A-Team*." She argued that *The A-Team* remained "classic right-wing American populism—patriotic, macho, anti-authority." Harron expressed the same fears as were voiced by so many others, that Reagan's rhetorical attempt to alter the narrative regarding Vietnam could be utilized by the president to lead the nation to war in Central America. "America sailed to Vietnam on a sea of comic book fantasies, and this is how she wishes it turned out. The dreams are being rewritten, at the worst possible moment, as she drifts towards a Central American war." She concluded, "Vietnam hurt so deeply that personally I've never believed that they could whip up popular fervour for El Salvador. However, *The A-Team* is a significant fantasy. There's a new generation of young men watching television now; and as the polls show, the vast majority of Americans don't know which side is which in Central America, they won't be well equipped for telling the good guys from the bad."[9]

As the Reagan rhetoric continued and *The A-Team* popularity crested in 1986, Frank Bies of *TV Guide* wrote of the danger involved in rewriting the past for a more palatable present. The commentator, a Vietnam veteran, argued that the pendulum marking the place of the Vietnam veteran in entertainment television perhaps had swung too far from the criminal image of the 1970s to the untarnished heroes of the 1980s. He cited the half dozen popular programs and postulated that network television "focused on Vietnam vets as an excuse for TV violence" in the past. Bies wrote, "What a difference a decade makes. Ten years ago Vietnam vets were the scourge of prime time." He continued, "They invariably were cast as psychopathic bustouts and homicidal maniacs." Bies utilized a key term from the Reagan rhetoric to make his next point. "No sooner had the Nation begun acknowledging that Vietnam veterans performed honorably during the war than television conveniently recycled them into acceptable forms." He quoted William Broyles, also a Vietnam veteran and former editor at *Newsweek* magazine, who had recently penned *Brothers in Arms*, a book about his Vietnam experience. "It is an improvement," Broyles said, "I'd rather see television romanticize us than vilify us. Even if the characters function in complete ignorance of what we're like, or what it was like for us over there." Reagan's oratory almost never called for open debate surrounding the causes of the war or frank discussions about the reality of the hardships of combat. Broyles seemed to welcome such ignorance for it exchanged vilification for idealistic imagery and positive prose. Bies certainly recognized the emerging danger of the revisionist reevaluation of the Vietnam veteran but ended his observations with a simple hope for a more realistic future for Vietnam veterans in the entertainment medium.[10]

The A-Team ranked in the top ten for the first three years before a move to Friday nights in the show's last two years where it did not match well with two rising family sitcoms on ABC: *Who's the Boss* and *Growing Pains*. The actors complained that the writing became stale and the episodes predictable. The series ranked a still respectable thirty-first in year four, nowhere near, however, the stratospheric highs of the first three seasons. Marketing studies, audience polls, and thousands of dollars in research attempted to return the program to the glory of the previous ratings.[11] The format of the show changed in season five, as the A-Team stopped traveling the country and actually worked for the US government. The move did not resonate with audiences and the network canceled the show in 1987.

The demise of *The A-Team* followed essentially the same pattern experienced by the series of *Rambo* films. The television series premiered to high ratings one year after the release of *First Blood*. The program had reached the pinnacle of its ratings success the same year as *Rambo: First Blood Part II* launched Rambomania. The network canceled the show one year prior to the release of the disappointing *Rambo III*. Thus the broadcast success of *The A-Team* revealed the emerging Reagan-influenced national second look at Vietnam veterans in the early 1980s, the national acceptance of the new narrative surrounding Vietnam and the veteran by the middle of the decade, and the continuing power of the president's rhetoric as Reagan changed his language in subject and tone.

No sooner had *The A-Team* left the airwaves in 1987 than American television turned its attention again to the Vietnam War with CBS's *Tour of Duty*. Similar to *Platoon's* reaction to *Rambo*, the new series attempted to distance itself from *The A-Team* and bring to the small screen a more realistic view of the war. While *The A-Team* dealt sparingly with the actual Southeast Asian conflict, the new program tackled the war directly. Issues such as drug abuse, sadistic officers, confused morality, and impossible missions ordered by faraway and faceless leaders were central to many episodes. Several characters died as the writers wished to maintain as much realism as possible. Episodes also detailed the soldier's post-Vietnam experiences as many were discharged and returned home.[12] However, the program followed the rhetorical pattern of Reagan by ignoring the politics and rationales surrounding the origins of the conflict and by design fully concentrated on the collective experiences of the people involved in fighting it.

L. Travis Clark, two-tour veteran of Vietnam and co-creator of *Tour of Duty*, recalled years later that the focus of the series remained relentlessly on the soldier. He believed that the American public would respond more favorably to a character-driven series as opposed to constant explosions and gunfire or a program that debated the conflict. "I didn't want to do a war piece. I wanted to do a story about people together, having to live together, under harsh conditions, different races, different parts of the country." He wished to produce "a relationship piece with the war as a backdrop." Clark concluded, "Because if you get to know a character, and get to like that character, you will want to follow that character to see what will happen to him. And relationships are much more interesting than shooting and being at war."[13]

Tour of Duty possessed the distinction of being the first television series actually to concentrate on the Southeast Asian conflict in a weekly drama format. Debuting in the fall of 1987, the show portrayed the men of Company B in 1967 Vietnam. Since the series planned to represent the experience of the veteran, the cast consisted of over twenty regulars, an unusually large ensemble for a weekly television series. The group of actors represented the diversity of American society. The soldiers consisted of a "by the book but down to earth" lieutenant, an "everyman" sergeant, a drafted pacifist and war protestor, a gung-ho All-American soldier from middle America Iowa, a tough Puerto Rican from the Bronx, and two black soldiers. Executive producer Zev Braun of *Tour of Duty* remarked at the time, "If anything we don't have enough Blacks. It was a Black Man's war at times. We have what I consider an absolute minimum of Blacks, Hispanics and Asians in the show, and I hope we have more." *TV Guide* also listed the complexities of the large cast in the 1987–1988 fall preview issue.[14]

Don Merrill, a reviewer with *TV Guide*, enjoyed the program. "*Tour of Duty* is CBS's serious, well-intentioned effort to do a series about the Vietnam War. It is carefully scripted and is directed and performed to achieve as much authenticity as is acceptable on broadcast television." He described each week's stories as "good ones" and "the men who play the soldiers do so with conviction, so that we come to feel for them and with them." He suggested that the overall theme of the program remained "the futility of war." Merrill addressed the critics who suggested that the lack of profane language, overt drug use, or gore hurt the reality of the series by suggesting that the addition of these elements perhaps would lend more reality to the show but would reduce the likelihood of its being broadcast into the country's homes. "Let's be grateful to executive producer Zev Braun [who] has been able to be so effective by indicating, rather than emphasizing, realities of war that many families would not consider appropriate for a living room audience."[15] Merrill's statement echoed the very type of method that allowed the Reagan language surrounding the Vietnam War to achieve success in helping to create a new national perspective regarding the veteran. The nation seemingly no longer desired to see the harsh negatives of the Southeast Asian conflict broadcast into their homes. However, a television show that diluted the horror of war for mass consumption while simultaneously broadcasting the innocence and heroism of the Vietnam soldier remained welcome.

L. Travis Clark recalled the initial response to the program: "It got great reaction. We were up against the *Cosby Show* when we first started, which was the number one show in the country." Clark added that the network placed *Tour of Duty* in such an unsympathetic timeslot for counter-programming. "But it worked for there were people who wanted to see it. The numbers weren't great but they were enough to let it stay on the air."[16] For the programs' three-year run, the ratings remained strong but never broke into the top twenty rated programs.[17] The show did gain a steady and loyal audience. One young Marine stated, "I'm interested in Vietnam, and the show really gets into the kinds of problems—black-white, officers versus men—that we have."[18]

Others in the viewing audience, however, did not have similar affection for the program. Some criticism arrived from former Vietnam servicemen and women who opposed what they perceived as a lack of realism. The comments revealed elements of the counter perception that emerged to oppose the new Reagan-influenced narrative surrounding the Vietnam War and veteran. One such criticism arrived from Kent Anderson, a veteran awarded two Bronze Stars for his Special Forces service in 1969–1970. The author of *Sympathy for the Devil*, a work of Vietnam combat fiction that mirrored much of the author's experiences in the war, Anderson lamented the lack of realistic emotion portrayed by the characters. He argued that the series failed to demonstrate the anger and dread that obsessed the soldier and thus drove many veterans to kill. He demanded the very elements that *TV Guide's* Merrill suggested did not need to be broadcast into America's homes. Anderson wrote of the passion needed to survive war: "It is an emotion born of terror and rage, that the producers of CBS's *Tour of Duty* have chosen to avoid." He described the characters as "too nice," people who at times shocked by the horror of war remained "concerned for the safety of Vietnamese civilians. That is a comforting concept of human nature, but it's not true."[19]

Anderson argued that the program failed to show the profound changes soldiers went through even after a brief time in Vietnam. He dismissed how the characters of *Tour of Duty* moved through the jungle, approached the enemy, fought battles, and set up camp. Anderson blamed a great deal of the problem on the show's cooperation with the Department of Defense. The government agency provided advisors for the program in exchange for the use of military equipment during filming. "These are people who, during the war, changed the term 'search and destroy' to 'search and clear' when Americans, seeing bodies and burned villages on the 6:30 news, began to consider the implication of the word 'destroy.' The people who 'neutralized' Communist cadres, 'sanitized' after-action reports, exaggerated body counts and kept telling us we were winning the war we were losing." He added, "Do you think they are going to deal in the truth now when they have a chance to tidy up history and present a positive image of the Army?" He even wondered, "If any of the DOD advisers were ever in combat in Vietnam?" Toward the end of the article, it seems, Anderson recognized the strength of the new interpretations surrounding the Vietnam War and veteran and the possible futility of his protest: "Americans, after all, may not want the truth about the war. They may not honestly *believe* the truth when they see it." He concluded with a return to his initial call for more realistic emotion in the show but lamented, "But how do you produce love stories for an audience that has never been in love? That is the problem facing *Tour of Duty*."[20]

For three years, *Tour of Duty* maintained steady ratings for CBS. Just prior to the start of the fourth season, in a move that stunned the program's creators, the network canceled the series. *E.A.R.T.H. Force*, a show described as "a kind of ecological A-Team," replaced the program. *Tour of Duty* fans felt grim satisfaction when the new series lasted just three episodes.[21] Fifteen years later, Clark remembered the cancelation: "CBS changed heads, a guy named Jeff Sagansky took over the network and he wanted to put his mark on the network itself. He made a big mistake in what he did." He added that the new president of CBS Entertainment arrived from NBC with a borrowed idea. "He brought over something called *E.A.R.T.H. Force* which was environmentalist but the show was patterned behind *The A-Team*, and he was part of that, and he thought that would work at CBS." Clark recalled that at the time of cancellation *Tour of Duty* still maintained solid ratings. "Our ratings were holding steady. And he [Sagansky] did it and put this silly show on and thinking it would take off like *The A-Team* did. And I don't think anybody even remembers the show, I remember it only because it replaced us."[22]

As the first weekly television series dedicated to the Vietnam War, *Tour of Duty* earned a place in television history. The producers opted to avoid the debates and controversy that surrounded the conflict and instead generated a program that focused on the experience of the Vietnam veterans. With this decision, the creators of the series mirrored a fundamental element of the Reagan rhetoric. Within a year of the cancelation, emerging scholarship on *Tour of Duty* revealed that researchers often detected the lack of political debate for a concentrated emphasis on the vet, the same approach as was initially reported earlier by television reviewers.[23]

Clark recalled that, while producing *Tour of Duty*, he remained aware of the Reagan language concerning the Vietnam vet. He recognized that in the 1980s the president often stood alone in praising the soldiers of that Southeast Asian conflict. "Sure I had heard it of which I was very much appreciative. Because at that time public figures really had not embraced us. For him to embrace us really meant something." He continued with phrases that closely matched the Reagan oratory concerning the veteran: "We were not at fault, we were just taken from our homes, thrown into a war, and told to go home you must stay alive." Clark continued on the impact of Reagan's words and revealed that at the time he had hoped the rhetoric would aid in producing change for many Americans. Additionally, he directly linked the president's effort with the content of *Tour of Duty*. "So to hear a national figure who was getting on the national stage, saying that this was noble, that we were noble people for being there, just gave all of us hope." He concluded, "Which meant, and when I was doing this [*Tour of Duty*], I was thinking that now there is a forum that people can watch and see what we went through and how we managed to keep ourselves sane. And how we were just young kids trying to make it."[24]

Network television of the decade ventured into the Vietnam War one final time with the 1988 debut of ABC's *China Beach*. Unlike *The A-Team*, which dealt with the Southeast Asian conflict only infrequently, or *Tour of Duty*, which concentrated singularly on the soldier's experience, *China Beach* examined the war from a female perspective. The cast consisted of strong female lead characters headed by actress Dana Delaney, and the show concentrated on the various events surrounding the lives of a group of young American nurses. The series mirrored both preceding programs, however, as the debate and controversy surrounding American involvement in the war was deliberately left unexplored. In step with the Reagan Vietnam interpretation, the creators of the show ignored larger geopolitical issues and concentrated instead on the combatants and nurses lost in a chaos not of their choosing.

The producers set the series in the late 1960s at a combination medical evacuation station and United Service Organization (USO) entertainment center near Da Nang, South Vietnam. The episodes examined various topics such as drug addiction, extramarital affairs by characters stationed far from their spouses, and the fathering of Amerasian children by US soldiers. The series also displayed the harsh realities of war as the 1968 Tet Offensive killed several characters. The later episodes included "flash forwards" as the principal players in the show looked back from the late 1980s on their wartime experiences. Echoing the image of the veteran portrayed by the Reagan rhetoric, *China Beach* often revealed the characters in the series as bewildered and overcome by the carnage surrounding them. Consequently, the principals maintained in the series a sense of blamelessness as they struggled to exist in the chaos of the Vietnam War.[25]

Much like CBS's *Tour of Duty*, the program earned critical accolades and a steady loyal audience, but during its three-year run, the series also never rated in the top twenty programs on television. The *TV Guide* reviewed the program in February 1989 and declared, "For *China Beach* we looked at the required three episodes and were so intrigued we watched two more in sheer admiration." The magazine added, "Not having served in Vietnam, we don't know whether *China Beach* portrays what happened there accurately. We do know that in an intensely dramatic and engaging manner the show emphasizes the horrors and futility of that war and its frightful effect on the minds and bodies of the people trapped in it." The reviewer described the show as a soap opera surrounded by the reality of war. *TV Guide* celebrated the effort by the architects of *China Beach* to achieve realism in the program. The periodical cited the research and interviews with veterans undertaken by producers of the show in order to tell a more accurate story.

Ironically, one of the creators of the series, William Broyles, had stated in *TV Guide* three years earlier that he would gladly sacrifice realism for a more positive portrayal of the veteran.[26]

More positive critical assessments found print. The *New York Times* reviewer, John J. O'Connor, praised *China Beach*, admitting that the show needed some additional work but adding, "When it's good, it's terrifically on target." The columnist described how the show concentrated on the experiences of those who had experienced the conflict firsthand. O'Connor wrote, "The crucial concept is summed up in a network press release: 'Their drama about the unsung heroism of American women in Vietnam is laced with the humor that allowed these participants to cope with bizarre realities of a conflict that soon polarized Americans at home.'" O'Connor wrote of the strong quality of the series in dealing with the frustration of the war. He described a scene in which a soldier, who tends to the dead, peers into a body bag and asks, "Gotta be a reason why you're in there but I don't know what it is." O'Connor concluded, "Tackling the still difficult and tender subject of Vietnam, '*China Beach*' could develop into a series worth having around."[27]

USA Today reviewed *China Beach* on the same day. The reviewer, Monica Collins, also made note of the absence of politics and the singular concentration on the female veterans of the conflict. "It's an unusual way to look back on the war, examining Vietnam through the gentler eyes of participants who did not carry heavy metal firepower but whose emotional firepower was persuasive." She concluded, "Vietnam becomes a much saner, safer place. So *China Beach* feminizes the war, without making it a feminist issue."[28] Collins's words acknowledged a softening surrounding television's portrayal of the Vietnam War. Writers replaced politics and debate with stories of actual participants, in the case of *China Beach*, female veterans. The same newspaper on the same day carried "Vietnam's Prime-Time Tour of Duty," a story penned by Matt Roush. This article examined network television's efforts in the late 1980s to bring the Vietnam War back to the small screen and pointed to the emphasis on characters over any controversy surrounding the conflict. Roush quoted Broyles of *China Beach* as stating, "It's about service, about how people make a difference." Broyles added, "These women were healers in a classic sense, and we're trying to tell that story in an unsentimental way."[29]

The same newspaper quoted co-executive producer of *Tour of Duty* Bill Norton, who also spoke about the significance of characters. In describing an upcoming episode in which a soldier who opposes the war is seriously wounded, he spoke of how the series planned to follow the character home as he joined the domestic antiwar movement. "We're trying to keep the show from being in the jungle every week. . . . And this is a good way to have a character we care about and use him as a tool to humanize the home front."[30] Again, by emphasizing the human element—the soldiers themselves—over the controversy of the war, networks closely mirrored the rhetorical pattern of the Reagan language.

Other periodicals complimented *China Beach* as the series won coveted industry awards. *Rolling Stone*'s reviewer seemed to take a swipe at both *Platoon* and *Rambo* and stated that the series "is not an acid trip down hallucination lane, nor is it a heavy-handed allegory of good and evil." The magazine quoted Broyles, who responded to questions concerning any relationship between the series and politics. His choice of words suggested an awareness of the conflict between the two battling interpretations surrounding the Vietnam War as well as a verbal standard in the Reagan rhetoric. "So many people have this fixed view of the war," Broyles said regarding national debate over Vietnam. "Some think it was a blot on our national record; other people think it was this noble cause. You may find neither of those in here, or you may find both." He concluded, "But you won't find any resolved."[31] *TV Guide* in 1990 wrote that the program received a string of praise from Vietnam veterans. In 1989 actress Dana Delaney won an Emmy for Outstanding Lead Actress in a Drama Series for her work on *China Beach*. The following year, later fellow cast member Marg Helgenberger took home the same honor.[32]

The producers of *China Beach* pressed the politics of the war to the background in order to concentrate more on the experiences of the veterans. In doing so, the show's architects unknowingly acted within an emerging perspective regarding the conflict that reflected a key element of the Reagan rhetoric. As a result, the program contained no debates surrounding American involvement in the war, only stories of brave American women and men doing an impossible job in an insufferable place. The narrative of the show thus matched exactly the tenor of much of the Reagan oratory.

At least one national media publication realized that, while entertainment television ventured into new subject matter with the Vietnam War, political debate did not necessarily follow. *Time* magazine in February 1989 noted that both CBS's *Tour of Duty* and ABC's *China Beach* focused on the vet and avoided any examination of American involvement in the Vietnam War. As a result, the weekly periodical concluded that the nation's attention moved away from revisiting the deliberations of the conflict and instead turned to the less controversial personal experiences of the veterans. *Time* also reported that both series dealt with the "disillusionment" and "frustration" so often applied to the American experience in Vietnam. "These sentiments, however, are largely denuded of their political context. Rarely are they linked to any specific complaint about the conduct of the war—a policy mistake or battlefield blunder." Both *Tour of Duty* and *China Beach* "add plenty of fabric softener to the abrasive material," and the article goes on to include how each show "fills its soundtrack with '60's pop songs, as if Vietnam was just another trip down nostalgia lane. . . . The angry pacifism once expounded by *M*A*S*H* has been tempered by sympathy for the average grunt."[33] *Time* recognized the shift in national attention, echoed in the Reagan rhetoric, concerning the Vietnam War.

Good reviews and critical support alone could not support a show, however, and ABC canceled *China Beach* in 1991. One year earlier, *TV Guide* had documented the program's difficulties in acquiring viewers as the series ranked forty-ninth out of ninety-six shows. The same magazine acknowledged the efforts of the program's stars to convince the network to renew the TV show. One constant tension between the network and the creators of *China Beach* appeared over how far to allow the program to portray accurately the misery of war. Drugs, blood, graphic triage, and surgery often remained the breaking points. Much like the debates over realism with CBS's *Tour of Duty*, the arguments suggested reluctance on the part of ABC to allow *China Beach* to go too far in depicting the horrors of the Vietnam War. Confused and innocent veterans playing out soap opera stories nevertheless remained acceptable. Similarly to *Tour of Duty*, scholarship regarding the show detailed how the programs looked to remove politics from the narrative, to legitimize American involvement in Vietnam with nostalgia, to eliminate any shame for the war, and how such an approach could make future military forays, such as in Nicaragua, easier for the American people to accept.[34]

Entertainment television in the 1980s portrayed the Vietnam War in a manner not dissimilar to that of the decade's motion pictures. *The A-Team* included cartoon elements reminiscent of the *Rambo* series. The series echoed several elements often repeated by Rambo and Reagan, namely, the innocence of the veteran as well as his betrayal and mistreatment by the government. Critics of the series, again comparable to the columnists who attacked the *Rambo* films, worried that the show paved the way for future military adventures. *Tour of Duty* and *China Beach* reflected an answer to *The A-Team* in much the same fashion as *Platoon* responded to *Rambo*. Reviewers praised the realism of both series and noted how each program focused on the experiences of the veterans instead of on the politics of the war. All three programs emerged from the revisionists' version of Vietnam. As a result, the approach that each series utilized followed the rhetorical pattern of the Reagan vernacular.

The Reagan Rhetoric and Marvel Comics' *The 'Nam*

The environment of the 1980s that allowed the Southeast Asian war to emerge in motion pictures and television found additional outlets in American popular culture. War has long been a staple of American comics. Compared to the thousands of World War II and Korean War stories in comics, however, illustrated stories about the Vietnam conflict prior to the 1980s numbered only in the hundreds. Smaller presses in the 1960s approached the war in stories that mirrored contemporary opinions. The enemy often remained a faceless coward, hiding behind women and children while fighting a guerilla war against brave American soldiers.

Although limited in their number, comics had dealt with Vietnam almost from the beginning. Dell Publishing Company launched *Jungle War Stories*, the first comic devoted to the Vietnam War, in the spring of 1962. The comic supported US involvement and echoed the containment policy of early 1960s America. In the late 1960s, Charlton Publications published a series of stories in *Fightin' Marines* that remained friendly to American efforts in Vietnam and harsh to those who opposed the war. The June 1967 issue labeled war protestors "fools" and stated that they "are helping the Viet Cong." Additionally, the November 1967 issue even chastised media coverage of the war. After witnessing the cruelty of the enemy firsthand, a fictional news reporter who initially opposed the war told an American soldier, "I was a gullible fool."[35] DC Comics initially mirrored the patriotic pattern of Dell and Charlton. In 1966, the company published the adventures of Captain Hunter in *Our Fighting Forces*, a story line that told of a retired Green Beret who returned to Vietnam to find his lost brother. The stories failed to gain an audience, however, and the series quickly returned to tales from World War II.[36]

Some projects did not reflect a pro-American view of the war. A small underground publisher, Last Gasp Press, published *The Legion of Charlies*. The work reflected the growing dissent from American involvement in Vietnam. The comic book employed a split-panel story titled "My Lai, Mar. 16, 1968" and "Hollywood, Aug. 9, 1969," a story that explored the similarities between the Lieutenant Calley and Charles Manson murders.[37]

Popular war comics of the larger publishers, DC and Marvel, did not directly deal with Vietnam. In the 1960s and 1970s, World War II series such as DC Comic's *Sergeant Rock* and Marvel Comic's *Sergeant Fury* portrayed stories from World War II that echoed the contemporary Vietnam conflict. The government sent the soldiers on difficult missions with ambiguous endings, and soldiers grew angry with superiors for leading men into deadly firefights where there was little chance for success. One such comic presented as cover art US troops angrily deserting a lieutenant who led them into an impossible battle while another soldier demands loyalty from his troops. Therefore, narratives directly concerning issues of the Vietnam conflict found explicit expression in smaller presses while the two larger national comic companies, DC and Marvel, changed names and locations and placed the accounts within less overtly controversial tales concerning World War II or Korea.[38]

As the conflict progressed, however, so did its representation in comic books. The books took a more serious look at the war and began to reflect the changing attitudes of the nation. Stories left the faceless enemy of communism and instead focused on the consequences of American involvement. Comics also underwent controversial cosmetic changes. In 1971 DC received criticism for ending all issues of its comic line with the message, "Make war no more."[39]

While realistic stories were still beyond the reader of the two big publishers, less realistic use of the war was still possible. Marvel Comics initially used the Vietnam War as a plot device for many of its superheroes. *Iron Man*, the popular comic that depicted the adventures of a brilliant playboy businessman/adventurer, Tony Stark, placed the origin of the hero in the Southeast Asian conflict. The 1963 debut issue found the munitions producer wounded by a piece of shrapnel while in South Vietnam on a fact-finding inspection of his weaponry. Stark then designed a suit of technological laden metal to keep himself alive but to fight also against an assortment of enemies. The Norse god of thunder, Thor, a popular Marvel Comics superhero since his inception in the 1960s, journeyed to Vietnam in 1965. He used his powers to rescue a family of peasants from the communists. At the end of the story he vowed to return, but subsequent writers never sent the character back to Vietnam. Iron Man, however, returned to Southeast Asia the next year to fight his Soviet counterpart, Titanium Man.[40]

Other superheroes got into the act. Marvel's *Captain America* contained a brief Vietnam adventure in 1970. The superhero rescued a kidnapped "peacemaker" seized by The Mandarin, an Asian villain who hoped to cause a wider war between the United States and communist nations. Captain America ignored direct involvement in the war and rescued the captive, thus allowing the fighting parties to resume peace negotiations.[41] In 1970 the company's flagship title *The Amazing Spider-Man* shipped one of the supporting players, Flash Thompson, on a tour of duty in Vietnam. The popular character had been with the series since its inception. As Spider-Man's alter ego, Peter Parker bid farewell to his friend. He lamented, "Which is worse? Staying behind while other guys are doing the fighting . . . or fighting in a war that nobody wants . . . against an enemy you don't even hate?" A few years later, Thompson returned from

Vietnam a changed character, tormented with guilt for his actions in the war. Thus, as the war dragged on and domestic support withered, Marvel writers began to alter how they portrayed Vietnam. The comic company still dealt directly with the controversial conflict only rarely, using secondary characters in prominent books to address the war.

Of all of Marvel's fantasy magazines, *Iron Man* reflected the domestic attitudes concerning the war. Tony Stark's link to weaponry created an easy target for those readers opposing the war. Marvel writers developed a sensitivity from the growing number of readers' letters that painted the character as an "enemy of the people" or a "profiteering, capitalist, war-mongering pig." In 1971, Iron Man argued with a conservative senator over the actions of war protestors. The following year, Stark transformed his weaponry factories into makers of peaceful products, and by 1975, the character had turned completely against the war, wondering "what right did we have to be there in the first place?"[42] For ten years, this 1975 *Iron Man* story remained one of the last to represent the Vietnam War. Most comics felt morally safer basing war stories on the less-controversial World War II. For the most part, Vietnam had left the American comic book scene until the mid-1980s.[43]

In the fall of 1986, Marvel Comics returned to the Southeast Asian conflict with a treatment of war unlike any other in comic history. *The 'Nam*, presenting a self-proclaimed intentionally realistic and gritty representation of the war, arrived at newsstands and specialty shops nationwide. Written by Vietnam veteran Doug Murray, the monthly comic concentrated on the experience of the average soldier in the field.[44] The magazine's approach mirrored the decade's motion pictures and television in bypassing any political arguments surrounding the controversial war. The portrayals of many of the characters—soldiers, war protestors, enemies—easily matched the descriptions that were common in the Reagan rhetoric.

The 'Nam approached the war in a way completely different from that of any other entertainment format before. The book moved in "real time," meaning that, as a month passed between issues for the reader, a month simultaneously passed in the lives of the depicted characters. By utilizing such an approach, Murray hoped to show changes in the lives of common soldiers over a one-year tour in Vietnam. Setting the origin of the series in 1966, the author planned to cover the American involvement until the 1975 evacuation of Saigon.

The first issue introduced Ed Marks, a young, blond, fresh-faced new recruit who suffers airsickness on his way to Vietnam. For the readers, the initial book contained a myriad of images that generated sympathy for the characters. Murray included scenes of leaving concerned parents, the

The action-packed December 1986 cover to the first issue of *The 'Nam*. *The 'Nam*: TM & © 2010 Marvel Characters, Inc. Used with permission.

unease with military medical examinations, and the miseries of kitchen patrol, exhaustive training, malaria, abusive officers, not to mention the horror of killing another human being.[45] The subsequent twelve issues followed Marks through his one-year tour in Vietnam. The reader saw events as Marks did and simultaneously witnessed the transformation of a young innocent kid into a battle-hardened soldier. They go with him as the clean recruit survives a violent mugging and the destruction of his hotel in Saigon, and as he witnesses the aftermath of a slaughter of a Vietnamese village. Readers learned quickly, along with Marks, as "friendly" Vietnamese suddenly turned deadly. The stories dealt with the difficulty that some Vietnamese experienced in supporting America while other accounts portrayed the dangers of Vietcong tunnels. Additionally, Marks and the readers who wrote letters to *The 'Nam* both reacted with sadness at the unexpected battlefield deaths of close friends. As his tour wound down, Marks observed the instability of the South Vietnamese government, the torture and murder of captured Viet Cong, and tension with new recruits. Finally, the young boy turned soldier returns home to an uncertain future. A subsequent issue recorded the difficulties Marks encounters as he tries to adapt to a nation he no longer recognizes, including a hostile encounter with war protestors. Subsequent story lines followed different characters and stories and at times ended abruptly with the death of established characters—chilling reminders sent to the reader that in war no guarantees exist.[46]

Marvel fully supported the unusual comic with patriotic enthusiasm. In 1987 *Comics Interview* included a behind-the-scenes look at how the comic company wanted retailers to market *The 'Nam*. Marvel specified a large exhibit, preferably in a storefront window. Besides posters, displayed comics, trade paperbacks, and a raised platform, the company also suggested the use of a US flag as a backdrop.[47] The marketing strategy was successful, and the comic itself opened to enthusiastic reviews. The *LA Times* stated that a comic book "has been attracting a large, unusual audience" and that mail to Marvel Comics suggested that half the readership consisted of veterans. The article added that "sales of *The 'Nam* are running about 400,000 copies each month, which makes it a best seller among comic books." The newspaper also printed approving remarks by Bob Duncan, an adjustment counselor at a veterans' center. His comments described what the comic book represented and what it did not: "*The 'Nam* doesn't Rambo-ize the war—it's closer to home. We had our heroes but Nam grunts like myself don't tend to look at the war as heroic: It became a matter of survival." Duncan offered his hope that *The 'Nam* would continue to remain as accurate as possible in a comic and took a swipe at a more recent Vietnam project, *Platoon*. "I think Stone did us a disservice by throwing all the negative stereotypes into the movie, instead of reinforcing some of the heroic things soldiers did in Vietnam—the way we took care of one another, and the camaraderie."[48]

Other reviews were equally enthusiastic. The *Washington Post* stated, "The Marvelized Vietnam is a darker, more surreal place than John Wayne or Stallone ever visited." The paper stated that *The 'Nam* "is outperforming" *The Uncanny X-Men*, Marvel's number one title, and the readership remained diverse, from those too young to remember the war to veterans who offered praise and constructive criticism of story lines. Murray stated that the killing of one of the most popular characters, Mike Alberto, generated "between 50 and 100" letters from irate fans. The writer added that the reader understood the death as *The 'Nam* promised not "typical" but "realistic" war stories.[49]

Other news outlets praised the new series. The *LA Times* article identified the innocence of new recruit Marks, calling him "a naïve young draftee." The *Washington Post* echoed the observation and described the young soldier as "fresh of face and square of jaw."[50] Former *Newsweek* editor, *Brothers in Arms* author, and future creator of *China Beach*, William Broyles, Jr., was quoted as praising the book. The Vietnam veteran stated of the creators, "They know what they are talking about. It has a certain gritty reality. And they are not going to shrink from the ambiguities." In fact, the *Washington Post* carried one dissenting opinion. Although appreciating the detail and realism of *The 'Nam*, Jan Scruggs, president of the Vietnam Veterans Memorial Fund, added, "Another side of me thinks, why should Vietnam be the subject of a comic book?"[51]

The popularity of *The 'Nam* grew quickly among comic collectors. A little over a year after the series began, retailers listed the seventy-five-cents first issue for fifteen dollars. The following month the price rose to sixteen dollars. Ads for *The 'Nam* labeled the book "Red Hot."[52]

Murray, writer and co-creator of the series, earned fame through the success of *The 'Nam*. Employed at the time as a full-time computer operations manager for Chase Manhattan Bank, the two-tour Vietnam vet and part-time comic writer hoped through the series to present the experience of those who served in the conflict to a new audience. An examination of his words in various interviews illustrates his recollections of returning from Vietnam, changes in the national atmosphere concerning the war, hopes for the comic series, as well as his responses to the new Reagan-influenced communal remembrances. "When I got back, the thing that I had problems adjusting to was the fact that, for the most part, no one seemed to give a shit about the guys who were in Vietnam and the guys who were coming back." He critically compared his generation's reception to that of his father's after World War II.[53] He spoke of the negative media attention of the war. "I'd sit by the TV and watch the six o'clock news, see reporting of the war: and what they were talking about was *nothing* similar to what I remember things like over there." While he understood the importance of broadcasting the horror and realities of the war, the author added, "But, I think, on the whole the press did more harm than good in Vietnam."[54] With these words Murray joined the thousands of Vietnam veterans who emerged from the war troubled by their lack of acceptance and subsequent portrayal in America's society.

Murray enjoyed the early success of *The 'Nam*, although he admitted that it surprised him. He recalled earlier, less successful attempts to bring the Vietnam War to the comic genre and the changes in the national mood that allowed such a comic to exist. In 1972 after returning from Southeast Asia, he had attempted to produce a Vietnam-focused comic for DC. "It just wasn't time–'72 was a bad time to do Vietnam stories because Vietnam was still going on, to a certain extent, and we were in the Nixon years and that was not a good subject. It really was a taboo subject."[55] By 1984 he had detected a change, as comic audiences seemed more receptive to the Vietnam War. He perceived a readiness in 1986 to examine the conflict, "a willingness that didn't exist 10, or even 5 years ago." Murray added that, prior to the 1980s, no one wanted to discuss the war; "I think that began to change around '82 or '83: Some healing has taken place."[56] Murray obviously understood the national reevaluation of the Vietnam War and veteran. His citation of the early 1980s as the origin of an alteration in the national mood represented the new opportunity encountered by Reagan to share his interpretation of the Vietnam War with a national audience as well as the appearance of popular culture examples such as *First Blood*. The way had been paved for him by the nation's acceptance of the president's rhetoric and by the hugely popular mass-media products being crafted from it.

Murray also expressed surprise at the vast media attention *The 'Nam* received, although "doing a Vietnam comic book was certainly going to get some kind of coverage." He added, "I think what happened was that a lot of the newspapers and TV stations took their cue from the *Washington Post*." He recalled how that newspaper had reviewed the first issue in a manner normally reserved for novels or scholarly historical text. "Their former Saigon bureau chief was the one who reviewed it, and he liked it, liked the way we'd handled it, and I think that when the various readers for TV companies and newspapers and whatnot saw the review, it kind of led them to look at the comic as press releases from Marvel."[57] Turning to the content of *The 'Nam*, the author added that he did not want the comic to glorify war, suggesting that enough of that had been done in the 1980s. He included a contemporary and a telling example as he cited a member of the Reagan administration: "I mean Oliver North is a fine example of a person who believes in the glory of war." At the time of this comment, North (a Vietnam veteran himself) was in the nation's news due to the Iran-Contra scandal. Murray later added that officers who glorified war in Vietnam often found themselves "fragged"—killed—by their own men.[58]

Murray spoke of the focus that *The 'Nam* placed on the experience of the veterans, and he admitted to utilizing some of his own experiences in the book. The creators of the book wished to avoid both the 1960s and 1970s debate and the subsequent 1980s fantasy imagery that surrounded much of the war. Accordingly, the architects of the series made a point to emphasize the realism of the stories and to distance the comic from debates surrounding the war and such contemporary projects as *Rambo* and *Platoon*. In tune with the changing mood of the nation, Murray added, "I'm curious to see how the third Rambo film does, simply because the climate has changed a little bit since the second one came out." *The 'Nam* comic book defeated *Platoon* for an Entertainment Award from BRAVO, a combined group of approximately four hundred veterans' organizations.[59]

Murray recalled how working on *The 'Nam* helped him to deal with his personal recollections of Vietnam. He suggested that the more difficult memories of Vietnam do not dominate his recollections of the war. As he put it: "but the human memory is a tricky thing to start with. The tendency is to remember the good stuff rather than the bad, so I guess the good stuff I still have in the forefront of my memory."[60] Murray's interviews, in a broad sense, revealed the canvas that allowed a new interpretation of Vietnam to flourish. The nation did not want to revisit the war in the 1970s, but by the early 1980s, the author found a receptive audience for his work by ignoring politics and concentrating instead on the individuals involved in the struggle itself. Reagan's rhetoric followed a similar path. He too ignored politics and concentrated on the men and women who served in the conflict. By doing so, the president's Vietnam language tapped into the "good stuff" within the American psyche, the nostalgia, and found a receptive audience for his version of the Vietnam War and veterans.

Comic book audiences often share their thoughts in the form of letters to the publishers. An examination of the letters page of *The 'Nam* during the first year shows that many of the readers appreciated the realism of the series. Many letters echoed the sentiments of Murray that the comic should avoid joining into the Reagan-influenced revisionist reevaluation of the Vietnam War. Early issues contained letters that criticized other 1980s popular culture projects while elevating *The 'Nam*. One reader wrote, "War is not a game, it is not *Rambo* or *G.I. Joe*." Another similarly added, "*The 'Nam* isn't super heroes, it's not *G.I. Joe*, it's not *Rambo*." One reader initially dreaded the release of a comic book based on the Vietnam War. "I envisioned four-color adaptations of such travesties as *Rambo* and *Missing in Action*. I feel it is a pernicious tendency in the popular media today to trivialize what was a very traumatic experience, not only for the U.S. but also the rest of the western world."[61] Other readers' letters contained direct references to Reagan. The correspondence revealed that some readers of the 1980s comic recognized Reagan as one of the key architects of the revisionist history surrounding the Vietnam War. One even echoed his rhetoric virtually word for word. After praising *The 'Nam*, one early letter writer added, "Now if you guys could only come up with 'Invasion of the Conservatives, starring Captain Ronnie' to show what life in the 1980s was all about." Another reader praised the comic and stated his loyalty to the company that produced the work by proclaiming, "Well, until Reagan goes back in time and changes the 'Nam so we would've won, Make Mine Marvel." Finally a veteran's letter printed in the second year of the series contained language from the Reagan rhetoric. "I am an avid fan of the series, which is doing an excellent job of portraying a very dirty, very tragic war, one we first weren't allowed to win and finally lost not on the battlefield, but in our home streets."[62]

The 'Nam ran from December 1986 until September 1993, short of the nine-year span originally envisioned by Marvel Comics. By the end of the 1980s, sales for the book slumped and interest waned. Murray bickered with Marvel Comics over the direction of the book as he hoped to present his Vietnam stories to a wide audience but Marvel insisted he still work within the Comics Code, a self-imposed industry regulation with ties to the 1950s Senate Subcommittee Investigations on Juvenile Delinquency in the United States. In 1954 there were concerns within the committee that comics had a detrimental effect on the nation's young, and it conducted investigations of the industry. Afterward, the comic book business closed ranks and adopted a self-regulatory code that, although much less strict, still exists today. Murray felt constricted under such limitations regarding violence and gore and after a series of confrontations left the comic.

Marvel attempted numerous gimmicks to save the project. The company redirected *The 'Nam* to a more central market with a 1988 change in distribution from national newspaper stands to the more limited direct sales through specialty shops and mail subscriptions. The marketing moves and price increases cut the readership from approximately 250,000 issues monthly to 100,000. Marvel continued to tinker with the book and hoped to lure readers back and generate new customers through persistent publicity stunts. The comic soon lost the originality that had endeared it to so many fans. The company dropped the month-to-month real-time format in order to concentrate on more multi-part stories. In a 1990 imaginary tale, Captain America, Iron Man, and Thor, all part of the comic company's superhero line, entered the war and forced Ho Chi Minh to the peace table. In 1991, the Punisher, Marvel's non–super-powered vigilante and Vietnam veteran, appeared in the series twice. The story involved flashbacks of the Punisher character and recalled his Vietnam adventures long before his superhero origin. Reader mail showed that some enjoyed the inclusion of Marvel's superheroes, while most did not. One 1987 letter from a fan begged Marvel never to include superheroes, and the editor gave assurances that he would not.[63] Nevertheless, a diminishing sales record encouraged the editorial changes, with the result that less than two years after the appearance of the Punisher, Marvel canceled the series.

Similar to the box office fate of *Rambo III*, the failure of *The 'Nam* comic book illustrated the popular culture power of the Reagan rhetoric surrounding the subject of Vietnam. The timing of the initial sales slump that forced Marvel to such drastic decisions as the abandonment of particular formats, distribution changes, and inclusion of superheroes coincided precisely with the last months of the Reagan administration. The national attention concentrated on the 1988 presidential election as Reagan prepared to leave office. For *Rambo III*, bad timing and a change in national dialogue directed in part by Reagan helped to kill the picture. For *The 'Nam*, a nation preparing to elect a new president had moved on to other subjects as the chief champion of the new Vietnam interpretation prepared to leave office. The new version secured, the nation moved forward.

For thirty years Reagan repeated his convictions that the Vietnam War remained a noble cause, he portrayed the conflict as but one part of a broader struggle against world communism, and he asserted that war protestors often remained dupes of America's enemies. Reagan described the veteran as an innocent warrior denied victory by the betrayal of an uncaring and uncommitted government. He compared Vietnam with other less controversial wars in US history and encouraged no debate concerning American involvement in Southeast Asia. From the mid-1960s until his 1994 departure from public life, his rhetorical pattern remained consistent as he reconstructed the past surrounding the war by creating more palatable images with his words.

Through the power of the Oval Office, Reagan had found an American audience willing to embrace some of the simpler and more attractive elements of his Vietnam interpretation. As a result the 1980s provoked for many Americans a fundamental change in perception concerning the veteran of the conflict. For many Americans, the vet became a betrayed blameless innocent, no longer liable for the folly of the Vietnam War. While the president did not actually convince all America that the war was a noble effort, overt debate in the 1980s over American involvement remained virtually silent.

The popular culture of the decade—detecting the changing mood of the nation—adapted around particular elements of the Reagan rhetoric and as a result nourished the new narrative. The film and television industry produced numerous formulaic projects concerning the Vietnam conflict that directly mirrored the language of the fortieth president. Comic books in the 1980s dealt seriously with soldiers' experiences for the first time. Regardless of either embracing or attacking the Reagan revisionist rhetoric, these projects presented new images of the experiences of the men and women who served in the conflict, and these images echoed his interpretation. Under Reagan's persuasive guidance, Vietnam veterans underwent a marked conversion from national failures to American heroes.

5 / Falling from Grace

The Inconsistency of Iran-Contra

> "We did not—repeat—did not trade weapons or anything else for hostages, nor will we."
> —**Ronald Reagan, November 13, 1986**

On March 4, 1987, President Ronald Reagan addressed the American people from the Oval Office at the White House. Cosmetically, the speech appeared like so many other previous televised remarks. Dressed in a pressed blue suit, Reagan smiled slightly at the camera, tilted his head and began speaking. In the past, his broadcast comments to the American people seemed to come easily, but at no time during his previous six years in office did so much depend on one speech. The administration was mired in scandal, and the president was now suffering low polls and had lost credibility with the American people. Many in the national media suggested that the very survival of his presidency depended on this address.[1]

Four months earlier, the scene had been very different. As the winter of 1986 approached, Reagan enjoyed a 63% approval rating. The national economy continued to grow during what was at the time the longest peacetime expansion in contemporary American history. In July 1986, during Liberty Weekend, a national celebration of the centennial of the Statue of Liberty was punctuated by the largest fireworks show in American history. President Reagan presided over the festivities and with a laser beam dramatically "relit" the statue's torch. By late October, the president had returned from a summit held in Reykjavik, Iceland, with Soviet premier Mikhail Gorbachev. Reagan refused to bargain over his space-based missile defense shield, the Strategic Defense Initiative, even when the Soviet leader offered significant cuts in his nation's nuclear stockpiles. *Time* reported that 69% of Americans agreed with the president. As fall turned to winter, the Reagan White House walked with a well-deserved swagger.[2]

On November 3, 1986, everything changed, however. A small Lebanese newspaper, *Al Shiraa*, reported that the Reagan administration had secretly sold military weapons to Iran. The Iranian government quickly confirmed the *Al Shiraa* story. Events moved rapidly and more revelations followed. Within two weeks, the story took on the atmosphere of a scandal. Reagan announced to a shocked nation the discovery of possibly illegal secret diversions of funds from the Iranian arms sales to the Contra rebels fighting the Marxist Sandinista government in Nicaragua. The story was no longer about sordid arms dealing with a sworn enemy of the United States. Now the narrative seemed to suggest impeachable offenses. The shaken president assured the nation he had not had any prior knowledge of the funneling of money to the Nicaraguan rebels.[3]

The episode shattered the blissful atmosphere and uniformity of message of the Reagan administration. The American people had grown accustomed to Reagan's rhetorical consistency during his first six years in office. With each new Iran-Contra revelation, the president appeared increasingly confused, both unsure and unsteady. At first Reagan offered contradictions and puzzling explanations. Then, with the scandal at fever pitch, he went silent to the questioning public for three months. Such a quiet was deafening. The president refused to speak about Iran-Contra because, he said, it would be inappropriate to comment during the numerous ongoing investigations, but he assured the nation he would return to the subject eventually. With Reagan quiet, however, new revelations and the national press drove how the nation perceived the story, especially regarding the president's role. Finally, in the spring of 1987, when investigations concluded that at best Reagan had done nothing illegal, the president began to speak. Remarkably, he was able to put the scandal behind him. Historiography and contemporary research on Iran-Contra offer various reasons that Reagan survived the crisis.

Scholars have long debated Reagan's survival. What is so far missing from that debate is an examination of how Reagan's use of language at first set him up not to be believed but then later aided in his political survival. At the beginning of the scandal, his own consistency condemned him. In a manner similar to his earlier 1980 visit to Neshoba County, Mississippi, Reagan's own words returned to haunt him. For the nation, his previous six years of rhetoric on the Contras positioned the president in an indefensible place. The American people easily remembered his years of constant support of the Nicaraguan rebels. They recalled his many battles with Congress regarding funding for the rebel groups. Since remembering the past always occurs within the context of the present, Americans within the ongoing scandal recalled his past Contra cheerleading. As a result it remained easy and almost automatic to connect the president to the illegal diversion of funds. The more Reagan professed his innocence, the more polls and surveys declared that the nation did not believe him. Americans questioned his credibility. Whispers of impeachment crept through the halls of Congress.

Later, however, in March 1987, Reagan found his voice. The release of the Tower Commission's official report echoed almost exactly the president's previous assertions of innocence. While not everyone agreed, Reagan received the report as vindication and moved forward. His important tool of consistency returned with a vengeance. He emerged with a polished script in hand, a fresh uniformity of message. Only then did his recovery begin. His emergence from the self-imposed rhetorical exile played a key role in his surviving. As months passed, the American people remembered the now past scandal under the persuasion of the present. Reagan's opponents tried to return to Iran-Contra, and congressional hearings continued into the summer. With no new evidence to counter the president's assertions, however, the press and the public had nowhere to go but forward. To be sure, his reconnecting with his audience is not the only reason Reagan survived Iran-Contra, but a reestablishment of rhetorical consistency must be included with any other considerations.

In November 1986, the arms-for-hostages story stunned the nation. There stood Reagan, staunch outspoken opponent of terrorism, apparently dealing arms to Iran, the same country that had once held fifty-two Americans hostage for 444 days, that had denounced the United States as the "Great Satan," and that remained widely suspected of supporting international terrorism. To many in the nation, Reagan seemed at best a hypocrite, at worst a lawbreaker. The law itself remained muddled. Reagan had indeed signed an extension of an arms-embargo against Iran that had first been initiated by President Jimmy Carter. On January 17, 1986, however, Reagan quietly signed an additional waiver, which permitted shipments to restricted countries that the president deemed to be in the national interest.[4]

In the early days of the scandal, Reagan seemed unsure of how to respond. Initially, he pleaded for the national press to stop reporting the story. He stated that silence from the press remained vital to keeping communications open with the moderates in Iran and to ensuring the safety of the remaining hostages in Lebanon. His protests fell on deaf ears. The story was one that the press simply could not ignore. For millions of Americans, Lebanon served as a mental tripwire. During the decade, the Middle Eastern nation maintained a prominent place in the national psyche. In August 1982 Reagan had sent US Marines into the war-torn country to act as peacekeepers—only to remove them two years later after 270 died in a series of terrorists' attacks. Additionally, Hezbollah, a militant Islamic group loyal to Iran's Ayatollah Khomeini, remained based in Lebanon. Through the latter part of the decade, the terrorist organization held captive no fewer than ten Americans.

Four days after the Iran story hit the newswires, Reagan met with newly freed hostage David Jacobsen at the White House. Originally a hospital administrator in Beirut, Jacobsen had been held since May 1985. What should have been a joyous celebration of Jacobsen's return soon turned into a verbal fencing between Reagan and the assembled press. The president refused to answer questions. He cited the possible risk to ongoing efforts to win the release of the other hostages. Jacobsen agreed, "Unreasonable speculation on your part can endanger their lives."[5] In subsequent days, the president admitted that only a few weapons had indeed been sent to Iran in an effort to show good faith to Iranian moderates. In the succeeding days, however, he often changed the amount. The uproar continued to grow. For many Americans, minuscule cracks slowly began to appear and then spread throughout Reagan's presidential consistency.

While the arms-for-hostages affair continued to dominate the national media, Reagan attempted to stay on more familiar rhetorical ground. He did not forget Nicaragua. On November 10, 1986, he sent the required letter to the Speaker of the House and the president of the Senate for the continuing of economic sanctions against the Sandinistas. Five days later, during a national radio address the president did not use the word *Contras*, choosing to substitute the more positively loaded phrase "freedom fighters" instead. Ironically, on November 18, while his administration struggled to regain credibility, the president addressed the Ethics and Public Policy Center Anniversary Dinner in the International Ballroom of the Washington Hilton Hotel. He railed against "the dying of the light in Nicaragua" and stated that America possessed a duty to stand by all freedom-loving people of the world.[6] Even though revelations continued to swirl around him, in none of these events did the president address the arms-for-hostages problem that was plaguing his presidency. The story of weapons to Iran gained momentum.

Reagan knew he needed to reclaim the initiative. He quickly decided upon a White House address, to be given on November 13, which gave his speechwriters only a few hours' notice. The preparation for the speech revealed a president directing the interpretation he wanted to portray to the

American people. The National Security Council and the speechwriting staff jointly prepared the remarks and presented a rough draft to Reagan. The speech may have been influenced by a series of "Talking Points" dated November 12, 1986. Written in the first person and meant for public use by administration officials, the two-page typed brief served as a script regarding the ongoing arms-for-hostages issue. The memo included lines such as "sensitive," and "for the time being we cannot go much beyond what has already been said," and instructions for pushing the geographic importance of Iran and the significance of diplomatic relations. The document provided assurances that no laws had been broken and that appropriate legal counsel had been utilized.[7] Evidence remains inconclusive if the Talking Points were typed from Reagan's notes or prepared for the president. Regardless, his November 13 speech closely followed the brief.

After looking at the early draft of the November 13 speech, Reagan sent a note to staff secretary David L. Chew. "I didn't try to rewrite knowing you were already rewriting," said the president, who then added, "I feel we dwell too much on the Iran history etc. & need *more* flat denials of such stories as the attached ABC item. RR."[8] The early draft concentrated a great deal on the past thorny relationship between the United States and Iran. While the president would try to explain to the American people his attempt at normalizing relations with Iran, this directive for "more flat denials" sought to regain the initiative from what he perceived as errors in the nation's press. He wished, instead, to push his side of the story.

Reagan also made changes to the speech's introduction, softening it to give it a more conversational feel. An earlier draft had started rather blandly with "I have requested this time to talk with you about an extremely sensitive and profoundly important foreign policy initiative: The renewal of a stable relationship with the nation of Iran." Along the top of the page and down the right margin Reagan rewrote by hand the introduction. "I know you've been reading, seeing, and hearing a lot of stories the past several days attributed to Danish sailors, unnamed observers at Italian ports and Spanish harbors, and especially unnamed government officials of my administration. Well, now you're going to hear the facts from a White House source, and you know my name." Later, Reagan himself added the strong denial, "We did not, repeat, did not trade weapons or anything else for hostages, nor will we."[9] His handwritten comments reflect a beleaguered president working to get his message out, trying to regain the initiative, and denying any sort of arms-for-hostages swap.

Six hours later he addressed the nation from the Oval Office. Reagan acknowledged the press frenzy of the "past ten days." He admitted that his administration had indeed sent "defensive weapons" and spare parts to Iran but only as part of a larger secret diplomatic initiative. He strongly denied any arms-for-hostages deal. Reagan went on to give a geography lesson to the audience, explaining in detail Iran's geographical importance in relation to the Middle East and the Soviet Union. He talked of reaching out to moderates in the Iranian government. He went on to compare his efforts with Richard Nixon's secret yet successful dealings with China twenty-five years earlier. Finally, the president assured the American people that his administration had broken no laws. He concluded with his own line, "We did not—repeat—did not trade weapons or anything else for hostages, nor will we. Those who think that we have gone soft on terrorism should take up the question with Colonel Gaddafi."[10] The final comment stood as a plea to the American people and recalled the April 1986 bombing of Libya in response to a Gaddafi-supported bombing of a West Berlin discotheque that killed two people, including one American.

Reagan's staff closely monitored the reaction to the speech. Many in the Reagan camp believed the November 13 speech a success. Chief of Staff Donald Regan sent a letter of "deep appreciation" to the writers for their efforts "with only a few hours notice" to prepare. For five days the White House tabulated positive and negative phone calls to the White House. At first, it appeared that the "great Communicator" had done it again. Out of 2,951 calls, finals numbers returned with "67%" positive. Memos also recorded international press reaction from fourteen nations. Ironically, Reagan received a congratulatory telegram from Carlos Garcia, director of the Nicaraguan Humanitarian and Patriotic Movement. He voiced his support for Reagan's speech and thanked him for his "unflinching support to our brave freedom fighters."[11]

Ultimately, White House phone calls and administration self-congratulation did not matter. Reagan's own words returned to haunt him. For six years, in words and actions, the president offered a tough stance versus terrorism. Now it appeared that he had lied and possibly broken the law by shipping arms to a nation that sponsored terrorism. The media dutifully reported the mistrust. *Time* complained of "dissemination of misinformation." *U.S. News and World Report* used the words "stonewalling," "uncertain," and "bitter," adding that, even though "Reagan's harshest critics concede that his original intentions were sound," he "will pay a price for his troubles."[12] An ABC News snapshot poll reported that 56% believed an arms-for-hostages swap had occurred and that 72% disapproved of the entire policy. Ironically and comically, an NBC News–*Wall Street Journal* poll asked Americans "Do you approve or disapprove of the Reagan administration's support of the rebels in Nicaragua?" The data returned with 26% who answered "yes," 54% "no," and 20% had "no opinion."[13]

On November 19, the arms-to-Iran story dominated a nationally televised East Room press conference. Reagan's speech six days earlier had not satisfied the reporters. So many questions remained unanswered, and a great deal of information did not add up. Reagan opened the meeting with a lengthy statement essentially repeating much of his November 13 national address, but the day went downhill from there. He recognized his damaged credibility but refused to admit mistakes in the policy toward Iran. Reagan professed innocence of any wrongdoing. He offered only inconsistency, using the word "minuscule" to describe the amount of weapons sent to Iran, although evidence suggested otherwise, and he stated no other nations were involved in the affair. Both statements required a post-conference correction by his staff. Later during the press conference, the president fielded only one question on Nicaragua, happy to return to a solid script, and simply repeated his belief that the Sandinistas had betrayed the 1979 revolution.[14] The press conference mercifully ended to the clamors of shouted questions. That same day, upset at the lack of clear information from his own staff regarding the entire affair, he asked Edward Meese, the attorney general and his longtime friend, to review the entire Iranian operation. To his aides Reagan remained personally confident, but he could read the numbers. His job approval rating had fallen ten points to 57% in one week. Most politicians would, of course, be happy with such a number, and the figure actually revealed just how popular the president was with the American people before the Iranian story broke. More disturbing numbers would roll in, though, as an ABC News poll reported that 61% of those surveyed simply did not believe the president, a one-week rise of five points.[15]

On November 25, the story exploded into a full-blown scandal. Meese told Reagan that evidence suggested the Iranians had been overcharged for the weapons. The excess profits then found their way into the pockets of the Nicaraguan resistance. Shortly thereafter, a solemn-faced Reagan, with Meese at his side, repeated the news of the discovery to leaders of Congress, and then the nation. The news shocked the country. As with Lebanon earlier, the mention of the Contras quickly struck a chord in American memory. Since the late 1970s events in Nicaragua had frequently played out in the nation's press. In 1979 the Sandinista National Liberation Front (FSLN) had toppled Nicaragua's Anastasio Somoza Debayle government. Led by a coalition that included Daniel Ortega, the victors of the revolution quickly opened close relations with Cuba and the Soviet Union. Opposition to the Sandinistas formed into a movement commonly called the Contras, which consisted of former members of the Somoza regime, disgruntled members of the Sandinistas, and other smaller groups. In 1981 the Reagan administration cut all economic aid to Nicaragua and obtained congressional support to begin funding Central Intelligence Agency (CIA) Contra military training in Honduras and Costa Rica. The director of the CIA, William Casey, told Congress that the operation's only purpose was to stop the supplying of El Salvadoran rebels with Cuban weapons funneled through Nicaragua.[16] Reagan constantly argued that funds for the Contras were meant to stop Nicaraguan arms from reaching the rebels in El Salvador, not for regime change in Nicaragua. This statement, however, was a clear contradiction, since the reason for the very existence of the Contras was to overthrow the Ortega government.

During Reagan's two terms, Congress authorized sporadic humanitarian and military aid. On December 8, 1982, the Democrat-controlled US House of Representatives had unanimously passed the Boland Amendment, a late attachment to the Defense Appropriations Act for the fiscal year 1983, and two additional versions of Boland were passed in 1984 and 1985. Named for Representative Edward P. Boland of Massachusetts, the 1982 amendment stated that none of the appropriated defense funds could be used covertly by the CIA or the Department of Defense to "furnish military equipment, military training or advice, or other support for military activities, to any group or individual, for the purpose of overthrowing the government of Nicaragua."[17] The legislation essentially made illegal any clandestine funding of the Contras. Many in the Reagan administration narrowly interpreted the Boland addition as pertaining only to intelligence agencies such as the CIA and not other government entities such as the National Security Council. Thus, this 1982 interpretation laid the groundwork for a key piece of the Iran-Contra scandal four years later. Indeed, even though the Boland legislation had expired in October 1986, the diversion to the Contras occurred well before that date.

With Ortega's consolidation of power in 1984, the CIA caused a national uproar with the illegal mining of several Nicaraguan harbors. Finally, on May 1, 1985, the Reagan administration placed a trade embargo on the country. In July 1986 with the Iran-Contra scandal fast approaching and Reagan still at a 63% approval rating, Congress awarded $100 million in additional Contra aid, most of it in the form of humanitarian support. Afterward, *Time* reported that even with new Congressional support "nearly two-thirds of the US public opposes the aid according to a recent ABC News/*Washington Post*" survey. In mid-October 1986, Congress restored full military aid to the Contras. Just days before the arms-for-hostages affair exploded in November, a *U.S. News and World Report* article quoted an overly optimistic State Department official as saying, "If things go well we might ask Congress for $300 million next year. After all, $100 million is just a start."[18]

Throughout his first six years in office, Reagan was obsessed with the Contras. The president constantly denounced the Sandinistas and praised the Contras and consistently accused the Sandinistas of supporting communist expansion in Latin America, betraying the Nicaraguan people and the original ideals of the 1979 revolution, and promoting violence in the region. He linked Ortega and the Sandinistas with groups and nations deemed dangerous by the United States: the Palestinian Liberation Organization, North Korea, Vietnam, and Moammar Gaddafi's Libya. Reagan described Soviet expansion in the region as a direct threat to the American economy. By contrast, he often called the Contra rebels "freedom fighters" and more than once likened the group to heroes and patriots of America's past. From 1981 to 1986 Reagan used various opportunities to share his interpretation of the Nicaraguan situation. Moreover, Reagan's private correspondence mirrored his public language. His rhetorical consistency was comparable to his treatment of subjects such as states' rights and Vietnam veterans.[19] The national media did not ignore Reagan's 1981–1986 rhetoric on Nicaragua. A cursory examination of just two national magazines reveals extensive coverage. *Time* and *U.S. News and World Report* reprinted the president's Nicaraguan language. Each magazine, like all other major media, dutifully reported Reagan's constant battle with Congress to receive financial support for the Contras.

The power of presidential political persuasion and the reporting of the press did not, however, translate into popular support. Reagan could never completely win the American people over to his side. Polling data revealed interesting conclusions. Various Gallup polls and other surveys reported that a majority of Americans, quite often over 60%, feared communism in Central America. The same margin viewed the safety of the region as vital to the national security of the United States. When questions turned to the subject of Contra support, though, Reagan ran into trouble, never achieving higher than 40% approval.[20] Americans did indeed recognize communist dangers in Central America, but the shadow of the Vietnam War lingered and the president could not overcome a lack of public support for any military ventures in the region. The jungles of Vietnam overshadowed the jungles of Nicaragua. To a certain point the American people agreed with him regarding the Contras, but only to a point. The most important thing is that the nation heard him, even if it did not agree with him wholeheartedly.

Thus, with Attorney General Meese's November 25 announcement concerning the diversion of Iranian arms funds, the arms-to-Iran story now possessed new and potentially criminal elements. The episode could no longer be explained away as misguided good intentions with a current enemy. Bad political judgment could no longer be an excuse. Reagan's past words echoed in the minds of millions and in the headlines, easily drawing from six years of presidential remarks and press coverage.

On November 25 at twelve noon, Reagan quickly entered the White House briefing room. He looked grim as he took the microphone. No cock of the head or crooked grin could save the moment; no jokes would work. This was deadly serious, and he knew it. Gloom floated over the White House in a manner not seen since the 1981 assassination attempt. The president stated of the diversion of funds, "This action raises serious questions of propriety" and "I was not fully informed." He announced a special review board to investigate the revelation, as well as the resignations of Vice Admiral John Poindexter from the office of assistant to the president for National Security Affairs and Lieutenant Colonel Oliver North, deputy director for Political-Military Affairs, from the National Security Council staff. "I am deeply troubled that the implementation of a policy aimed at resolving a truly tragic situation in the Middle East has resulted in such controversy," he proclaimed, ending his prepared remarks. The assembled press attacked in a jumble of shouted questions. An agitated Reagan placed his hands up in front of him, almost in a defensive posture, and firmly said, "Hold it!" The shouting continued in a chaotic mass of voices. The president, as he left the podium, answered two. He stated that he did not believe his initiative to Iran was a mistake, and no one had been fired.[21]

Reagan's defense of his Iranian policy should have surprised no one. Before entering the press room, he made one quick change to his prepared remarks. He said to the media, "The information brought to my attention yesterday convinced me that in one aspect implementation of that policy was seriously flawed." The original speech read, "However, the information brought to my attention yesterday convinced me that *the* implementation of that policy was seriously flawed."[22] Reagan refused to condemn the entire strategy. He refused to concede, as he would for the duration of the crisis, that the initial opening to Iran was a mistake.

The president refused to answer any additional questions and introduced his attorney general to explain the diversion discovery. With that, he left the room to a continuous roar of questions. Meese stayed behind to face the press. A shocked nation watched the entire episode on television. In his words and action, Reagan did not provide the consistency so many millions had grown to expect. In the past, the president did not duck tough questions. To be sure, in the past, humor and changing the subject had proved useful tools in avoiding uncomfortable moments. The American people, however, could not recall when Reagan had left a room so quickly or left a subordinate to face a crisis alone.

The colder temperatures in Washington, DC, mirrored the feelings in the White House. On December 1, Reagan appointed a commission to investigate the entire affair. The panel consisted of former senator John Tower, former secretary of state Edmund Muskie, and former national security adviser Brent Scowcroft. The media took the opportunity to fire questions at the president, but Reagan answered only one, offering yet another assurance that he knew nothing of the diversion of funds. The White House continued to monitor the increasingly negative press reports to gauge appropriate response to coverage of the scandal.[23] *Time* saw the scandal as being on a par with Watergate and wrote of broken laws. Reagan sat for a phone interview with his old friend Hugh Sidey, the magazine's Washington contributing editor. He defended his initial policy toward moderates in Iran and shifted blame to the "great irresponsibility" of the press for first reporting the arms-for-hostages story. Reagan then provided a rhetorical preview of his survival strategy: "I'm not going to back off, I'm not going to crawl in a hole. I'm going to go forward. I have a lot of things to do in this job."[24] *U.S. News and World Report*'s coverage seemed more forgiving. While noting the seriousness of the revelations, the magazine asserted that the scandal did not approach the seriousness of Watergate, although Reagan "had been badly damaged."[25] Both magazines saw the upcoming congressional investigations dominating the domestic agenda in the near future.

Poll numbers continued to reflect Reagan's damaged credibility with the American people as his positives and negatives exchanged places. Some surveys reflected a drop of more than twenty points. An ABC News poll showed that 80% of Americans "believe Reagan knows more about the Iran-Contra affair than he has admitted to date." Reagan's job approval fell to 54%, down thirteen points from the *U.S. News* 67% rating just before the arms-for-hostages story broke.[26] As the days passed and more revelations reached the American people, the numbers continued to plummet. In early December, ABC News–*Washington Post* and CBS News–*New York Times* surveys placed Reagan's popularity below 50% for the first time in five years. He held at 50% in a NBC News–*Wall Street Journal* poll. Copies of many of the survey results circulated throughout the White House offices.[27] Reagan's impressive November job approval rating had disappeared within a month and increased discussion of the Contras did not help their cause. American support for them remained below 30%.[28]

Reagan continued to deviate from his past rhetorical patterns. On December 2, he again addressed a national audience from the Oval Office. He kept his remarks very brief, less than five minutes. Bombarded by dropping public support and a determined press, the president avoided the usual trappings of an evening broadcast. Instead, choosing to draw from the best traditions of the western cowboy, he faced the press at noon. With the address he gave with Meese on November 25, the timing of noon appears coincidental. Reagan could argue that he brought the news to the American people as fast as possible. On December 2, the choice of the hour was intentional. Midday would find most Americans at work and guarantee a smaller audience. Reagan's choice of a four-minute noon speech in front of a much smaller audience further revealed his unsteadiness and hesitancy on the Iran-Contra issue. The best anyone could hope for would be coverage on the evening news. During the short address, the president promised to get to the bottom of the episode, agreed that an independent counselor should be appointed to look into the entire affair, praised the Tower Commission again, and promised to work with congressional investigations. The president finished by announcing the appointment of Frank Carlucci as assistant to the president for National Security Affairs. With this, the president signed off.[29] Reagan satisfied no one. His short five-minute address was a complete change from hundreds of previous speaking engagements, and this change in approach only added to his ongoing problems. For a national audience accustomed to much longer speaking engagements, Reagan's staccato presentation appeared rushed and therefore suspicious. Poll numbers continued to sink. An early December Gallup telephone survey revealed Reagan's job rating at 47%, and less than half of those surveyed (45%) thought Reagan was handling Iran-Contra better than Nixon dealt with Watergate. Bad news for the Contras continued as 58% of Americans believed that the "U.S. government" should not be giving assistance to "the guerrilla forces now opposing the Marxist government in Nicaragua."[30]

Reagan saw his quickly dropping poll numbers. He had suffered low numbers in the past but never such a precipitous drop. He recognized the unease of the audience and knew the scandal had damaged his credibility. Against a deluge of bad press, Reagan was determined to continue trying to sway the Iran-Contra narrative. On Saturday, December 6, Reagan addressed the nation during his weekly radio address. Similar to his noon remarks a few days earlier, he chose a venue that promised a smaller audience. Of course, with Washington awash in scandal, press coverage of the radio broadcast promised to be high. Speechwriter Anthony Dolan wrote the original draft of the radio address. After reviewing the draft, Reagan kept the first paragraph and then rewrote the entire middle portion. The new speech carried a much more detailed explanation of why he reached out to Iran. Despite this effort on his part, none of it was new information, and again it failed to persuade.[31] His previous dogged consistency completely worked against him. He continued to push a disastrous version of events. As questions swirled around him,

Reagan insisted on presenting his explanation of events. He fell back on his previous statements and once again rhetorically walked the country through his initial initiative to Iran. He reminded the country that he had revealed the diversion to the nation. He assured listeners that the truth would be found out and anyone involved in illegal actions would be brought to justice. With this, he signed off.[32] *Time* quoted one former aide who stated that Reagan was going to look like a "fool" or a "liar." The magazine printed a "Credibility Gap" table that compared Reagan's assertions to known facts; he did not do well in that comparison. The story included a CBS News–*New York Times* poll that showed Reagan's approval rating had dropped in four weeks from 67% to 46%, the most dramatic one-month drop in fifty years.[33] *U.S. News and World Report* echoed that the "public isn't buying" much of Reagan's explanations and the twenty-point plummet in popularity felt like "a cup of ice water in the face."[34] Polls continued racing to the bottom.

The Washington winter grew colder. Buffeted from all directions, Reagan seemed confused and lost. The Iran-Contra scandal dominated headlines, surveys, Sunday morning talk shows, and conversations around office water coolers. Echoes of Watergate seemed so clear: a popular Republican president, two years removed from a forty-nine-state landslide reelection victory, mired in a second-term scandal that threatened his presidency. Since the early November announcement of arms to Iran, Reagan had tried and failed four times to stop the bleeding. His incredible gift—the power of communication and connection—now had deserted him, it seemed.

As the uproar reached a towering crescendo, Reagan made a bold and dangerous choice: he went silent. The first four weeks of the scandal had produced four national presidential addresses. Reagan made it clear that for the foreseeable future there would be no more. Citing ongoing investigations, he withdrew from the subject and essentially tried to ignore the entire affair. Whether he actually believed his own explanation or not, he really had no choice. With his rhetorical connection broken, the president floundered, openly in crisis. Words could not save him this time. Under the influence of the present scandal, Americans remembered his past speeches. Reagan's explanations of his arms-to-Iran strategy served only to cultivate confusion and anger directed at a president supposedly tough on terrorism. His constant proclamations of innocence regarding the diversion of funds to the Contras fostered disbelief in a nation that, for six years, had grown used to hearing his ardent pleas for rebel support.

Reagan's decision backfired. He completely misjudged the national reaction. He may have believed that investigations warranted his silence, but his decision produced only suspicion and outrage. For the American people, it was a new experience. Regardless of popularity or polls, the president had never before chosen to be silent on a subject. Supporters and opponents alike had always been able to count on him to be out front, pushing his policies, cheering his programs. Silence was a new tactic, and it only increased the national apprehension. For the next eleven weeks, Reagan revisited the issue only in the briefest way, always asserting his failed narrative that he knew nothing of the diversion. As a result, his brief December 6, 1986, radio address remained his last national comment on Iran-Contra until March 1987. His silence ceded the initiative on this scandal to the emerging evidence, to continuing events beyond his control, and other voices, which were then free to dictate and revise the account of what had happened as they saw fit, causing his credibility with the American people to disappear.

Reagan's decision frightened many of those closest to him. Longtime friends wrote and asked for him to return to the subject in an address to the nation. California friend Shirley Waldman wrote in December, "I believe the American people need to hear from you." Reagan responded to his friends' concerns, but his opinion about the right way to handle the situation remained unchanged. He wrote that he, too, wanted the truth to come out, that he was the one who announced the diversion of funds, but it would be better to wait until the investigations were over. He watched the CBS News Dan Rather interview with former President Jimmy Carter on December 11, 1986, and wrote a letter to his predecessor, in which he defended his approach to the Iranian moderates, reminded Carter that the announcement of the money to the Contras had come from his own White House, and offered hope that the current investigations would find answers. On December 19, White House communications director Patrick Buchanan sent a three-page memo to Chief of Staff Regan. He worried over Reagan's absence and suggested many "dramatic" and "bold" moves that Reagan might make.[35] Even Nancy, his wife and most trusted advisor, implored Reagan to do something. He did not. In the subsequent days and weeks, the president publicly and privately declared that it would be inappropriate to comment on the matter during an ongoing investigation. Reagan continued to give the American people nowhere to go. Faced initially with confusing statements and then with a suspicious silence, and always remembering his past rhetoric, the American people judged Reagan guilty. As revelation after revelation came out in print, Reagan's credibility and poll numbers continued to suffer, his own Contra rhetoric continuing to boomerang against him.

In December Reagan may have gone publicly silent concerning the issue of Iran-Contra, but his staff did not. Behind the scenes, aides scrambled to keep his message in front of the American people. Senior staff members made great efforts to maintain consistency with Reagan's earlier remarks.

Many took on the role of defending their boss. Just because Reagan chose silence until investigations ended did not mean that the press or the American people followed his lead. In early December, different versions of "Talking Points" bounced around within the White House. Staffers prepared possible responses to media questions and sent them to Thomas Gibson, special assistant to the president and director of public affairs. No evidence exists to suggest that Reagan ever saw the memos. Early versions included reminders of the president's reasons for reaching out to Iranian moderates, his personal disclosure of the diversion of funds, the appointment of the Tower Commission, the selection of Carlucci, and support of an independent counsel. Lines that described reaching out to Iran as a mistake were replaced with the "implementation" of a "flawed" strategy. Peter Wallison, counsel to the president, questioned whether the funneling of monies to the Contras actually broke any law. Richard Wirthlin offered a dissenting voice and argued that Reagan's claims of reaching out to Iranian moderates "were an absolute bomb."[36] While Reagan remained silent, his surrogates worked hard to put forth his message.

Administration talking points did not satisfy the nation's media. *Time* magazine reported Reagan's silence and the frustration of many Reagan confidants. The magazine reported that Reagan addressed the scandal only once in those tension-filled days. He began his December 12 remarks to the American Legislative Exchange Council with a joke, "Let me just add a few words about the controversy in Iran, or haven't you heard about it?" The magazine reported "nervous laughter." Finally, the magazine echoed recent polls that revealed diminished support for the Contras and almost half of the nation believed the president was "lying." Other surveys revealed similar results.[37]

Reagan's national silence notwithstanding, he did make small gestures that generated media coverage. On December 16, he issued a low-key written statement to the Senate Select Committee on Intelligence asking for limited immunity for North and Poindexter. The exception would only protect the men from prosecution for what they testified to Congress. An earlier Buchanan memo suggested such a move. While not a declaration of amnesty or clemency, the president believed such a gesture important "in order that the whole truth—all of the facts on Iran—may be told. This is essential because of the controversy surrounding the Iranian matter. There is an absolute need to get on with the business of government." *Time* reported that Republican leader Robert Dole deemed the move premature and that with his quiet rhetoric and inaction Reagan "has become a silent participant in the scandal."[38] On December 19, Congress appointed Lawrence Walsh as independent counsel to investigate Iran-Contra. In a written statement, the president warmly greeted the move and promised full cooperation.[39] With that, Reagan remained essentially silent on the issue, at least in any public way, for the rest of the month and into the next year.

With the arrival of 1987, Reagan continued his pattern of silence. On the surface, he had stopped the freefall of his poll numbers. No longer offering confusing statements, he settled in at just below 50%, not good numbers for a president who had long been used to the heights of popular support but not the earlier nosedive, either. The White House did not celebrate the surveys. Many feared that the stability reflected only a brief respite from further political damage. The national clamor continued for him to end his rhetorical exile regarding the scandal. The same request came from overseas. Reagan aides monitored the Western European press, examining 215 editorials and 81 papers from fourteen countries. The assorted papers all but begged Reagan to emerge from isolation and at least admit that mistakes had been made. Still, he remained quiet.

Meanwhile events went forward, and others seized the headlines and thus the momentum of the story. In January, Congress created the Joint House-Senate Select Committee on Secret Military Assistance to Iran and the Nicaraguan Opposition. The group sought to investigate the entire Iran-Contra affair. Americans cringed at the thought of new revelations the investigation would surely discover. Additionally, the president's Tower Commission continued to investigate. The national press continued to detail Reagan's silence, each new revelation, and the network television and Gallup low poll numbers reflecting lack of presidential credibility and the public response to Contra support.[40]

No one could declare with any certainty when Reagan would end his Iran-Contra silence. Millions, however, knew with confidence when he would hold his next national address, on January 27, 1987, the annual State of the Union address. Reagan could not hide from the calendar. A year earlier he had delayed by one week his State of the Union remarks because of the explosion of the space shuttle *Challenger*. Now, mired in a political tragedy rather than a national one, he would speak to the nation again. Experiencing very different emotions, the country and world awaited his words.

Reagan understood the importance of his remarks. He sensed the country's apprehension. He knew he had to return to his rhetorical roots and to use the gifts that had helped win him the presidency. As a result, he prepared carefully, writing and rewriting the words. He wanted to convey to the nation that, although recent weeks had been difficult, he was moving forward as president. He looked at three drafts of the speech, including his own. In the end, however, he brought in a former speechwriter, Ken Khachigian from California. The author of Reagan's 1981 inaugural speech, and of several key speeches since then, Khachigian returned to bring back Reagan's rhetorical consistency.

The January 27, 1987, address was vintage Reagan. He took great pains to look and sound great. His confidence had seemingly returned, and it found expression through his voice. The recent confusion and unsteadiness disappeared, and for forty minutes he returned again and again to old themes and ideas. He pointed out a need to put God back in the classroom, warned of "Big Government," and praised the returning pride of America's armed forces. The president even returned to damning the Sandinistas and praising the Nicaraguan "freedom fighters." The national media took notice of the return to rhetorical consistency. The words seemed so familiar to everyone who heard them—and they should have. *U.S. News and World Report* wrote that the "Big Government" portion came "almost word for word out of his 1986 [State of the Union] speech" and the assertion of military pride "was in his 1982 State of the Union, among other places."[41]

The American people clearly heard him, but they still wanted explanations. The nation longed for clarity on Iran-Contra, but Reagan did not offer that clarity. Millions turned off their televisions in disappointment. Reagan had barely touched upon the subject uppermost on everyone's mind. Early in his speech, in only the fifth paragraph, the president spent seven sentences on the ongoing Iran-Contra scandal. He explained again his rationale for reaching out to Iran. He defended the policy and admitted no personal mistakes, saying, "The goals were worthy. I do not believe it was wrong to try to establish contacts with a country of strategic importance or to try to save lives. And certainly it was not wrong to try to secure freedom for our citizens held in barbaric captivity. But we did not achieve what we wished, and serious mistakes were made in trying to do so." Reagan assured the nation that, when the numerous investigations reached their completion, he would take appropriate action. Once again he offered nothing new. He made it very clear that Americans waiting for any new details would continue to wait.[42]

After the speech, the White House watched anxiously for reactions. Marlin Fitzwater, White House press secretary, collected a series of newspaper editorials. He presented the findings to Chief of Staff Regan. The January 28 *Cincinnati Enquirer* called the speech "vintage Reagan," but the next day the *Oregonian* used the words "meager" and "half-hearted." The January 29 *Cleveland Plain Dealer* wrote of "rejected ideas" and "populists clichés." A January 30 *Chicago Tribune* editorial called Reagan a liar three times as "his sweet words were largely devoid of any nutrition, and they left a sour aftertaste."[43] *Time* made note of the "few words" on Iran-Contra and reported, "If the calendar could have been turned back a year or two, the speech might have been one of Ronald Reagan's most effective." The weekly periodical also remarked that the president's words "indicated little awareness" of how trouble now affected his administration. *U.S. News and World Report* agreed and stated that Reagan did not seem "aware how much the dynamics have changed since the Iran arms scandal exploded like a TOW missile over the White House." The story quoted an unnamed Reagan advisor: "The state-of-the-union speech didn't do very well in the way of substance."[44] As January turned to February, polls continued to present grim news. Reagan's job approval ratings remained in the low forties. The press complained that the president had not held a full press conference in three months. The howls of protest fell on deaf ears. Reagan declared he would only address Iran-Contra upon the conclusion of the investigations, and he meant what he said. As a result, he continued the December–January rhetorical strategy, and the Oval Office remained essentially silent on Iran-Contra for the remainder of the month.[45]

On February 26, 1987, the Tower Commission released the results of their investigation. After interviewing almost one hundred witnesses and swimming through thousands of pages of documents, Tower, Scowcroft, and Muskie presented their findings to the president. While small in size, barely three hundred pages, the report presented a damning indictment. The panel strongly criticized Reagan's hands-off management style and stated that he remained largely out of touch with the operations of his own National Security Council. "President Reagan's personal management style places an especially heavy responsibility on his key advisors." The panel continued: "The President did not seem to be aware of the way in which the operation was implemented and the full consequences of U.S. participation." The final conclusions placed blame on the president's top advisers for a chaotic environment that, the commission found, led to the entire affair. On the matter of the funneling of money to the Contras, the commission agreed with Reagan and concluded: "The President said he had no knowledge of the diversion prior to his conversation with Attorney General Meese on November 25, 1986. No evidence has come to light to suggest otherwise." With harsh and painful words the commission criticized but simultaneously vindicated Reagan's earlier assertions.[46]

In the Old Executive Office Building while the national press watched, a grim-faced Reagan accepted the commission's report and thanked the panel. He took the opportunity again to remind the nation that he had personally formed the panel and asked for the investigation. "I'm proud to have appointed this distinguished Board, because it fulfills my commitment to get the facts and share them with the American people." He remarked that he would "carefully" study the report in the coming days, since "I consider their work far too important for instant analysis." Reagan

President Reagan speaks after receiving the final report of the Tower Commission in Room 450 of the Old Executive Office Building. The fact that the podium is lacking the presidential seal is an unintended yet subtle reminder of Reagan's diminished stature in the eyes of many Americans. Seated from left to right: Edmund Muskie, John Tower, and Brent Scowcroft, February 26, 1987. Courtesy Ronald Reagan Library.

announced that he would address the nation the following week. To a loud chorus of reporters' questions, the president left the room. A quick Gallup telephone poll for *Newsweek* magazine showed how far the president had to go. Reagan's job approval stood at 40%.[47]

On March 9, *Time*'s cover pictured Reagan holding the Tower Commission Report under the caption "Can He Recover?" The story centered on the report's "sorry picture of the lack of presidential leadership." The magazine labeled Reagan's upcoming address to the nation "probably the most important speech of his presidency." *Time* wrote that serious problems now existed with Reagan's ability in gaining future funds for the Contras. The article ended with a call for an engaged and active president, not a leader "befuddled" and "intellectually lazy."[48] The same week *U.S. News and World Report*'s cover displayed a similar photo under the headline "The Teflon Is Gone." The story reported, "Many friends and foes believe that Reagan's moment has passed—that after the damage done by the Tower report, the consequences now preclude any significant comeback."[49] Such judgments would prove to be premature.

6 / Iran-Contra and Reagan's
Return to Consistency

"A few months ago I told the American people I did not trade arms for hostages. My heart and my best intentions still tell me that's true, but the facts and the evidence tell me it is not."
—Ronald Reagan, March 4, 1987

Many in the nation's press and population had dropped the lame duck gavel too soon. Six days later, Reagan broke his self-induced nine-week national silence on Iran-Contra. The comeback had begun. For the first six years of his administration, Reagan had offered rhetorical consistency to the American people. In the case of the Nicaraguan Contras, he presented an unchanging message even in the face of constant low poll numbers. The revelation of arms being sold to Iran made many Americans feel angry and betrayed. The news of an illegal diversion of funds to the Contras immediately took the nation back to numerous memories of Reagan's support for the Nicaraguan rebels. His own words set him up not to be believed. His job approval plummeted as his credibility disappeared. Offering first only confusing answers and then silence, Reagan allowed others to dictate the scandal's narrative. With the release of the Tower Report, however, Reagan began his rhetorical return to consistency and as a result began to put the scandal behind him.[1]

At nine o'clock in the evening, Eastern Standard Time, March 4, 1987, Reagan appeared on millions of televisions across the nation. The Tower Commission report had been out for a week. The press and the public continued to examine the findings. Newspapers, magazines, and television news programs contained no shortage of opinions. Prior to the address, Reagan and his staff knew well the importance of the president's first public reaction to the Tower Commission Report. A March 4 multi-page document prepared for the White House staff and titled "Today's News Events" quoted a United Press International (UPI) citation that "tonight's speech will be a 'turning point.'"[2] The American people and the world watched and listened closely. So much hinged on this moment; the president would either regain lost momentum and begin a recovery or continue the downward spiral in which he seemed to be locked. For three months the president had assured the American people that at the conclusion of the Tower Committee's investigation he would address the country. On March 4, he kept his promise. Sitting behind his Oval Office desk, looking more fresh and confident than in recent weeks, Reagan used the occasion rhetorically to reconnect with the American people and relieve a scandal that simultaneously cost him credibility and threatened his presidency.

In the twelve-minute March 4 address, the president acknowledged the pounding he had received in the past three months in the national polls and explained his silence. "For the past three months, I've been silent on the revelations about Iran. And you must have been thinking: 'Well, why doesn't he tell us what's happening? Why doesn't he just speak to us as he has in the past when we've faced troubles or tragedies?'" He continued, "I felt it was improper to come to you with sketchy reports, or possibly even erroneous statements, which would then have to be corrected, creating even more doubt and confusion. There's been enough of that. I've paid a price for my silence in terms of your trust and confidence."[3]

Once again, Reagan thanked the Tower Commission and praised the efforts of the panel. "Its findings are honest, convincing, and highly critical; and I accept them." He continued to deny any personal knowledge of the diversion of funds to the Contras but accepted responsibility for the actions of his administration. "First, let me say I take full responsibility for my own actions and for those of my administration. As angry as I may be about activities undertaken without my knowledge, I am still accountable for those activities." Reagan remarked, "And as personally distasteful as I find secret bank accounts and diverted funds—well, as the Navy would say, this happened on my watch." He added, "As I told the Tower board, I didn't know about any diversion of funds to the contras. But as President, I cannot escape responsibility."

Reagan concluded with an admission that his personal concern for the hostages in Lebanon affected his policy toward Iran, assured the families of the captive Americans that his administration would continue to seek their release, confessed mistakes in his management style, promised changes, and announced long-demanded new faces in the offices of chief of staff, national security advisor, and director of the Central Intelligence Agency. He remarked, "Now, what should happen when you make a mistake is this: You take your knocks, you learn your lessons, and then you move on. That's the healthiest way to deal with a problem. This in no way diminishes the importance of the other continuing investigations, but the business of our country and our people must proceed." He concluded by saying, "You know, by the time you reach my age, you've made plenty of mistakes. And if you've lived your life properly—so, you learn. You put things in perspective. You pull your energies together. You change. You go forward." With this combination of accountability and determination, Reagan had taken his first steps toward surviving the scandal.

The most revealing lines of Reagan's national address, however, actually came early in the speech. "A few months ago I told the American people I did not trade arms for hostages. My heart and my best intentions still tell me that's true, but the facts and the evidence tell me it is not." What appeared on the surface to be an obvious linguistic contradiction actually remained vital to understanding Reagan's survival of Iran-Contra and his ability to regain credibility with the American people. He denied personal culpability and yet accepted administrative responsibility. In the president's mind, he did nothing wrong personally. Unlike Presidents Nixon and Carter who had seemed distracted and politically compromised by the issues of Watergate and hostages, Reagan used his words to depict a man with a clean conscience moving forward with his presidency. In doing so, he helped to consign the scandal within a year to the back pages of the press.

Congressional investigations began on Iran-Contra and continued throughout 1987, but the president turned his focus to more familiar subjects. After March 1987, he rarely returned in any true detail to the arms-for-hostages scandal and considered his role in the matter closed. When required, he would comment on the subject but almost always in a dismissive way that resorted to the explanation found in his March 1987 speech. On broad themes, the president always returned to script; on specifics he stated that he either could not recall details or remained silent and cited ongoing investigations. With Reagan now back out front and rhetorically consistent regarding his role in the scandal, polls revealed a gradual increase in the president's job approval rating. Furthermore, after his March 1987 national address, the president quickly felt comfortable enough to return to the subject of the Contras. Never completely quiet on the subject of his "freedom fighters" even during his three-month Iran-Contra silence, Reagan nevertheless had not pounded the Contra drumbeat as fervently as before, during that time tempering his language. After the March address, however, his Contra language quickly reappeared. In 1987 he publicly spoke thirty-seven times on the subject; the following year, fifty-four. With rising poll numbers and a nation moving past the scandal, Reagan perceived no danger of returning to a key element in the entire affair in his speeches. The president continued to ask for financial support for the Nicaraguan rebels. As he had in the first six years of his presidency, Reagan found any venue suitable for sharing grand accolades describing the Contras and requesting additional funds from Congress.

While Reagan considered his role in the entire affair fully explained, the national media did not. The press continued to concentrate on Iran-Contra and reported each new revelation. Reagan never changed his basic story-line of the Iran-Contra story, which left the press and the public nowhere new to go with respect to his role. The Tower Commission had printed the details of the investigation and its subsequent conclusions. Reagan had responded by accepting responsibility. For millions of Americans, that was enough. Other events soon began to dominate the nation's attention: the public fall of televangelist Jim Bakker and Democratic presidential hopeful Gary Hart, the accidental Iraqi attack on the USS Stark, Reagan's "tear down this wall" declaration in West Berlin, the Senate rejection of Reagan Supreme Court nominee Robert H. Bork, the October stock market crash, and the continuing thaw in the Cold War brought on by the growing relationship between Reagan and Gorbachev. By 1988 hard questions regarding Reagan's role in the Iran-Contra scandal—in large part because of his rhetorical treatment of the issue—had faded from the nation's consciousness.

As the president signed off on March 4, the White House breathed a collective sigh of relief. The speech seemed to go well, but it had been publicly described as a rush job. Since the release of the Tower Report one week earlier, White House speechwriters had worked feverishly to offer the president different versions of what to say and some read more contritely than others. Since the Tower Commission did not provide any new evidence to challenge Reagan's account of his role in the affair, he ignored any drafts that challenged his earlier pronouncements in any way. The president was now back on message. Reagan made sure that what had been a scattered rhetorical defense in November and early December now emerged as a well-rehearsed consistent message. One draft, written on February 27 and titled "NSC Draft," contained great remorse. Of the Tower Commission's findings the speech offered, "I'm ready to take my medicine as I promised I would." That speech criticized Reagan's policy toward Iran by offering the admission, "It was a gamble, and it failed." Of the aides who disagreed with the course of action, Reagan would have said, "they were right and I was wrong." The draft played on the president's emotions regarding the hostages, "It's a very human reaction, but it's the wrong policy." The NSC draft also had Reagan admitting error in his management style and declaring that his Nicaraguan critics "are right" and "private enterprise" should not fund the Contras. Finally, at the end of the proposed draft, the president was to talk of moving forward and of placing the entire "episode" in the past.[4] Other than the call to move ahead, the remarks contradicted almost every Reagan assertion since the beginning of the entire affair. Needless to say, this apologetic version of the speech was not the one he gave in public.

Reagan ignored another apologetic speech that spent only a few paragraphs on Iran-Contra and the Tower Commission and instead focused on the future. The remarks were unnamed, but the writer may have been Patrick Butler, a former speechwriter for President Gerald R. Ford. In 1987, Butler worked for Senator Howard H. Baker, Jr., who had become Reagan's chief of staff on February 27. If Butler was the author, the speech reveals that the new chief of staff wasted no time in putting his surrogates to work on helping to save the Reagan presidency. The remarks had Reagan defending his policy toward Iran but admitting that emotion for the hostages blinded him to the danger. "I was human when I should have been president." The speech briefly pointed out the commission's conclusions, again stated that the president knew of no diversion of funds, reminded the nation that Reagan himself named an independent counsel, and finally pointed out Baker's appointment as chief of staff. With that, the speech moved Reagan on to issues of deficit control and forging better ties with the Soviet Union.[5]

The March 4 remarks Reagan used came from the pen of Landon Parvin. He had worked for a public relations firm before joining the Reagan White House. He had been with the president since 1981, and he wrote for Nancy Reagan as well. After a few years, he was burned out and left the White House in 1985 to serve as executive assistant to the US ambassador to Britain. Nancy Reagan liked Parvin and his rapport with her husband. She once called him "one of our best speechwriters."[6] On paper he seemed to find Reagan's style easily. She suggested his name to her husband and played a key role in his return to help craft the president's remarks.

Of the March 1987 address Parvin recalled the president's allegiance to consistency: "The president was in denial" about what had actually occurred and initially just wanted to "rehash" what he had said earlier. Parvin added that the "hard part" of writing the speech remained finding words and phrases that were honest to the president's beliefs but that also remained something the nation wanted to hear. Parvin pointed to the syntax-straining lines, "A few months ago I told the American people I did not trade arms for hostages. My heart and my best intentions still tell me that's true, but the facts and the evidence tell me it is not." Those two sentences are as close as Parvin could manage to a Reagan apology. He remembered, "We were trying to embrace the Tower Commission Report" instead of "picking [our] way through." Parvin concluded that the tone of the remarks had to "accept the findings without denial so the administration could move on." Parvin recalled being in the residence with Reagan the very night that Chief of Staff Don Regan resigned. Tower arrived and "briefed the president on the findings of the Tower Commission." He added that with Regan's departure and Baker's arrival the administration got back on track, which helped add a "tone of acceptance" and "taking responsibility" to the March address.[7] On March 4, Parvin's words and Reagan's personal additions returned the president to his earlier and more consistent Iran-Contra message, an account that took advantage of the Tower Report.

Parvin's speech lacked consistency in one key area, namely, following the pattern of usual presidential speech preparation. A review of early drafts of Parvin's March 4 address raises several questions. Reagan's speechwriters usually worked on drafts for several days—sometimes even weeks, depending on the importance of the occasion at hand—prior to the event. The speeches would then be reviewed by Reagan and several members of the president's staff. The various drafts usually displayed the month, day, year, and time in the upper right-hand corner. Since speeches went through numerous rewrites, such a practice kept everyone current as to which of the numerous versions circulating through the White House offices had precedence. According to the public story, speechwriters working on the various Iran-Contra addresses had only one week (from the February 27 release of the report to the March 4 address) to prepare the remarks.

Reagan biographer Lou Cannon wrote that Parvin did not begin to work on the March 4 address until "the last week of February." In his 1990 memoir, Reagan wrote himself that he began working on the March 4 speech after Don Regan submitted his resignation on February 27. This fits perfectly with Parvin's memory of being with Reagan when Regan resigned. One problem exists. The Parvin speech draft on file at the Reagan Presidential Library clearly displays in the upper right-hand corner the date, "1/1/87," almost two months before the Tower Commission submitted their final report to the president. The date is problematic because the draft contains information not yet officially released by the Tower Commission. The "1-1-87" draft followed very closely Reagan's March 4 address to the nation.[8] Subsequent copies retained the original date, an uncommon practice, even when reviewed by staff members in late February. It is only one day before the television broadcast that the date changes to the more common month, day, and year pattern. On one of the later drafts, in the top right-hand corner of the remarks, "Parvin" is typed with "RR" added in longhand. Since other Reagan speeches displayed authorship in the same location, the names signify that both the speechwriter and the president worked on the script.

Parvin's "1-1-87" rough draft, like Reagan's March 4 remarks, contained the line "for the past three months I have been silent on the revelations about Iran."[9] The phrase suggests a deadline for the commission's findings. Other evidence, however, does not. Reagan appointed the Tower Commission on November 25, 1986, and stated, "I anticipate receiving the reports from the Attorney General and the Special Review Board at the earliest possible date" and "I hope the Board will conduct its review in a prompt and thorough manner."[10] An examination of *Time* and *Newsweek* magazines at the time found no evidence of deadlines, although *Newsweek* did cite in March that "the commission also was handicapped by limits on its time and investigative resources."[11] The Tower Commission cryptically declared that while "the president gave the board a broad charter," the "short deadline set by the president for completion of the Board's work and its limited resources precluded a separate and thorough investigation."[12] Again, other than the Tower Report's own words, no evidence of any prearranged deadline has been discovered. Yet Parvin's draft of the speech—dated two months before the report's findings reached the president—talked of Reagan's three-month silence.

Additionally, upon receiving the Tower Commission's final report, the president stated that he did not know what the information contained, saying, "Whatever this report may say, I have appointed—or I'm proud to have appointed this distinguished Board, because it fulfills my commitment to get the facts and share them with the American people."[13] Yet Parvin's "1-1-87" speech detailed what the committee concluded and many of the president's subsequent reactions.

Reagan's own diaries add to the time-line confusion. Passages reveal a White House seeking to craft a strong speech in response to the Tower Commission and private meetings between Tower and Reagan regarding the language of his remarks. In one of his diary entries, the president described a February decision to bring Parvin back to the White House and meetings with Tower in regards to speech preparation. He wrote on Monday, February 2, "I've told Don Regan to see if we can augment the speech writers by bringing back Landon Parvin." On Wednesday, February 4, he wrote, "Telephoned Landon Parvin about returning to the White House as a speechwriter."[14] Reagan wrote on Thursday, February 26, that he had received the Tower Commission Report that day, but "I won't know what's in it 'til I've read it." The next day he wrote that "early evening John Tower came by and we discussed my next week speech about the Tower

Commission Report, etc." Reagan added on Sunday, March 1, that he had "finished reading" the report and "now it's up to me to say the right thing Wednesday nite [sic] on TV." The next day Reagan wrote that he hoped to get Tower to take the job of director of the Central Intelligence Agency and anticipated receiving an answer from him on March 3.[15]

Other evidence supports a direct line between Reagan and John Tower. Cannon revealed in 1991 that Tower himself, along with Parvin, helped Reagan prepare his March 4 address to the nation. Cannon added that Tower's role remained secret because aides "thought it was unwise to advertise that the chairman of the board that had just passed judgment on Reagan's activities was now assisting him in his response to the Tower Report." Longtime Reagan political advisor Stuart Spencer wanted Tower's help, since "the only guy who knew what the hell was going on that I trusted was John Tower."[16] Amazingly, it would appear that the very person appointed to investigate Reagan's role in the Iran-Contra affair aided the president in preparing his public remarks in response to the committee's findings. Spencer and others were wise to hide such information. If the public or Congress had known of such a connection, the uproar no doubt would have been tremendous. Incredibly, it seems that Reagan not only utilized Tower to help him craft his response but then hoped to elevate the same person to be head of the CIA.

The "1-1-87" Parvin draft seems to suggest two incredible scenarios. One option remains that Reagan, confident that the Tower Commission would not find anything to counter his assertions of innocence, had Parvin start an early draft. The president and the speechwriter then worked on the speech during the eight weeks, retained the "1-1-87" date in the upper right-hand corner, and very early in the process fashioned exactly what Reagan wanted to say. Both men would then have added timely information as events warranted, such as the February appointment of Howard Baker. There is a problem with this theory. None of the other speeches prepared for Reagan through his administration, regardless of subject, maintained the original draft date in such a manner. Second, according to all accounts, Nancy Reagan brought Parvin back to the administration in February, long after any "1-1-87."

The alternative explanation is more sinister. The "1-1-87" date could imply that the president privately knew more about the ongoing investigation and subsequent findings of the Tower Commission than was publicly known. As a result, he could work two months early on a speech because he was already aware of the final outcome. Evidence clearly reveals that Reagan and Tower talked much more than was known at the time. Cannon's suggestion that Tower aided in writing the March 4 remarks does not completely clarify the "1-1-87" date. It does for some, however, make at least plausible an assertion that Reagan possessed foreknowledge of the commission's findings, which were then incorporated into early drafts as they became known.

Two days before Reagan's address to the nation, the Parvin draft still displayed the original January dates and staff members described the document as "1-1-87 Draft of 'Initial Address of the Nation.'" Two memos raise additional questions surrounding Reagan's reactions to the Tower Commission. One full week before the committee released the findings— on February 19, 1987—a memo from David Abshire, special counsel to the president, to Chief of Staff Regan and national security advisor Frank Carlucci contained, "In my judgment, the Tower Board Report will be devastating in its criticisms of process, and will reinforce an image of the President as detached and not in command." Abshire's "judgment" antici- pated, by two weeks, exactly the conclusion of the commission. He added that, as a first step to recovery, "the President would give a nationally televised speech soon after the Tower Board is released, but under no cir- cumstances should the President give a hastily prepared speech." He then lists three parts that should be included in the speech. Abshire wanted an explanation of initial Iranian policy and wrote that Peter Wallison (counsel to the president) was "drafting such points." Abshire also asserted that the speech must include an admission by Reagan that his policy degenerated into arms-for-hostages, an acceptance of the Tower report, and a discus- sion of the nation's future. Abshire's points followed exactly the pattern in both the "1-1-87" draft and Reagan's March 4 address.[17]

For all the confusion and supposed conspiracy of the "1-1-87" speech draft, Parvin himself explained the entire episode as a simple error on his part. He stated that when he began to work on the speech he meant to record 3-1-87 but, by mistake, wrote 1-1-87 instead. He explained his dif- ference in numerically writing the month instead of spelling it out, as was traditional, "because I was not a member of the White House staff at that time and did this [the speech] totally independently." As a result, Parvin utilized his own citation style to record the drafts of the speech and did not use the normal White House format. He stated that he did not know why, in the few days prior to Reagan's March 4 remarks, the "1-1-87" date remained on the early drafts of the speech. In regards to Tower's role in helping with the speech, Parvin explained that Tower did not help with any actual writing but instead was utilized during the February 27 White House meeting to help explain to the president what the Tower Report meant, the seriousness of the findings. Tower had taken no role in the actual writing of the speech.[18]

On March 3 Parvin's "1-1-87" date finally disappeared, as the remarks changed to the more standard practice of including the current date in the upper right-hand corner. In the second important memo, one day before Reagan's address a "5:00 p. m. Master" copy, with "(Parvin/RR)" in the upper right-hand corner, revealed that the speechwriter handwrote a presidential public apology into the final draft. Someone, possibly Reagan, crossed it out in blue ink. Parvin wrote for Reagan to say that, "As the Tower board reported, what began as a strategic opening to Iran deteriorated, in its implementation, into trading arms for hostages. . . . There are reasons why it happened, but no excuses. I made mistakes and I am sorry." In the March 4 broadcast Reagan repeated the lines until he reached the end and stated, "There are reasons why it happened, but no excuses. It was a mistake."[19] Thus he dropped "I am sorry" from the broadcast copy and matched his earlier consistent refusal to apologize publicly for his role in the affair.[20]

As technicians turned off the floodlights in the Oval Office, the waiting began. News of reactions arrived quickly. Not surprisingly, Reagan defenders celebrated the speech. Telegrams and phone messages arrived first, full of praise and of support. Many of the president's celebrity friends cheered the speech, including Efrem Zimbalist, Jr., Charlton Heston, Al Davis of the Oakland Raiders, Ray Charles, Fess Parker, the prime minister of Japan Yasu Nakasone, and Congressman Jack Kemp. The Reverend Billy Graham praised Reagan's "brevity and clarity" and added, "This is exactly the method Jesus used in the Sermon on the Mount." On March 5, a brief note arrived from Richard Nixon. The letter simply read, "Dear Ron, Bingo!! Dick."[21]

Reagan's White House carefully gauged the initial public and media reaction to the speech. After the broadcast, the press secretary Marlin Fitzwater sent a memo to Reagan that included complimentary quotes from the media and added, "The speech was very well received by the press." Memos to Chief of Staff Baker found a "six-fold increase" in telegrams sent to the White House in one day and of those received "93%" supported the president. Another memo recorded over five thousand phone calls in twenty-four hours with again "93%" offering praise for the speech. Another report described the reaction of the foreign press. Pollster Richard Wirthlin told Parvin a couple of days after the speech that his words and Reagan's delivery had "stopped the slide."[22]

Time reported Reagan's March 4 rhetorical return from a self-induced exile: "For three months the president refused to speak out on the crisis that swirled about him." The magazine reminded the readers that the president's one major appearance since early December remained the "recycled" State of the Union address in January. Of Reagan's March remarks

Time declared, "For the old trooper it was a masterly performance." The magazine declared the president as "repentant" yet "proud," "regretful" but "determined." The story stated, "Reagan looked to the future, assuming the tone of a grandfatherly sage," and that, "by summoning his tremendous skills as an orator, Reagan once again managed to swing events his way." *Time* reported that some overnight polls rose by as much as nine points but wondered if the trend would last. The magazine recognized Reagan's exile was over and declared that, with the revelations of the Tower Commission behind him, the president planned a "burst" of public appearances. *U.S. News and World Report* reported similar reactions.[23]

At first glance, all seemed well. The first official investigation offered nothing to contradict Reagan's claims of innocence. The "Great Communicator" had flawlessly delivered a well-received speech. The president planned now to move forward. He had stopped the political hemorrhaging, but he realized he had no time to lose. His poll numbers still hovered just below 50%.[24] Reagan quickly went on the offensive. His attitude was, "I told the country in November and early December I was innocent, I was quiet while investigations did their work, and I have been vindicated by the Tower Commission, now I will tell them again." His consistency of message returned as he began to repeat portions of his March explanation at virtually any opportunity.

Additionally, Reagan no longer worried about rhetorical linkage and providing fodder for the news media and political opponents. With his role in the scandal now behind him, the president returned to one of his favorite subjects, the Contras. Just a few days after a nationally televised speech many Americans believed vital to saving his presidency, Reagan returned unabashedly to praising key players in that scandal.[25] He continued, throughout the year, publicly sharing his Nicaraguan/Contra rhetoric on no less than forty occasions, but his words did not translate into American Contra support. Public approval for the Contras remained low and would not top 40% for the remainder of his presidency. Polls recorded 38% just after North's July testimony to Congress.[26]

With a polished script in hand, the president engaged the nation. One day after the March 4 speech, during remarks at a White House briefing for members of the National Newspaper Association, he said, "As you know, last night I addressed the American people and talked about the initiative to Iran. One thing that has made our Republic great is that we don't hide from our mistakes. We learn from them; then we go on and do things better than we did before." He added, "The investigations will continue, and they should. And the committees will continue to meet, and they should. I've said the administration will give them every cooperation, and it will. But so far as I'm concerned, the American people sent me here to do a job, and there are just 2 years left to get it done."[27] Reagan's words revealed a great deal. He called the Iran-Contra matter the "initiative" to Iran and twice talked of moving forward with his administration.

On March 19, Reagan held his first nationally televised news conference in four months. He faced an anxious press. As expected, Iran-Contra dominated a great deal of the questions. Reagan may have considered the issue closed, but the media did not agree. A great many issues surrounding the scandal had yet to be answered. Nevertheless, the president used the opportunity again to display his post-Iran-Contra rhetorical pattern that would be his script for the next two years. Helen Thomas of UPI asked if the president knew of the diversion of funds to the Contras. The president repeated that he did not. He took the opportunity to remind the nation that he personally informed the leaders of Congress regarding the diversion of funds. He reminded the assembled media that the moment he discovered what had been done he alerted Congress and the press. Sam Donaldson of ABC News pushed the president on specifics regarding Israel's role, and Reagan replied he could not recall. Bill Plante of CBS News quoted Reagan's recent national speech: "Mr. President, you said that in your heart you still believe that it wasn't an arms-for-hostage deal, but that the weight of the evidence presented by the Tower commission convinced you that it was. In your heart, do you now believe that it was an arms-for-hostages deal from the beginning, as the Tower commission said, and that the policy was flawed?" Reagan stood ready. In words very similar to those of the March 4 speech, he again walked the national audience through his explanation of why he reached out to moderates in Iran, of how he hoped that better relations with the Iranians could lead to possible release of hostages in Lebanon, and how he did not realize until he had read the Tower Report that the entire endeavor "had disappeared completely" into a direct swap of arms for hostages.

Even though they sensed no new information from the president, the press refused to let go. Chris Wallace of NBC News pressed Reagan on obviously "misleading" statements he had made early in the scandal regarding the role of Israel. The president called the information "misstatements" and reminded the reporter that he quickly issued corrections. When pressed by Wallace as to why the president tried to knock down reports in early November when the Lebanese newspaper *Al Shiraa* first reported the story, Reagan replied once again he did it to save lives. Reagan responded to a question about polls revealing that many Americans simply did not believe him: "Well, in view of what they've been reading and hearing for all these several months, I can understand why they might think that." The president refused to accept blame. He viewed low poll numbers as a consequence of negative reporting, not just the actions of his administration.

As the news conference drew to a close, Reagan received a question that dealt directly with administrative support for the Contras. "Long before the diversion of funds to the *contras*, the Tower board has documented 2 years of an extensive U.S. military support for the *contras* at a time when Congress ruled that to be illegal—air strips, phony corporations, tax-exempt foundations—all directed by Oliver North and John Poindexter and, before them, Robert McFarlane, out of the White House. And the question is, how could all this be taking place—millions and millions of dollars—without you having known about it, especially at a time when you were calling the *contras* the moral equivalent of our Founding Fathers?" Reagan simply replied that he remained aware of private groups funding the Nicaraguan rebels, cited past examples such as the Abraham Lincoln brigade in the Spanish Civil War, and cited how Congress can "turn on a president" when he asked for funds. Reagan did not believe the Boland amendments applied to private individuals or groups. As a result, he saw no problem or illegalities with these types of groups supplying monies to the Contras. When pressed for more details on how he could not have known about the money to the Contras, Reagan retreated, cited the ongoing investigations, and refused to comment further.[28]

Time reported "well-rehearsed answers" as the magazine detected the rhetorical strategy; "the president said little that went beyond statements he had already issued in other forums." In describing the president's prep for the conference, "the object was to make certain that Reagan would stay consistent, no matter how sharp the examination."[29]

A week later, in a very unusual setting, Reagan continued his new rhetorical offensive. While visiting a Columbia, Missouri, elementary school the president decided to share with the sixth-grade students, in uncomplicated language, his reasoning for reaching out to Iran. "You know, there was a revolution in a country called Iran, and the Ayatollah Khomeini took over and became the dictator of that country. Before that, it had a royal family, the Shah, the King. And he was thrown out of the country." He continued, "Then, this revolution decided that we, the United States, we were the Great Satan, we were the evil force. And yet, that's a very strategic country there in the Middle East, where there is so much trouble, and yet, where so much trouble for the world can be caused. And we got word that some people there in the government would like to talk to us about maybe reestablishing a friendly relationship between the two countries."[30]

Reagan's story time went on as he described Iranian moderates, "They asked us to sell them some weapons. We hadn't been doing that because they're engaged in a war. But these people said they were opposed to the war themselves, and they would like to see it ended." The president concluded, "And I'm afraid it wasn't carried out the way we had thought it would be. It sort of settled down to just trading arms for hostages, and that's a little like paying ransom to a kidnapper. And, finally, all of this came out into the open. Up until then, we'd had to keep everything very secret because we felt that the people who were talking to us from Iran would be executed by their government if they were found doing this." *Time* magazine took notice of the odd location for an Iran-Contra justification, saying derisively that "he is so spooked by the Iran controversy" that after an eleven-year-old student asked a question about being president, "Reagan lumbered into a five-minute Iran defense, the very thing he was trying to get away from."[31] *Time* missed the point completely. Reagan's rhetorical strategy was still to repeat consistently the same simple story until it became the accepted version of events. He no doubt hoped that the simple language explaining his actions would enter the media mainstream and then find easy acceptance by the American people.

In April 1987 Reagan continued to follow the script. On April 8, the White House announced that the president willingly turned over to the independent counsel and congressional investigating committees any notes concerning the Iran-Nicaragua connection from January 1, 1984, through the appointing of independent counsel on December 19, 1986. During an April 28 interview with White House newspaper correspondents, Reagan dismissed any personal involvement with the diversion of funds to the Contras and again reminded correspondents that it was his administration that had announced the diversion to the media. Reagan addressed the public distrust of his administration during the same interview, stating, "Well, I don't think the mistrust is justified." He then repeated his "saving lives" defense and suggested it had helped to feed the perception of a coverup.[32] Various poll numbers lagged behind the president's offensive. His job approval still hovered at just below 50%.[33] The bleeding was over, but the press and American people were still not yet onboard with his version of events, so recovery had begun but was still painfully slow.

During May, Reagan soldiered on with his rhetorical offensive. On May 3 during an informal exchange with reporters in New York City, he again stated that he had not known of any diversion of funds to the Contras. The same day during remarks to the hundredth annual convention of the American Newspaper Publishers Association, he placed the Nicaraguan government in league with the Soviet Union and pressed for more funding for the Contra rebels. On May 15 during a question-and-answer session with Southeast Regional Editors and Broadcasters concerning the

Iran-Contra scandal, Reagan admitted his difficulties, saying, "Yes, I'd been wounded," but then going on to repeat his pro-Contra rhetoric and cryptically stating that, on some details of the scandal, "it's awfully easy to be a little short of memory." When asked about his poll numbers, Reagan responded with observations asserting the questionable wording of survey questions, stated that his own polling showed him at "53%," and pointed out that President Dwight Eisenhower had held the same number in the sixth year of his presidency.[34] In spite of Reagan's defense, May polling data continued to tell a story of a president in a holding pattern. CBS News–*New York Times* and NBC News–*Wall Street Journal* surveys reported Reagan at or just below 50%. Only the ABC News–*Washington Post* presidential job approval poll found good news for the Reagan administration. The president's rating according to their survey (52%) reached above 50% for the first time since October 1986.[35]

Poll numbers notwithstanding, throughout May 1987 Reagan continued to repeat his Iran-Contra story. As the congressional hearings began, Reagan sat for an interview with *U.S. News and World Report*. He assured the reporters that nothing illegal had happened. He added his belief that the Boland Amendment did not apply to private citizens who wanted to donate to the Contras or the National Security Council since it was not an intelligence operation. Both *U.S. News and World Report* and *Time* repeated his argument a few weeks later.[36]

In the weeks since the March 4 address, no new evidence emerged to challenge his narrative. To be certain, revelations continued to buffet his administration. The ripple effects did reach the president, but no smoking guns emerged, and no one discovered any evidence that openly contradicted the president's story. As a result, three months after the March address, Reagan remained in full rhetorical stride. During a June 11 news conference, the president simply reiterated a great deal of his post–March 4 language. He even continued his defense that private funding of the Contras did not necessarily break any laws. Once again he reached back seventy years for an example, saying, "we can go clear back to the Lincoln Brigade in the Spanish Civil War." Iran-Contra did not dominate the June press conference as the subject had in March. It seemed the president's rhetorical strategy was working. A consistent message from Reagan and no contradictory evidence gave the nation nowhere else to go. To continue hounding the president with Iran-Contra questions would seem like badgering. Of thirty-two questions asked of Reagan, only nine dealt with the scandal. By comparison, the March 19 news conference contained thirty questions, of which twenty-four were related to Iran-Contra. By June, the nation had begun to turn the page, and unless the upcoming congressional hearings brought anything new, the country would continue to move forward.[37]

The congressional hearings began, and individuals such as Oliver North and John Poindexter dominated the headlines. The nation tried to understand the complicated story of arms shipments, shredded documents, secret bank accounts, and third-party countries. *Time* reported, "The Iran-Contra mess has been more complex and difficult for Americans to follow than the Watergate tragedy." Three weeks later, the magazine recounted the 1981–1986 lack of national support for the Contras. After North's theatrical testimony in full-dress uniform, however, the magazine reported that the Marine colonel "won more support for the *contras* in four days of testimony than Ronald Reagan has been able to stir up in six years." Poll numbers revealed that many Americans, in one survey as high as 71% of those surveyed, continued to believe Reagan held back information. In all 57% stated that they believed the "president knew money was being diverted from the Iranian arms sales to fund the *contras*." Significantly, the identical number responded that the congressional hearings "are motivated more by politics than by the evidence."[38] More important even than poll numbers, however, was the fact that during the two-month congressional hearings, no one's testimony openly contradicted the president's definition of his role in the scandal.

Reagan's strategy continued to work. His poll numbers continued a slow tick upward. A June ABC News–*Washington Post* poll on Reagan's approval rating broke at 55%. A telephone Gallup Poll conducted during the second week of June showed Reagan's job approval at 53%. Additionally, *U.S. News and World Report* printed numbers that revealed an American public more ready to forgive Reagan for any role in the scandal.[39] The survey numbers revealed a great deal. Since the congressional hearings offered only suspicion of the president's knowledge of the diversion of funds and without credible evidence to indicate otherwise, Reagan's explanations began to be accepted widely. Additional surveys continued to tell a story of presidential survival. As the summer passed, poll data continued to show a slow but steady increase in Reagan's popularity. It seemed 60% remained far away, but so thankfully, too, did the low thirties of several months ago.[40]

The congressional hearings ended with no direct evidence to contradict Reagan's self-described role in the entire Iran-Contra affair. On July 15, Poindexter told the House and Senate Iran/Contra Committee that Reagan did not know of the diversion of funds to the Contras. "I made a very deliberate decision not to ask the President so that I could insulate him from the decision and provide some future deniability. The buck stops with me." *Time* reported, "What? No Smoking Gun?" The magazine described the president's reaction. Reagan seemed "nonchalant" and replied, "What's new about that? I've been saying that for seven months."[41] No doubt pleased with Poindexter's admission, the president stuck to script.

Reagan personally sensed a turning tide in public opinion. A July 29, 1987, letter from his old friend Henry Salvatori suggested to the president that, because of the ongoing congressional hearings, Reagan needed to return to television to talk to the American people. Reagan wrote a reply on August 4 and observed that large crowds at several recent rallies convinced him "that the recent carnival on TV hasn't won the people's hearts or minds. Nevertheless, I'll be glad when it's over. Then I'll make a statement. Meanwhile, we're getting on with the business of government."[42]

The congressional hearings ended on August 3, 1987. The same day, *Time* published the reaction of Marshall, Arkansas, to the Iran-Contra affair, measured by a visit to the local barbershop. The piece contained various points of view, some supporting the president, others not so friendly. The story ended when one patron who had been silent the entire interview suddenly said, "Don't matter how worked up you get about the whole mess people'll just forget it, just like always."[43] The customer was more right than he could have known. Regarding the president's role in the scandal, the American people had begun to accept his explanation. No contradictory evidence meant two choices: a person could either believe the president or not. The process of moving forward continued, and very soon the entire affair would fade from the nation's collective consciousness.

On August 12, the week after the conclusion of the congressional hearings, Reagan planned to address the nation. Now that the hearings had exonerated him from personal knowledge of any diversion of funds, the president wished to put the entire mess behind him. His diary revealed that on Sunday, August 9, Reagan met at the White House "with Howard Baker, Senator John Tower (R-TX), and speechwriter Landon Parvin to discuss Wednesday speech."[44] Once again, as in March, Parvin and Tower sat together in the same room, speechwriter and committee chair, making sure consistency remained the key to success.

Before facing the nation as a whole, Reagan had already delivered a one-two Iran-Contra rhetorical punch during a late afternoon Oval Office interview with Hugh Sidey of *Time* magazine. During both events, Reagan offered no new information and instead stuck to script. Therefore, the interview and address provided the president a forum for repeating much of his phrasing regarding the Sandinistas, Nicaragua rebels, and the Iran-Contra affair. Sidey asked how history would remember Iran-Contra. Reagan responded, "Well, it is my hope that, once everything is settled and known, history will deal with it as the big investigation that finally discovered the President was telling the truth from the very beginning." Sidey asked if that would happen while Reagan still resided in the White House, to which the president replied, "Well, I would like to see it established very quickly." The interview concluded with Reagan again looking ahead and discussing what he wished to accomplish in the remaining two years of his presidency.[45]

The president faced the nation a few hours later. The August 12 address borrowed heavily from Reagan's March 4 remarks and echoed his consistent language of the past five months. From the Oval Office, he quickly reminded the country that the time had arrived to move forward. He addressed his audience's concerns and yet sought to guide the nation beyond them, as he stated, "I've said on several occasions that I wouldn't comment about the recent congressional hearings on the Iran-Contra matter until the hearings were over. Well, that time has come, so tonight I want to talk about some of the lessons we've learned. But rest assured, that's not my sole subject this evening. I also want to talk about the future and getting on with things, because the people's business is waiting."[46]

Reagan talked of his personal cooperation with the investigation of the scandal and admitted again that his initial outreach to moderates in Iran had deteriorated, without his knowledge, into an arms-for-hostage swap, stressing, "And this was a mistake," and "I was stubborn in my pursuit of a policy that went astray." He strongly denied any knowledge of the diversion of funds to the Contras but admitted, "I am the one who is ultimately accountable to the American people." The president then outlined several changes made in his administration to ensure that the conditions that begat Iran-Contra could not occur again. Past matters thoroughly covered as far as he was concerned, he continued, "But now let me turn to the other subject I promised to discuss this evening—the future. There are now 17 months left in this administration, and I want them to be prosperous, productive ones for the American people." With this, the president turned to issues such as Supreme Court nominees, relations with the Soviet Union, and the economic future of the nation. Of course, during his address Reagan could not but help revisit Nicaragua and the Contras. "As you know, I am totally committed to the democratic resistance—the freedom fighters—and their pursuit of democracy in Nicaragua." The president revisited his Nicaraguan betrayal theme. "My administration and the leadership of Congress have put forth a bipartisan initiative proposing concrete steps that can bring an end to the conflict there. Our key point was that the Communist regime in Nicaragua should do what it formally pledged to do in 1979—respect the Nicaraguan people's basic rights of free speech, free press, free elections, and religious liberty. Instead, those who govern in Nicaragua chose to turn their country over to the Soviet Union to be a base for Communist expansion on the American mainland."

In his conclusion Reagan again reminded the nation that, as far as he stood, the time had arrived to place the scandal behind him: "My fellow

Americans, I have a year and a half before I have to clean out this desk. I'm not about to let the dust and cobwebs settle on the furniture in this office or on me. I have things I intend to do, and with your help, we can do them."

A review of a rough draft of the speech reveals very few changes. An original line in the remarks, however, read, "Well, of course, I'm angry; at times, I've been mad as a hornet." Reagan personally dropped "I'm angry."[47] By changing the tense of the statement, the president again showed an effort to move forward and place Iran-Contra in the past. Parvin called Reagan's August 1987 remarks a "do nothing speech" that did not go as far as the earlier March address on the subject. He recalled that the second major Iran-Contra speech offered nothing new in policy and that Reagan missed an opportunity to go a "step before" what he stated in the March address. Part of the problem remained that Reagan "really believed" his explanation for Iran-Contra, that no arms-for-hostages-swap ever took place, even though the facts supported other conclusions. As a result, it remained very difficult to push the president beyond his oft-repeated comments on the subjects.[48]

Time detected the Reagan rhetorical strategy and cited his persuasive powers. Of the speech, the magazine reported, "nothing had changed" and "Reagan is calling for the nation to forget and move into the future." The story concluded, "Reagan is free because he did not know"; the president's "eyeball-to-eyeball insistence can sway any voter." *U.S. News and World Report* wrote that Reagan's address to the nation "added little new and ignored much." The magazine added that an ABC News poll reported that "three quarters" of America "agrees to put the scandal aside." The president's actions for the next eighteen months and the fading of Iran-Contra from the nation's consciousness supported both magazines' reports.[49] It seemed that, as far as America was concerned, Reagan had the right idea. It was time to look to the future.

On August 12, 1987, Reagan made what would be his last national address on Iran-Contra. He considered the matter closed and moved forward with his presidency. For the most part, the scandal earned only brief mentions in his speeches and usually only after specific questioning. Old habits and subjects returned to his dialogue. With words that echoed his pre-scandal language, Nicaragua and the Contras dominated a great deal of his oral arsenal. As fall turned to winter, the nation's interest in any possible Reagan role in the Iran-Contra affair began to fade. News accounts faded, and after September 1987, Gallup did not conduct any additional Iran-Contra surveys. On October 22, Reagan held another press conference. Of thirty-five questions asked, not one question dealt with the Iran-Contra affair. Perhaps not wanting to tempt fate and return to the subject of the scandal, the president did not mention the Contras or Nicaragua.

On November 18, with the official release of the congressional investigation of the scandal, Reagan did not even respond in person. There was no need. Marlin Fitzwater, assistant to the president for press relations, released a statement, announcing that the recently concluded congressional investigation supported the president's assertions that he had not known of any diversion of funds. Fitzwater quoted extensively from Reagan's March and August national addresses. He concluded with a nod to the continuing investigation of independent counsel Lawrence Walsh, but he also made a plea to move forward: "This report is but another step in the investigatory process. But, it does culminate the long summer of self-examination for America and for the administration, and now we are through it. We are moving on, and we trust that out of this experience has come a new wisdom about the process of governing in America."[50] *Time* gave only one page to the release of the congressional report. *U.S. News and World Report* did not allow even that much and instead gave the story a half-page box.[51]

Polls throughout the end of 1987 continued to show, for the most part, stability and a slow uptick for Reagan's job approval numbers. The president had crept into the mid-fifties by October, before the November release of the Congressional Iran-Contra Report brought a brief return of the scandal to the public's attention. In some surveys Reagan briefly slid below 50%. By December 1987, Reagan had regained lost ground and was back in the mid-fifties.[52]

As 1987 closed, Reagan had experienced a year of presidential extremes. The year had begun with his popularity floundering in the low thirties and many Americans wondering if he would last the year. Twelve months later, he enjoyed a twenty-point turnaround in poll numbers and had put the scandal behind him. In late December, journalist David Frost interviewed the president for *U.S. News and World Report*. Frost asked, "Irangate, I suppose, was a mistake?" Reagan comfortably launched into his reliable script. When Frost then asked him to compare the scandal to Watergate, the president gave a wandering answer about money exchanging hands for weapons and did not answer the question. Former President Carter possessed no such restraint when interviewed in the same issue. He said that indeed Iran-Contra remained far worse than Watergate since the credibility of America's foreign policy suffered great damage. He offered his own opinion of Reagan's survival and added that—because of the impact of Nixon's scandal—Congress, media, and "of course" the American people did not want to punish Reagan.[53] Carter's frustration mirrored his irritation of seven years earlier regarding Reagan's Neshoba County Fair visit. The former president's words expressed disbelief that his Oval Office successor had survived another much graver mistake. While Carter's conclusion that Watergate tempered the nation's anger toward Reagan should not be dismissed, the former president had simply expressed frustration at the fading of the scandal from the nation's collective attention.

During 1988, Iran-Contra seemed forgotten and seldom did the president return to the scandal. When he did, his remarks stayed completely on message and echoed the long-ago March 1987 speech. Similar to his spring 1987 confidence in returning to the subject of the Contras, Reagan in his last year in office felt confident enough to add a new rhetorical twist to the entire episode. He stated several times that the affair did not deserve the label of a scandal. He would repeat such a claim often in the future.[54] Additionally, with Iran-Contra barely on the nation's radar, Reagan increased his Nicaragua rhetoric. In 1988 he publicly shared his now-eight-year-old championing of the Contras on no less than fifty-eight occasions.[55] Reagan had reason to feel confident. A February 1988 survey by the Gallup organization found that 55% of respondents believed "the Reagan administration's overall record for honesty and ethical standards" remained the same or better than other recent presidential administrations.[56] Incredibly, one year after a speech he gave to save his presidency, over half of the Americans surveyed gave the president a passing grade on honesty and ethics.

On March 16, Independent Prosecutor Walsh handed down four indictments for four participants in the scandal: Oliver North, John Poindexter, Richard Secord, and Albert Hakim. *Time* stated that for Reagan and the public the scandal had "dropped from sight" since the summer of 1987. The story called Iran-Contra a "half-forgotten drama."[57] Reagan's job approval numbers, while not achieving the pre-scandal highs of the mid-sixties, nevertheless remained respectable for a president at the end of his second term. Surveys by Gallup in 1988 revealed lows of just below 50% and peaks ten points higher. The data reported also that, by late 1988, over half of Americans believed Reagan would go down in history as an outstanding or above average president. Gallup pointed to financial optimism in the nation and approval in the president's handling of relations with the Soviet Union as factors in Reagan's upswing.

In his final year in office, Reagan may have successfully avoided Iran-Contra, but the scandal did not go away completely. Vice President George Bush, seeking to follow his boss into the Oval Office, endured a great deal of questioning on the subject. Bush lacked Reagan's rhetorical survival skills and quickly ran into trouble. On January 25, CBS News anchor Dan Rather interviewed the vice president on live television. The exchange soon turned heated between the two men, when Rather pressed Bush on Iran-Contra. *Time* reported that almost 80% of Americans believed Bush knew more about the arms-for-hostages deal and 60% supported Rather in pushing Bush for explanations. The story did not make a single mention of Reagan, clearly showing his distance from the scandal in the minds of many Americans. Reagan offered "no comment" when asked about the Bush-Rather altercation.[58]

Lingering Iran-Contra questions did not stop Bush. Reagan's vice president easily defeated the Democratic nominee, Michael Dukakis. Gallup conducted a poll just after the 1988 presidential election regarding the importance of Iran-Contra during the election. Not surprisingly, only 8% of Bush voters perceived "Bush's role in the Iran-Contra affair" as "very important." Supporters for Massachusetts governor Michael Dukakis replied that 51% viewed "Bush's role in the Iran-Contra affair" as "very important."[59] Although a majority, the numbers told an important story; for the American public, regardless of political orientation, Iran-Contra continued to grow fainter in the national awareness. One month later, in a December 8, 1988, news conference, Reagan denied that Bush had any role in Iran-Contra and expressed confidence that a Bush administration would continue to support the Contras.[60]

As Reagan packed for California and Bush prepared to take over occupancy in the White House, the national media began to say good-bye to Reagan. As is common, the nation's press took the measure of the departing president. Reagan made it easy. His poll numbers were up and a sense of goodwill surrounded his two terms in office. What the media did not write about told just as much as what they did. Iran-Contra generated no coverage. Questions regarding Reagan's knowledge of the diversion no longer earned any ink. Reagan's rhetorical strategy had worked; the nation had moved forward.

Newsweek stated that Reagan was in "87 another failed president" but that "in 1988 [he was] so great he even elected Bush" and added, "Reagan will depart with a reservoir of good will almost unheard of in the modern presidency." In two successive issues, *Time* covered Reagan's last days in office. Reporting his job approval back at 64%, the magazine included a detailed survey of America's thoughts on the fortieth president. The poll asked, "What kind of president was Ronald Reagan?" The results returned that 11% of Americans answered great, 37% good, 37% average, and 15% poor. The same poll asked, "Is the U.S. better or worse off as a result of Reagan's eight years in office?" The numbers returned a confident "60% Better Off" and "27% Worse Off." Finally, the poll asked, "If Reagan could have run for another term, would you have voted for him?" The respondents answered that if given the opportunity 41% would put Reagan back into the White House while 54% would not. Not bad numbers for a politician who less than two years earlier had been fighting to survive his second term. Hugh Sidey of *Time* concluded, "Rarely if ever in 100 years has there been such an affectionate farewell from the nation and from the White House staff."[61] As Reagan left office on January 20, 1989, Gallup recorded his job approval rating back to the level just prior to the arms-for-hostages story. With numbers in the mid-sixties, he left office with the highest approval rating of any outgoing president since Franklin Roosevelt.[62]

A key component to Reagan's survival of the Iran-Contra affair remained his post–March 1987 return to a consistent message on the issue. When the scandal broke in the fall of 1986, his 1981–1986 persistent championing of the Contras had made it easy to believe Reagan knew more than he initially told. His November and early December uncertainty and wavering on the subject cost support and credibility with the American people. His three months of silence allowed others to dictate the narrative and describe his role in the scandal. By spring 1987, however, Reagan returned with a polished script in one hand and the Tower Commission vindication in the other. Uncertainty disappeared as he offered an unwavering account regarding his responsibility in the affair. The success of his new rhetorical initiative allowed the president to return to praising the Contras frequently and fearlessly, a key element in the Iran-Contra crisis. The press, with no new evidence to counter the Reagan description of events, initially continued to ask questions but could only report the president's consistent responses. By the summer of 1987 the president's job approval rating slowly began to rise from the low numbers of late 1986 and early 1987. The Iran-Contra scandal continued as a media story but slowly faded as any real danger to the Reagan presidency. Congressional hearings and independent investigations answered some questions, offered opinions on others, but produced no evidence to suggest the president's involvement in any diversion of funds. By the time Reagan left office sixteen months later, his job approval ratings once again reached pre-scandal levels. A story line concerning his Iran-Contra role established, in part by Reagan and in part by evidence, the scandal as an issue soon disappeared, not only from the national press but also from public consciousness.

7 / Reagan's Death and the Enduring Power of Collective Memory

"He has a legacy that is greater than his presidency."
—Cokie Roberts, June 9, 2004

"Reagan used to say that it took twenty years of saying something before it got into the nation's consciousness."
—Landon Parvin, August 16, 2010

ABC News broke the story first, on Saturday afternoon, just after four o'clock eastern time on June 5, 2004. Anchor Elizabeth Vargas announced, "We have been notified that the LA Police Department has been notified that President Ronald Reagan has died this afternoon in Los Angeles in his home in the Bel Air suburb of Los Angeles."[1] Rumors had circulated for weeks that the ninety-three-year-old former president had taken a turn for the worse. Spokesmen for the Reagan family officially dismissed such claims. Privately, though, the family had been notifying friends that the end, indeed, was at hand. A life begun in the early twentieth century neared an end early in the twenty-first. Reagan had not been seen in public since the late 1990s. As his battle with Alzheimer's disease progressed his wife, Nancy, began to limit access to him. A few years after the 1994 announcement to the public that the former president had Alzheimer's, she told close friends to arrange final visits, that contact with Reagan would soon be restricted only to family and necessary medical staff. By the late 1990s, any recent photographs of Reagan came from the family and these images were tightly controlled: birthday celebrations, a carefully staged 1998 spread for *Vanity Fair* magazine. To be certain, determined photographers still found opportunities and snapped photographs as Reagan ventured out for walks with his Secret Service detachment or attended church. Nancy's tight controls and careful precautions, however, kept any embarrassing images out of the hands of the national media. Always his protector and greatest champion, she ensured that the nation remembered Reagan at his best, not as a man struggling with an incurable disease.[2]

His 1994 Alzheimer's announcement removed him from the national stage, a broken hip in 2001 severely limited his mobility, and in June 2004, pneumonia ended his life. And then there began a weeklong marathon of media coverage. The twenty-four-hour news networks, CNN, FOX, and MSNBC devoted the vast majority of programming to Reagan's death. The traditional "big three" networks—ABC, NBC, and CBS—broadcast the key moments of the week. Reagan seemingly dominated every channel, and the media coverage brought the Reagan presidency back to the center of the nation's attention.

On Sunday, the day after his death, his presidential library hosted a private family memorial service and then allowed public viewing of the flag-draped casket until Tuesday. On Wednesday, his body was taken to Washington, DC, for a formal procession to the Capitol Building, complete with horse-drawn caisson. After a state funeral ceremony that evening, the Rotunda opened to the public for another viewing that continued through Thursday. President George W. Bush declared Friday, June 11, a national day of mourning as an honor guard transported the president's body to the National Cathedral for a funeral service. Following the ceremony, Air Force One flew Reagan back to California for a sunset interment at his hilltop presidential library overlooking the Pacific Ocean. The press detailed every ceremony. In the era of twenty-four-hour news coverage, even Reagan's hearse received airtime. As his body traveled from location to location, helicopters hovered overhead and broadcast pictures.

Members of his past two administrations, now a little grayer and a bit slower, suddenly found themselves in demand once again. On television, in newspapers, and in magazines they retold old stories and then retold them again. The scenes documented in the mass media took on the appearance of a 1980s political reunion. Millions of Americans paused from their daily lives to reflect on Reagan's presidency and to remember events from two decades earlier. Many wrote letters to the editors who, in turn, composed editorials. Many spoke into television cameras, which broadcast their recollections. Good or bad, it seemed everyone had a Reagan story to tell.

The nation remembered Reagan as the country last saw him or, more important, how millions recalled seeing him. At his last major public appearance, the April 1994 funeral of Richard Nixon, Reagan did not look his eighty-three years. His hair looked a little grayer but had not thinned at all. Dressed in a dark suit, his skin tanned by the California sun, he carried the same squared shoulders. He still looked like a president. He did not speak at the service, gave no opportunity to hear again the strength of the Reagan rhetoric. No real concern. The two primary speakers, after all, had compelling reasons to stand at the podium. Senator Robert Dole had a long relationship with Nixon, and Bill Clinton was the current president. A few months later, the November 5 Alzheimer's letter shocked the nation, and Reagan disappeared from public life. An era definitely had ended. There would be no more speeches, no more rhetoric.

Nancy did her job well. The nation remembered Reagan at his best: strong, confident, smiling. The media coverage also revealed that many key elements of Reagan's rhetoric offered twenty years earlier had now passed into accepted collective memory. America did not watch Reagan grow old and feeble. In memory, the country had nowhere to go but back to better days, nowhere to look except back through the lens of nostalgia. This communal remembering took place under the influence of the commemorative present. The national collective memory naturally gravitated to a point almost two decades old. Fifteen years after he left office, dominant precedents set years before suddenly reappeared in force. Reagan's words once again echoed across the national headlines and airwaves. Like twenty years earlier, voices of protest found expression but gained little ground opposed to an established national collective. Press coverage of Reagan's death, as well as subsequent reflections on his presidency, exposed familiar patterns of collective memory. The five-day media marathon offered numerous opportunities for national reflection. Within the many stories, the American public and the press shared memories regarding Reagan and Neshoba, Vietnam, and Iran-Contra.

The Neshoba County Fair Revisited

Even in the weeks prior to Reagan's death, some continued to argue that Reagan began his 1980 campaign in Philadelphia, Mississippi. The *Raleigh (NC) News and Observer* printed a story on the inequalities of society fifty years after the landmark 1954 decision *Brown v. Board of Education*. The article observed that in 1976 at Madison Square Garden Democratic candidate Jimmy Carter had joined hands with Martin Luther King, Sr., but "Only four years after civil rights symbolism helped a white peanut farmer from Georgia gain the White House, candidate Ronald Reagan employed a different kind of symbolism to open his bid for the presidency in 1980." The story continued, "Speaking in Neshoba County, Miss., a site chosen because three civil rights workers had been murdered

I KNOW IN MY HEART THAT MAN IS GOOD
THAT WHAT IS RIGHT WILL ALWAYS EVENTUALLY TRIUMPH
AND THERE IS PURPOSE AND WORTH TO EACH AND EVERY LIFE

RONALD WILSON REAGAN
FEBRUARY 6, 1911 ~ JUNE 5, 2004

President Reagan's final resting place at the Reagan Library.

there in 1964, Reagan called the Civil Rights Act of 1964 'bad legislation,' the Voting Rights Act of 1965 'a humiliation to the South,' and declared his devotion to Strom Thurmond's old cause of 'states' rights.'"[3] The story had many problems. Reagan did not choose the Neshoba location because of the 1964 murders or "open his bid" at the fair. Nor did the candidate invoke the name of Strom Thurmond as the story suggested. Regardless, the article revealed how—even before Reagan's death returned attention to his August 1980 visit—the erroneous campaign kickoff story remained a part of the collective memory surrounding his Neshoba visit.

As there had been a national and a regional interpretation of Reagan's visit to Neshoba, the media throughout the country tended to follow the same pattern, with the national media far less concerned about the fair visit than were local and regional media outlets. The *New York Times* and *USA Today* coverage of Reagan's death do not mention the August 1980 Reagan visit. On more than one occasion, the two national newspapers did print stories regarding the president's controversial record on civil rights, but the visit to Philadelphia, Mississippi, did not attract a single citation. Other national papers with less circulation did revisit the issue, but only briefly, in separate stories, and never in the coverage of Reagan's funeral. The June 9 *Chicago Tribune* reported the erroneous story that the president began his 1980 campaign in Mississippi. On June 10, the *Boston Globe* did the same, as did the *Atlanta Journal-Constitution*, which wrote: "One of Reagan's first campaign stops after the Republican convention was at the Neshoba County Fair in Mississippi, a few miles from where three civil rights workers had been murdered in 1964." In a June 13 article in the *Washington Post*, Donna Britt wrote, "Newt Gingrich suggested Wednesday that Reagan, surrounded for decades by wealth, simply didn't know poor black people [were] hamstrung by racism's effects." She then asked, "Does that explain why he kicked off his campaign by talking about 'states' rights' in Philadelphia, Miss., where three civil rights workers were slain in the 1960s?"[4]

Regional media, however, spent more time on the subject of Reagan and Neshoba. The coverage recalled President Carter's September and October 1980 refusal to leave the issue. Approaching the subject, as Carter did from a more localized memory, the smaller presses devoted more time to reminding the nation of Reagan's August 1980 visit. On June 6, one day after Reagan's death, an Associated Press story from Jackson, Mississippi, reported the reaction of Mississippi officials. The piece declared that Reagan had begun his 1980 campaign in Neshoba.[5] On June 9, 2004, the *Raleigh News and Observer* printed a passionate letter from a reader still angry over the Mississippi visit. On June 10, journalist Juan Williams also repeated the campaign-origin story.[6] The next day Derrick Jackson of the *Boston Globe* stood closer to the truth and revisited Reagan's "first major speech after receiving the nomination for president in 1980." He continued, "The fair was a more comfortable fit for Reagan than the mainstream press has ever admitted."[7] With his words, Jackson noted the "pass" Reagan had received from the national media in 1980. He, like others, wished for more attention to what he perceived as the true meaning of the trip.

Three days later, the *Washington Post* carried an editorial by Pulitzer Prize–winning columnist William Raspberry. A native of Mississippi and in his late twenties at the time of the 1964 murders, he approached the 1980 visit through the prism of local memory. He, more than most, could understand the fervor over Reagan's words. Raspberry began his work respectfully, "I don't mean to be graceless, but I would like to inject a slightly off-key note in the praise-fest following the death of former president Ronald Reagan." He shared with the readers that he heard of

Reagan's death, ironically enough, while he was in Mississippi and just one day after he had learned that the state's attorney general, Jim Hood, had asked the US Justice Department for help in introducing new evidence in the still open 1964 murder case. He added, "Philadelphia, county seat of Mississippi's Neshoba County, is famous for a couple of things. That is where three civil rights workers—Michael Schwerner, James Chaney and Andrew Goodman—were murdered in 1964. And that is where, in 1980, Republican presidential candidate Ronald Reagan chose to launch his election campaign with a ringing endorsement of 'states' rights.'"[8]

Raspberry reflected on Reagan's political seizure of the South and the importance of the Neshoba trip. "The essence of that transformation, we shouldn't forget, is the party's successful wooing of the race-exploiting Southern Democrats formerly known as Dixiecrats. And Reagan's Phila-delphia appearance was an important bouquet in that courtship." Rasp-berry refused to accuse the former president of racism, but he did point out Reagan's "indifference" to blacks, his "refusal" to act against South African apartheid, and even his tutelage of a "political progeny" in Mis-sissippi senator Trent Lott. The native Mississippian referred obviously to Lott's infamous December 5, 2002, comments at the one-hundredth birth-day celebration for Senator Strom Thurmond. The Mississippi senator expressed pride for his state's 1948 support for Thurmond and concluded, "If the rest of the country had followed our lead, we wouldn't have had all these problems over all these years, either." Less than three weeks later Lott resigned his post as Senate Republican Leader.

Raspberry concluded that Reagan "did have a grand way of expressing what was an unquestionably grand vision of America's place in the world. But in some ways, including racially, he left us a more divided nation, in part by making division seem legitimate. That's the legacy of Philadelphia." Although long gone from Mississippi and working for the *Washington Post* at the time of the murders, Raspberry approached the 1964 deaths as a local. He, more than most, understood the ramifications of Reagan's words. Raspberry recognized who in the region would appreciate Reagan's language and who would not. He also sensed where the true power lay within the region, and how two words at a Mississippi fair could alter the state's political direction.[9]

The Neshoba visit continued to generate more passion in the smaller presses as the 1980 campaign kickoff story continued to find print. On the fortieth anniversary of the murders, June 21, 2004, Jane Wallace Claymore of the *Charleston (WV) Gazette* strongly criticized Reagan's trip.[10] She offered harsh words, but again the article only found print in a regional newspaper.

Finally, the incorrect assertions surrounding the 1980 presidential campaign and Neshoba showed no sign of diminishing and continued to appear five months after Reagan's funeral. On November 15, 2004, the *New York Observer* printed an article by Jim Callaghan trying to assuage fellow Democrats who were upset over the reelection of President George W. Bush. The writer listed several past instances when the future seemed dark for Democrats. He included, "Ronald Reagan, the 'affable' charmer, was cruel in his attitudes toward cities, except the one where he opened his 1980 campaign to get across his obvious code-worded message: Philadelphia (Mississippi, not Pennsylvania)."[11] Callaghan's words, or lack thereof, remain telling. The erroneous campaign kickoff story surrounding Reagan and Neshoba remained so ingrained in the minds of some Americans that the columnist did not even have to define "his obvious code-worded message" of states' rights.

For the most part, the subject of Neshoba remained absent from the national newsmagazines. Of the mass-circulated weeklies, only two mentioned the August 1980 Mississippi trip. Matching the pattern of the nation's newspapers, the account of the trip found print in secondary stories, but not in the funeral coverage. The June 14 *Newsweek*, in a story by editor and writer Jon Meacham, repeated the erroneous assertion that Reagan began his 1980 campaign at the fair. *U.S. News and World Report* included in the June 21 issue the observation that Reagan experienced tense relations with blacks due to his Neshoba trip.[12]

The absence of the Neshoba story on television mimicked the pattern of the national newspapers and magazines. Thus, television news organizations ignored the 1980 Neshoba County trip, not only in live televised coverage of Reagan's death but also in the more scripted cable news programs. CBS remained the closest any major network came to Philadelphia, Mississippi. In the weeks after Reagan's death, the network published *Ronald Reagan Remembered*, a commemoration book with an accompanying DVD. Partly a Reagan biography and partly a record of the media coverage of his death, the work simply reprinted the June 14 *Newsweek* Meacham piece stating that Reagan began the 1980 campaign in Neshoba.[13]

During the days after Reagan's death, media coverage painted a clear picture. Reagan's success in defusing the "states' rights" controversy in 1980 remained intact. The pattern of the press coverage revealed that national newspapers, magazines, and television media essentially ignored the trip, relegating the Neshoba remarks for the most part to editorials that could only propagate a false campaign-origin story. More detailed accounts of the August 1980 speech could find print only in smaller presses. While the erroneous campaign-kickoff story continued in both national and regional coverage, only the smaller press communicated any real anger regarding the visit. To be fair, part of this media inattention could be explained by the fact that the press was eager to focus on the more celebratory achievements of the Reagan presidency. What is certain, however, is that Reagan himself deserves the vast majority of the credit for having successfully neutralized the issue over two decades earlier. The majority of the nation remembered the Mississippi speech exactly how Reagan wanted them to—in other words, not at all. Similar to the initial August 1980 reaction, in the days after Reagan's death the nation simply moved forward regarding Neshoba while smaller and more regional recollections protested from the fringes.

The Memory of Vietnam

A great deal of the media coverage, reflecting the popular culture of the 1980s, often placed Reagan and Vietnam in the same sentence. The press, either national or regional, through news coverage or editorials, talked of a pre-Reagan America, racked with domestic problems and international uncertainty. Often citing Vietnam specifically, the reports consider Reagan the one individual who lifted the United States out of the doldrums of the 1970s beyond the Vietnam Syndrome and who returned confidence to the country. Upon his death, the press continued to repeat the Reagan Vietnam interpretation.

The June 6 *New York Times* obituary remarked, "To a nation hungry for a hero, a nation battered by Vietnam, damaged by Watergate and humiliated by the taking of hostages in Iran, Ronald Reagan held out the promise of a return to greatness, the promise that America would 'stand tall' again." The same day, the *Washington Post* wrote of Reagan's 1980 campaign and two subsequent election victories, "It had been 20 years since a president had completed two full terms. Five administrations had been cut short: by assassination, Vietnam, Watergate, rampant inflation and civic malaise. In a sense, Reagan's signal achievement was that he restored in Americans their hope for normalcy."[14]

Regional newspapers joined in praising Reagan's two administrations for moving the nation past the shadow of Vietnam. The June 6 *Chicago Sun-Times* stated on the editorial page, "It's difficult now to recall how bad things seemed in America when Ronald Reagan entered the White House in 1981." The editorial continued, "Post-Vietnam America seemed in retreat," and concluded, "The conventional wisdom, for once right, is that Ronald Reagan was one of the two most consequential presidents of the 20th century, the other being Franklin Roosevelt." The same day, the *Columbus (OH) Dispatch* offered, "After the long, difficult ordeal that was the 1970s, after Vietnam and Watergate, after an energy crisis and a hostage crisis, this nation was desperate for something to feel good about. The time was ripe for Ronald Wilson Reagan."[15] On June 7, the *Richmond (VA) Times-Dispatch*, the *Norfolk Virginian Pilot*, and the *Lancaster (PA) New Era* all printed stories that praised Reagan for moving the nation past painful memories of Watergate and Vietnam.[16]

Two days later, the *Washington Post* took Reagan and Vietnam from the editorial page to the financial section. "The Reagan defense buildup was a hallmark of his presidency, a free-spending crusade that lifted the nation's military industry out of the doldrums after the Vietnam War." The same day, the *Boston Herald* ran an editorial that described America prior to Reagan's 1980 victory, cited the impact of Vietnam, and added that "Reagan strode forth with clear beliefs, a strong sense of right and wrong, and an unbending willingness to get his way, no matter what the cost. His was a philosophy of sunny optimism, not grim moralizing. And his sense of sureness was so powerful that people followed."[17]

On June 11, Steve Otto in the *Tampa (FL) Tribune* remembered hearing Reagan offering "strength" when "the conflict in Vietnam was spinning out of control, and there was a sense of helplessness in the country." The *Washington Times* recalled a pre-1980 America in an editorial, his role in turning the nation around, and that "in all of American history, few presidents did as much as Ronald Reagan to advance the cause of freedom and make the world a safer place."[18] As funeral services concluded in California, the tributes continued throughout the country. On June 12, Georgia columnist Dick Yarbrough in the *Augusta (GA) Chronicle* echoed the oft-repeated assertion that Reagan brought the nation back after Vietnam. The next day the *Lancaster (PA) Sunday News* in an editorial wrote, "It may be hard for younger generations to imagine how disheartened Americans were as the Vietnam decade dragged into the stagflation years" and how "Ronald Reagan, the GOP's own happy warrior, renewed a nation's confidence in itself."[19]

Media reports continued to contain praise for Reagan's confidence in a post-Vietnam America. Some writers, only children when Reagan served as president, longed for his consistency of message. Syndicated columnist Collin Levey on the opinion page of the June 10 *Seattle Times* wrote of memories of Vietnam, and the calming effect of Reagan's words, comparing those bygone days to the contemporary unease regarding the war in Iraq. She added that Reagan's clarity of message would be welcome in the current situation, saying, "The antidote to the intellectual mushiness then wasn't subtlety or coercion; it was clarity. Reagan's success and the endurance of his legacy are a reflection that Americans respond best to big ideas." Levey admitted, "As somebody who was 5 when Reagan took office, I belong to a generation that already has to make an effort to recall the despair and pessimism that preceded him. Had Reagan died in a quieter time, we surely would have known his value and honored him still. But we wouldn't have needed him nearly so much."[20]

Meanwhile, news coverage reported Reagan's pre-presidency support for Vietnam veterans. On June 11, 2004, an Associated Press story for the wire service, dateline Honolulu, detailed Reagan's personal connections with Vietnam veterans. Reporter Bruce Dunford depicted a recent memorial service held at a cathedral in Hawaii and the reaction from former prisoner-of-war Navy Captain Gerald Coffee. The veteran remembered visits with then Governor Reagan of California: "Receptions that were memorable even more than the elegant sit-down banquets the Nixons provided to us a month or so later, memorable because they were like family. He was eager to hear our stories." Captain Coffee then walked to the lectern and tapped out a message to Reagan from a secret prisoner code learned while he was a captive in the infamous Hanoi Hilton. The veteran rapped "G-N" for goodnight and "G-B-U" for God bless you.[21]

National newsmagazines also joined in describing a pre-Reagan America. The periodicals echoed a great deal of the national and regional dailies. In *Newsweek* Jon Mecham wrote of a nation lost because of Vietnam and Watergate. He then added, "Then along came Reagan." The following week the magazine covered the former president's funeral and included a two-page-spread photo of a teary-eyed Vietnam veteran, Hubert Jordan, saluting Reagan's caisson in Washington, DC.[22] The June 14 *Time* magazine talked of "a U.S. still licking its wounds from Vietnam" as Reagan came into office and recalled that, "from the first, Reagan moved aggressively to undo the 'Vietnam syndrome.'" That same week the *Economist* offered, "The Carter years were a period of American self-doubt: about the economy and about American power (with the memory of Vietnam still tormenting many policymakers). Mr. Reagan set about wiping this away."[23]

Hour upon hour of television coverage displayed the same pattern regarding Reagan and Vietnam. The day of his passing, CNN broadcast a special live weekend edition of *Larry King Live*. Columnist George Will cited the loss of Vietnam as one of many problems depressing the country and recalled Reagan's optimism and approach to the nation.[24] The following day, NBC's highly popular *Meet the Press with Tim Russert* devoted the entire program to the subject of the president's passing. Arizona senator John McCain, asked about his first meeting with Reagan, spoke of the connection between the former president and Vietnam veterans: "When I came home from a Vietnamese prison camp. And it was the first time—

chance I had to meet him face-to-face. But I knew prisoners who were shot down after I was were very well aware of his commitment to the POWs and to our release and his extreme affection that he and Nancy had displayed to the families of those who were in prison." McCain continued, "He was very curious about what had happened to us. But most importantly, he was committed to the belief that America was still great. He believed that the men and women who served in Vietnam, including the POWs, were the best of America." McCain concluded with a nod to Reagan's position on Vietnam and veterans, a viewpoint that had been years ahead of the nation's: "And, you know, America was very divided in those years. When I came home from a time warp, from '67 to '73, America wasn't sure of itself. A lot of people think we'd lost our way. And he had an unwavering belief and faith in the greatness of the nation."[25] On June 7, *Larry King Live* guest Dan Rather of CBS News cited Vietnam as one of many problems sapping the nation's will. He concluded: "And whether one liked him or not Ronald Reagan from the first second he came to the presidency brought that sunny, smiling, optimism and hope."[26]

Finally on June 11, as Reagan's body arrived back in California for burial, ABC News anchor Peter Jennings pointed out a *Wall Street Journal* story by Gerald "Jerry" Seib: "The president was giving masterful, elegant speeches full of irresistible Reaganisms and powerful lines. And they were directed not at us the reporters but at Middle America beyond us." The news anchor continued, "'He headed to places that others avoided and said things they wouldn't dare. He gave a speech saying the Vietnam War had been a noble cause and shockwaves ensued . . . [when] a pack of reporters chas[ed] Mr. Reagan's most-trusted aide, Ed Meese, down a hotel hallway to find out what the candidate really meant. And he looked back at us blankly as if he were shocked that we were shocked.'"[27] Jennings's singling out that particular portion of the Seib story and the reaction of the press at the time clearly revealed, again, that Reagan's "noble cause" Vietnam language remained well ahead of the comfort level of the country.

Influenced by a now entrenched collective memory that had been established two decades earlier, national and regional newspapers, weekly newsmagazines, and the television media all echoed the same description of events. Almost to a source, each remembered and reported a disheartened America, crippled by the war in Southeast Asia. Reagan received accolades in print or broadcast for moving the country past Vietnam. Reagan's consistent version of the Vietnam War and veterans—greeted with anxiety early in his presidency, and later a key part of a national reevaluation of Vietnam veterans—was accepted reality by 2004. Deviant voices to the collective memory remained silent or unreported.

Reagan's exit music could not have been more fitting. As the June 11 National Cathedral service concluded, a military honor guard carried the former president's casket to a waiting hearse for his final journey back to California for burial. The large church echoed with the strands and chorus of "Mansions of the Lord," a recent hymn composed by Nick-Glennie Smith with words by Randall Wallace. Individuals who personally knew Reagan could only smile as the music began. The song gained popularity as the soundtrack of the 2002 film, *We Were Soldiers,* based on the 1993 memoir *We Were Soldiers Once, and Young* by Lieutenant Colonel Harold T. Moore. The book recounted Moore's experiences as an American soldier in Vietnam.

After the picture's release, *Chicago Sun-Times* critic Roger Ebert wrote that the film waved the flag and recognized that "American troops were better trained and better equipped, but outnumbered, outmaneuvered and finally outlasted." John Patterson in the *Manchester Guardian* stated that the film attempted to "rewrite history" and "remake John Wayne's naive and ghastly 1969 flag-waver *The Green Berets*, with all its delusions of honour and valour intact." Patterson added, "If it's a remake of anything, it's a remake of *Rambo: First Blood Part Two.* 'Do we get to win this time, sir?' Sure we do, son. Sure we do." Peter Travers in *Rolling Stone* called *We Were Soldiers* "unabashedly pro-military" and A. O. Scott in the *New York Times* added that in the film "soldiers are presented without blemish. The domestic world they inhabit—of station wagons and whitewashed houses, patient wives and obedient children, where racism is a rumor and sex the vaguest of notions—seems mythical and unreal, a nostalgic projection of American innocence that has existed only in the movies." Thus the critics all offered observations laced with sarcasm that Reagan himself would have had no trouble in embracing as reality.[28]

It was most fitting that the individual most responsible for pushing the shift in the nation's views of the veteran of its most controversial war was borne to his grave to the very soundtrack of that nation's altered memory.

Obscuring the Past: Iran-Contra

The extensive media coverage of Reagan's passing paid much more attention to Iran-Contra than either the 1980 Neshoba visit or the president's relationship with the Vietnam War. The scandal was frequently mentioned in numerous outlets, and the media recognized the seriousness of the entire affair. In echoes from sixteen years earlier, however, Reagan was largely absolved of responsibility. Thus, in a way not dissimilar to the entire timeline of 1986 and 1987, in death, Reagan rose above the scandal while a small group remained behind to debate his actions. The contrary recollections remained too weak to sway or otherwise alter the more established 2004 collective memory regarding the entire scandal.

The June 6 *New York Times* obituary reported the entire account of the Iran-Contra scandal, including Reagan's early November 1986 denials and his March 1987 admission of responsibility.[29] The obituary told an important story both in what it said and in what it did not say. While the account criticized Reagan for the actions of some in his administration, he personally remained above any charges of illegal wrongdoing. Thus, the report echoed late 1986 and 1987, offered nothing new, and illustrated that the collective memory surrounding Reagan's role in Iran-Contra remained intact. The *New York Times* acknowledged this pattern in their assessment of the media's funeral coverage. On June 7, the paper recounted the first two days of televised media coverage: "Some commentators raised Iran-contra and other Reagan missteps, but most television tributes dwelled on his greatest speeches and most endearing ad-libs." On June 11, the paper returned to the national pattern and wrote that Iran-Contra had "dented" Reagan's popularity and that his inattention to detail hurt him at times, "as when Oliver North ran amok in the Iran-contra affair, for instance." Once again, the story gave the impression that while Iran-Contra hurt Reagan, others like North actually broke the law. Two days later, columnist Frank Rich called the overall media coverage of the president's passing an "orgiastic celebration of Reagan's presidency" and "an upbeat Hollywood epic that has glided past Iran-contra, Bitburg and the retreat from Lebanon with impressive ease."[30]

Other national papers, like the *Chicago Tribune*, printed similar coverage, while, initially, the *Washington Post* June 6 obituary did not even mention Iran-Contra. Even in subsequent reporting of the events surrounding Reagan's funeral and reviews of his presidency, the *Post* paid only passing attention to the scandal, as in a June 6 editorial that covered the entire affair in a single sentence—in relation only to Reagan's lack of attention to details. The same day in a story regarding Reagan and the Cold War, the *Post* wrote of the president's opposition to the Sandinistas: "In Reagan's second term, it was disclosed that he had bypassed congressional restrictions on aiding the rebels, known as the Contras, in part by diverting $3.8 million from the secret sale of 2,000 antitank missiles to Iran." The use of the term "he had bypassed congressional restrictions" was the closest any national press ever came to pointing an accusing finger at the president directly.

Five days later, the *Washington Post* detailed the numerous veterans of Reagan's two administrations returning to Washington, DC, for the funeral services. The paper reported that Oliver North planned to skip the services, quoting the Marine: "At that point, when I walk into the cathedral, all the cameras go to Ollie North, and that's not what this is about."[31] The former member of the National Security Council was right more than he knew. The national coverage of Reagan's death remained about the man, not his mistakes. The national media coverage centered on positive coverage, and Iran-Contra remained a fading backstory, still present for brief recollection but for the most part located in the deep recesses of a nation's collective memory.

Regional newspapers continued to reflect the larger national coverage regarding Reagan and the scandal. The *Chicago Sun-Times* on June 6 dedicated an entire story to the scandal and concluded, "Polls indicated that most Americans didn't believe Reagan but thought he was well-intentioned in seeking to rescue the hostages."[32] The same day, the *San Diego Union-Tribune* called Iran-Contra "the biggest crisis of the Reagan presidency" but offered no verdict on the president's role. The *San Francisco Chronicle* added about the scandal, "Reagan not only survived but was essentially forgiven—by the country and, in a way, by the special prosecutor who went after him." In the same article, former independent prosecutor Lawrence Walsh stated, "He was a very understandable, humane person, and his instincts for the country's good were right." The story concluded with an unconscious acknowledgment of the nation's Iran-Contra collective memory: "Even decades after he left office, much of Iran-Contra was relegated to the history books, while Reagan continued to top national popularity polls."[33] On June 10, the *St. Paul Legal Ledger* recalled, "Reagan is remembered more for defeating communism abroad and spurring economic growth than for the Iran-Contra scandal and the huge deficits of the 1980s." The *Boston Globe* reported, "Reagan's legacy is the subject of vigorous debate. Conservatives revere him as the anticommunist champion who won the Cold War and remade the Republican Party in their image. Liberals say he shredded the social contract with the poor and disenfranchised, and got off scot-free in the Iran-Contra scandal."[34] On June 15, the *Augusta Chronicle* printed an editorial that stated Reagan "was ill-advised by his assistants and cabinet members." Two days later, a reader in the *Springfield (IL) State Journal-Register* reported on the scandal: "I think it's been a difficult process for liberals to reflect this week and realize that this man really did change the world and the country for the better. Even if you look at his darkest moment—Iran-Contra—at the heart of it was his desire to release Americans from oppressors." That same day, in California, a letter in the *Ventura County (CA) Star* defended Reagan's actions regarding Nicaragua.[35]

The regional newspapers of the nation produced more detailed stories concerning Iran-Contra but the perspective, for the most part, echoed the larger dailies. Reagan's role in the entire affair remained exactly what the nation as a whole had concluded, with Reagan's rhetorical guiding, in 1987. The stories and editorials all seemed to say that while Iran-Contra remained a dark time for the Reagan White House, the president had justly survived the scandal and moved forward with his presidency.

The national newsmagazines essentially followed the pattern of the larger newspapers. The weeklies reported the scandal, and the damage done, but with no contradictory evidence having been presented in the past sixteen years the critical questions of what Reagan really knew had been answered long ago. *Time* magazine spent two pages on Iran-Contra but ultimately concluded, "At the height of the Iran-Contra scandal, there was some anxiety in the White House that Reagan might actually be impeached, and yet many Americans seemed to forgive him as easily as he forgave himself. When he left office just a year later, his approval rating with the public stood at 63%." *Newsweek* added, "in the Iran-Contra scandal, [he] came perilously close to—and may have committed—impeachable offenses," and "Reagan will answer to history for Iran-Contra. His motives may have been admirable, but his means were not."[36]

U.S. News and World Report gave a large amount of coverage space to Iran-Contra, but this merely enforced the nation's collective memory regarding Reagan's role in the scandal. Of Iran-Contra the periodical cited Reagan's humanity and stated, "Some think his actions [in the Iran-Contra affair] were softhearted rather than softheaded—the sight of the American hostages held in Lebanon made him cringe—but the outcome was a mess that nearly crippled his presidency." Later, the magazine relegated the whole affair to the periphery and called the entire episode "a strange sidebar to the main story of the Reagan era—his role as catalyst in breaking up the Soviet Union." Reagan, then, was excused for possible illegalities because he possessed a soft heart or enjoyed success in relations with the Soviet Union. A special issue focused entirely on Reagan called his March 4 speech "vintage" and reminded the nation, "no credible evidence was found to contradict him." The magazine concluded that even if proof had surfaced, Reagan would have survived. Such thoughts matched the opinion of former independent counsel Lawrence Walsh. For seven years he had investigated Iran-Contra, not releasing his final report until election eve, 1992. During the media coverage upon Reagan's death, Walsh observed, "I don't think he would have been impeached by the House, let alone tried and convicted by the Senate, he was just terribly popular, and this was a very questionable action by the Congress."[37] Walsh's words in June 2004 proved that remembering past events is done through the lens of the present. Walsh's claims—"he was just terribly popular" and "this was a very questionable action by the Congress"—remained memories constructed directly under the ongoing celebration of Reagan's life. Reagan's job approval rating never reached above 48% for the first six months of 1987.[38] In June 2004, surrounded by favorable reporting, the former independent counsel could recall the scandal only in a more sympathetic light.

The following week, *U.S. News and World Report* suggested that while the crisis "stained his presidency" Americans lost interest in the scandal because of their continued prosperity and security. The magazine observed the recent positive press coverage of Reagan and the press's passing nods toward Iran-Contra as "the nonstop lovefest put on by the mainstream electronic and print media during the week of Reagan's death" included "almost obligatory" references to the scandal. The magazine reported that Reagan's constant professions of ignorance of the diversion of funds merely reinforced what his critics believed was an "out-to-lunch image." Even *People* magazine recounted that Reagan's role in the entire affair remained "never clearly defined."[39]

The television media echoed the national newspapers and weekly news-magazines. The scandal received airtime, but any critical analysis of Reagan's role in the affair remained on the periphery. An ABC News special report, aired the day Reagan died, contained observations by Barbara Walters. She reminded the audience of the scandal and the trials of McFarland, North, and Poindexter but remained silent concerning any judgments regarding Reagan's role. The same day, CBS News spliced video clips of the president as longtime anchor Dan Rather walked the viewers through the eight years of the Reagan administration. When he reached Iran-Contra he said: "Later he was embarrassed by a national security aide, Oliver North, and others who admitted secretly trading arms to Iran, diverting the proceeds, via Swiss banks, to Nicaraguan Contras and lying to Congress to cover it all up. Investigators said President Reagan approved at least some of these secret dealings, but he pleaded ignorance." Rather concluded, "What became known as the Iran-Contra scandal tarnished his second term, but did not destroy his popularity. Riding horseback and doing chores on his ranch, he kept his all-American image intact, and his optimism never flagged."[40] Rather's description of Reagan's embarrassment by aides immediately moved the viewer away from any questions of the president's role in Iran-Contra. The reporter did not mention any lingering questions regarding Reagan's knowledge of the diversion of funds to the Contras. Rather's admission that Reagan suffered damage from the scandal but then regained his popularity echoed, with the same tempo, the national collective memory of the entire episode.

That night, NBC aired a special episode of the weekly newsmagazine *Dateline*. The program used a popular culture reference to treat the scandal as a simple bump in the road: "At times, Reagan's achievements matched his soaring rhetoric. It would take more than a recession or a James Bond adventure run amok, like the Iran-Contra scandal, to derail this president." The next day on *Meet the Press with Tim Russert*, the host offered his observations regarding Iran-Contra: "A real scandal in the Reagan administration, where weapons were sold to the Iranians. In return, hostages released from Lebanon and the profits from the weapons sales were used to fund the Nicaraguan rebels, and Ronald Reagan insisting to the country it didn't happen, later coming on and using very interesting words. He said, 'My heart and best intentions tells me it's not true, but the facts and evidence tell me otherwise.'" Russert, without a hint of sarcasm, concluded, "Very believable." His guest agreed. NBC State Department correspondent Andrea Mitchell stated, "Well, it is believable because he didn't really believe it had taken place." She continued, "He wanted the hostages out, and they just carried the ball, Ollie North and the others, and ran with it." Again, with blame pointed directly at Reagan subordinates, the president received absolution from the national press for any major role in the Iran-Contra scandal. During the same broadcast, Reagan's last chief of staff, Ken Duberstein, offered his own view of Reagan's survival of the scandal by saying, "He survived it because he knew what he had done. He knew what he had created. He was willing to take responsibility." Duberstein talked of questioning Reagan for months concerning his role in the scandal, but the president never wavered. "And we went through it for months asking the questions until we became convinced. And I think the American people again finally became convinced that he was shooting straight with them."[41]

On June 7, 2004, CNN's *Larry King Live* again focused on the death of Reagan. The guests that night included Bob Woodward, Dan Rather, and Ted Olsen. The latter represented Reagan as a private attorney in connection with Walsh's post-presidency Iran-Contra investigation. Woodward—of Watergate fame—looked at Reagan's role in Iran-Contra for his 1999 book, *Shadow*. He called the scandal a "blemish" on the presidency but praised how Reagan handled the entire affair. "He hired two very good lawyers. They interrogated Reagan thirteen times. Looked through 200,000 pages of documents and found they could not prove that he hadn't done anything illegal but they found nothing that would implicate him in any crime and that was, for all practical purposes, the end of the Iran-Contra scandal." He added that Reagan professed, "I didn't do anything wrong. And that's what the lawyers found out. And, in fact, that's what history's going to show, at least, based on the record we have now." Olsen agreed with Woodward and added that several judges connected with the investigation and even Lawrence Walsh complimented Reagan on his openness and cooperation. Both men then recounted Reagan's sworn 1992 Iran-Contra testimony. Each recalled the president's failing health and difficulty in remembering the most basic facts and the independent counselor's patience. Olsen added, "And I think that—there's no question that at the end of the day, Lawrence Walsh agreed, as Bob Woodward did, after looking into all of this, that Ronald Reagan had been honestly truthful in everything that he said."[42] Olsen, a Reagan defender, predictably shielded his old boss. Woodward, although more careful with his words, agreed that with no new evidence any new questions regarding Reagan's role would remain unanswered.

On June 11, while Reagan's hearse approached Andrews Air Force Base for the final trip to California, an NBC special report broadcast the proceedings. Anchor Tom Brokaw, Tim Russert, and others reflected on the past week of tributes and the Reagan presidency. Russert spoke of talking to average Americans about Reagan, and how many simply did not want to remember any negative feelings toward the man. "You're talking to them and you say, 'Well, what do you think of Ronald Reagan?' And they say, 'Well, I like him.' What does that mean? 'No, I like him. I think he's a good guy.' What about Iran-Contra? What about the deficits? 'No, I like him.'" Russert's account revealed that, while some in the media continued to perceive the scandal as an episode worth mentioning, in regards for Reagan, many Americans simply made their minds up long ago and no longer cared about the entire episode. Brokaw called Iran-Contra a "great scandal," but "the people knew all of that about him, and nonetheless he remained a revered figure." Former Reagan Chief of Staff Duberstein, sitting with Brokaw, agreed, "Even during those dark days of Iran-Contra people were willing to give him the benefit of the doubt because they liked him and they trusted him."[43]

The dominant Iran-Contra collective memory, however, did not escape unchallenged. Similar to what had happened in 1986 and 1987, opposing interpretations challenged the established recollections. What many saw as a lack of media coverage on the scandal generated concerns of another missed opportunity to answer lingering questions. Many who believed that Reagan had escaped justice once did not wish to sit back quietly and watch it all happen again. The regional newspapers and magazines, much more than the national press, contained more direct testing of the national collective judgment regarding Iran-Contra. Angry words filled many editorials.

Two national magazines, albeit with substantially lower circulation numbers than *Time* or *Newsweek*, gave Reagan's role in the scandal more than just a quick glance. The *Economist* called the entire affair "the worst episode of the Reagan presidency" and claimed scathingly, "The whole thing involved much lying, some blush-making quibbles when the lies were found out, and—if you believe the official story—a president who did not know what some of his officials were up to. This week's nitpickers do have some genuine nits to pick."⁴⁴ The *Week*, a magazine that collected the stories from the United States and international media, printed British columnists Christopher Hitchens's column from Slate.com. "'Reagan sold heavy weapons to the Iranian mullahs and lied about it,' and he 'diverted the profits of this criminal trade to an illegal war in Nicaragua and lied about that too.' So let's not get carried away in our grief."⁴⁵ On June 8, the *Washington Times* included a scalding attack by actor and activist Danny Glover. "We all know Reagan's legacy, from the Iran-Contra affair to the funding of the Nicaraguan military, in which over 200,000 people died." Three days later, the *Madison Wisconsin State Journal* printed on the opinion page, "We should remember his acts of treason in dealing with Iran to get the hostages back. Too bad he was never prosecuted for his crimes for that and Iran-Contra."⁴⁶

On June 13, a *Chicago Sun-Times* editorial pointed to fading memories regarding the scandal but reminded readers, "Iran-contra was not a much-used name a week ago. Now, history has been refreshed." The editorial then used the scandal to attack the current president. "Reagan was a happy warrior and, again unlike Bush, Reagan used his alleged mental low-wattage to insulate himself from the nefarious doings of his underlings, especially during the Iran-contra period."⁴⁷ The reporter's use of the word "alleged" suggests a disbelief that the Iran-Contra scandal arose from the president's lax management style and inattention to details. The same day, Philip Gailey, a columnist in the *St. Petersburg (FL) Times*, took notice of what the media failed to report, commenting, "Republicans canonized Reagan as the progenitor of the modern conservative movement and the terminator of the 'evil empire,' as he once called the Soviet Union. Their Reagan had no flaws as a leader, no failures worth mentioning (I have my own list, starting with Iran-Contra scandal and his record on civil rights)."⁴⁸ Erik Mink stated in a *St. Louis Post-Dispatch* editorial on June 23, 2004, that "The lawlessness of Iran-contra shows his administration scorned the Constitution." Mink went on to lament the lack of media coverage regarding the scandal. The critical editorial generated a passionate pro-Reagan response from a reader two days later.⁴⁹

The regional newspapers—with their different news coverage requirements and targeted audiences—contained many more points of view that ran in opposition to what the nation as a whole had determined regarding Reagan's role in Iran-Contra. These different opinions and recollections battled the larger collective for attention. Anger-filled stories cried out with tough questions concerning the president's part in the scandal, but ultimately, these attempts were scarcely heard and produced little. The counter recollections remained where they were seventeen years earlier: washed out in the background, unable to break through the Reagan-influenced national consciousness, and unable to sway the national collective memory, which judged any questions regarding Reagan's role in Iran-Contra as both asked and answered.

Conclusion

Ronald Reagan changed how many Americans looked at the present through his use of consistent rhetoric during his presidency. Upon his death in 2004, it remained clear that Reagan had also influenced how millions of Americans remembered the past. With his communication skills honed as both an actor and a politician, he shared his version of reality with the nation. His 1980 election to the presidency vastly widened his audience and offered new opportunities to share his interpretations on a myriad of issues and events. Reagan joined other twentieth-century presidents, among them Franklin D. Roosevelt and John F. Kennedy, who connected with the American people through powerful language used at the critical moment. Unlike past chief executives, however, Reagan's words not only entered the country's consciousness and altered the understanding of present events, his rhetoric in time also directly affected the nation's memory of certain periods in its past and helped to shape perceptions of the present.

Strong in his personal beliefs, Reagan knew what he wanted to say and exactly how he wished to say it. His consistency of message forced a staff of White House speechwriters to learn his style and practice his cadence. Speeches showed revisions and additions, often written in his personal handwriting, reflecting his dedicated control of the crafting of his message. Staff memos detail reminders that talking points had to match the president's rhetoric.

Reagan understood the power of language, but he did not always possess perfect timing. More than once during his presidency, while concerned aides and poor polling data suggested a needed change in course, Reagan merely dug in his rhetorical heels. The legacy he has left behind has proved that he was right more often than he was wrong. When trouble arose, at times in direct relation to his rhetoric, his use of language produced a connection to the nation that aided in its becoming a tool for political survival.

Reagan's consistent message acted as an element of change with results detectable throughout his presidency. Hearing his words, many in the nation lost a clear understanding of the line between history and memory, between proven facts and the chosen collective perception. Under the Reagan effect, many Americans replaced the memory of past racial murders with contemporary economic issues, soldiers of an unpopular war gained a moral reevaluation, and Reagan himself survived a direct threat to his presidency.

After Reagan's death on June 5, 2004, the press spent an entire week covering the various services and ceremonies. The twenty-four-hour news cycle went into overdrive. The media coverage revealed that patterns of collective memory surrounding Neshoba, Vietnam veterans, and Iran-Contra that were offered as new interpretations during Reagan's presidency still existed decades after he left office.

Reports contained many examples of two separate perspectives, still struggling over the Philadelphia, Mississippi, murders of 1964 and his 1980 visit. The nation's larger newspapers barely touched the subject, since Reagan had set the tone for the nation's group recollection twenty-four years earlier. The more regional press, operating under the influence of a local perception, dealt out more criticism. With the larger collective memory established, however, any cries of protest possessed little power.

Additionally, press coverage showed that the reevaluation of the Vietnam veteran remained entrenched in the nation's consciousness. Praise from vets found print as many remembered Reagan's consistent support. The media reported a pre-Reagan America and pointed to the president as the man who moved the nation past the Vietnam Syndrome and the crippling memory of military defeat in Vietnam. No deviant voices arose to challenge the collective judgment that the Vietnam vet remained an innocent soldier deserving of national respect.

Iran-Contra received more press attention than either Neshoba or Vietnam. The national media did not ignore the issue and often reprinted the particulars of the scandal. Reports, however, detailed the entire episode as a survived crisis, not an administration-ending scandal, and Reagan for the most part remained above the entire affair in 2004 as he had seventeen years earlier. As they had in 1987, some Americans asked critical questions, but this call for reexamination carried little impact against an ingrained collective style of thinking established by Reagan and accepted by a nation that considered the subject closed.

President Reagan in
Statuary Hall.
Courtesy Amanda Myers.

For years, Reagan's rhetoric offered the nation a consistent view of his convictions. Once he was in the White House, his words often challenged past narratives and offered new perspectives on contemporary issues. Certainly not all Americans accepted his language. The rhetoric did not always match the facts. This being said, three issues clearly display his rhetorical fingerprints, as through repetitiveness and personal conviction he provided the nation with new story lines. Millions of Americans accept his rhetorical offerings, continuing to remember past events under the influence of Reagan.

On June 3, 2009, past and present political dignitaries attended the unveiling of a seven-foot five-hundred-pound bronze statue of Ronald Reagan in the US Capitol's Statuary Hall. Sculpted by forty-two-year-old North Carolinian Chas Fagan and commissioned by the Ronald Reagan Presidential Foundation, the statue stands on a three-foot marble pedestal, which appropriately contains a piece of the Berlin Wall. Each state in the Union is allowed two statues in the hall, and immediately after Reagan's 2004 death many Californians pushed for Reagan to represent the state. Getting the statue approved had been a long process involving private citizens, the California state government, and the federal government.

Present as she was during so many important moments in his life, Nancy attended the ceremony. Roughly one month before her eighty-eighth birthday, she delivered a warm speech of thanks to those responsible for the statue. She said that the sculpture was a "wonderful likeness of Ronnie. And that he would be so proud." She then paused, choked back tears, and reminded the assembled audience that the last time she had been in the rotunda was during her husband's funeral service. She paused and then said, "So it's nice to be back under happier circumstances." *Wall Street Journal* opinion contributor and former Reagan speechwriter Peggy Noonan remarked of all the statues in Statuary Hall, "The Gipper will be the only statue in the rotunda that is smiling."[1]

Nancy's words and Noonan's observation proved that the unveiling ceremony was yet another Reagan moment to influence and persuade. To be certain, Reagan is remembered and honored around Washington: an airport bears his name as does a trade center and a medical facility. A statue in Statuary Hall is different. Nancy's words about "happier times" and the statue's likeness and smile are vital. For generations to come, people with no first-hand memories of Reagan will approach the statue. They will see the tall man in the suit. They will learn that the pedestal contains pieces of the Berlin Wall. They will see the smile, and they will ask questions, and they will seek answers from those who remember.

Appendix A / Ronald Reagan and the Vietnam War

Pre-presidential and Presidential Rhetoric

One consistent rhetorical element concerned Reagan's conviction that Vietnam remained one part of a much larger struggle versus world communism. From Skinner, Anderson, and Anderson, *Life in Letters,* see "1971 Reagan letter, Young Americans for Freedom," 174, and "1975 Reagan letter, Air Force Captain Wayne P. Spiegel," 268. From Skinner, Anderson, and Anderson, *Path to Victory,* see "April 1975 Radio Broadcast," 25–27; "July 1975 Radio Broadcast," 43, 44; "July 1977 Radio Broadcast," 175, 176; and "March 1979 Radio Broadcast," 422–24.

For more examples of Reagan's rhetoric comparing the war in Vietnam to a larger world struggle, see Skinner, Anderson, and Anderson, *Path to Victory,* 21, 22, 25–27, and *In His Own Hand,* 479. From *PPRR 1983,* see "Interview, *USA Today,* April 26, 1983," 1:587–93. From *PPRR 1985,* see "Remarks, Interview, Representatives of Soviet News Organizations, October 31, 1985," 2:1331–42. From *PPRR 1986,* see "Remarks, Question-and-Answer, Regional Editors and Broadcasters, United States Assistance for the Nicaraguan Democratic Resistance, March 11, 1986," 1:316–20, and "Address, Joint Session of Congress, State of the Union, January 27, 1987," 1:56–61.

A second consistent element of Reagan's pre-presidential rhetoric concerned the Vietnam War protestor. Reagan often portrayed the dissident as misguided, uneducated, and usurped by the enemy. Reagan often portrayed the activists as troublesome deviants, more selfish than strong. He often argued that many protestors simply sought disruption and not actual change. Reagan also described the dissenters as dupes of America's enemies, at times helping the North Vietnamese achieve victories denied on the battlefield. He never wavered in his belief that the protestor was wrong to oppose the war and avoid military service. Finally, he reminded his audience that the war protestor's convictions ultimately remained shallow and self-serving. See "March 1969 Reagan letter, Bob Crane," in Skinner, Anderson, and Anderson, *Life in Letters,* 582–83; "October 14, 1969 Eisenhower College Fundraiser," in Ronald Reagan, *Speaking My Mind: Selected Speeches,* 40, 42. From Skinner, Anderson, and Anderson, *Path to Victory,* see "Campaign Reminiscence: November 16, 1976 Radio Broadcast," 88, 89; "Pardons: November 30, 1976 Radio Broadcast," 95, 96, 103; "February 2, 1977 Radio Broadcast," 114, 115; "Vietnam I and II: February 1978 Radio Broadcasts," 390–93; "Vietnam War, May 29, 1979," 453–54; "Joan Baez I: June 1979 Radio Broadcast," 456–59. See also "June 1977 Address to the Foreign Policy Association," in Balitzer, *A Time for Choosing,* 209–10 (also 140, 148–49, 176); and "Suicide Lobby: April 1978 Radio Broadcast," in Skinner, Anderson, and Anderson, *In His Own Hand,* 140. See Cannon, *Governor Reagan,* 285, and for a concise narrative concerning the tensions between students and Governor Reagan, 271–96. For other works that contain examples of Reagan's rhetoric concerning the Vietnam War protestor, see "Remarks, Presenting the Presidential Citizens Medal to Raymond Weeks at a Veterans Day Ceremony, November 11, 1982," in *PPRR 1982,* 2:1445–47; and "Remarks, Memorial Day Ceremonies Honoring an Unknown Serviceman of the Vietnam Conflict, May 28, 1984," in *PPRR 1984,* 1:748–50.

A third rhetorical element that Reagan did not waver on was his belief that the Vietnam War remained a noble effort worthy of being remembered with pride by the American people. He repeated a constant pattern of praising the war and honoring the vets while criticizing the method with which America's elected leaders had fought the battles. In his perception the government had failed the veteran, and he asserted that the American people would accept the towering responsibilities of defending freedom if the nation's leaders would explain the challenges and present a clear strategy. He believed this did not happen with the Vietnam War. See "April 1971 letter to Lorraine and Elwood Wagner," in Skinner, Anderson, and Anderson, *Life in Letters,* 771. Lorraine's correspondence with Reagan began when she was Lorraine Makler, a thirteen-year-old serving as president of the Philadelphia chapter of his fan club. The correspondence between Reagan and Lorraine continued for over fifty years, growing to include Reagan's wife, Nancy, Lorraine's husband, Elwood, and other members of both families, who seemingly spared no subject matter in their writings. See Skinner, Anderson, and Anderson, *Life in Letters,* "December 1979 Open Letter to the Nation," 591, and "1973 Address, convention of Southern Republicans," 94, 395, 620, 778. See Balitzer, *Time for Choosing,* 140, 148–49; from Skinner, Anderson, and Anderson, *Path to*

Victory, "Vietnam: June 1977 Radio Broadcast," 165, 166, and "Vietnam I and II: February 1978 Radio Broadcasts," 390–93 (also 107, 114, 115); and from Skinner, Anderson, and Anderson, *In His Own Hand*, "March 13, 1980, Speech to the Chicago Council on Foreign Relations," 479 (also 24).

For more examples of Reagan's oratory defending the American veteran, containing the betrayal thesis, and portraying the Vietnam conflict as a noble effort, see "Remarks, Memorial Day Ceremonies Honoring an Unknown Serviceman of the Vietnam Conflict, May 28, 1984," in *PPRR 1984*, 1:748–50; "Remarks, Dedication Ceremonies for the Vietnam Veterans Memorial Statue, November 11, 1984," in *PPRR 1984*, 2:1820–22. From *PPRR 1981*, see "Proclamation 4841—National Day of Recognition for Veterans of the Vietnam Era, April 23, 1981," 381, and "Statement, Signing the Veterans' Health Care, Training, and Small Business Loan Act of 1981, November 3, 1981," 1011–12. From *PPRR 1982*, see "Remarks, Presenting the Presidential Citizens Medal to Raymond Weeks at a Veterans Day Ceremony, November 11, 1982," 2:1445–47, and "Address, Nation, Strategic Arms Reduction and Nuclear Deterrence, November 22, 1982," 2:1505–10. See also "Remarks, Conservative Political Action Conference Dinner, February 18, 1983," in *PPRR* 1983, 1:249–56; "Remarks, Memorial Day Ceremonies Honoring an Unknown Serviceman of the Vietnam Conflict, May 28, 1984," in *PPRR 1984*, 1:748–50; "Remarks, Dedication Ceremonies for the Vietnam Veterans Memorial Statue, November 11, 1984," in *PPRR 1984*, 2:1820–22; "Remarks, Question-and-Answer Session with Regional Editors and Broadcasters, April 18, 1985," in *PPRR 1985*, 1:451–57; and "Radio Address, POWs and MIAs in Southeast Asia, July 19, 1986," in *PPRR 1986*, 2:974–75.

Reagan linked Vietnam with other less controversial struggles in America's past. From Skinner, Anderson, and Anderson, *Path to Victory*, see "October 1976 Radio Broadcast," 74, 75, and "January 1977 Radio Address," 107. From *PPRR 1981*, see "Remarks, Presenting the Medal of Honor to Master Sergeant Roy P. Benavidez, February 24, 1981," 155–58, and "California, Proclamation 4878—Veterans Day, 1981, October 26, 1981," 989–90; from *PPRR 1983*, see "Proclamation 5100—Veterans Day, 1983, September 19, 1983," 2:1299–300, and "Radio Address, America's Veterans, November 5, 1983," 2:1549–50; and from *PPRR 1984*, see "Proclamation 5268—Veterans Day, 1984, October 19, 1984," 2:1576.

Appendix B / Reagan and Contra Support, 1981–1988

This appendix provides an extensive review, which reveals Reagan's increasing rhetorical pattern regarding Nicaragua and the Contras throughout his two terms.

1981

From *PPRR 1981, January 20 to December 31, 1981*: "Interview, Walter Cronkite, CBS News, March 3, 1981," 191–202; "State Dinner, President Luis Herrera Campins, Venezuela, November 17, 1981," 1059–62.

1982

From *PPRR 1982, Book I—January 1 to July 2, 1982*: "News Conference, February 18, 1982," 180–89; "Question-and-Answer Session, Newspaper Editors and Radio and Television Directors, February 19, 1982," 193–97; "Interview, Oklahoma City, *Daily Oklahoman,* March 16, 1982," 309–12; "Interview, New York City, *New York Post,* March 23, 1982," 362–69; "News Conference, March 31, 1982," 398–405; "Bridgetown, Barbados, Luncheon Meeting with Leaders of Eastern Caribbean Countries, April 8, 1982," 448–49; "Proclamation 4941—Modification of Quotas on Certain Sugars, Sirups and Molasses, May 5, 1982," 562–64; "Remarks, President Reagan and President Luis Alberto Monge of Costa Rica, June 22, 1982," 802–3.

From *PPRR 1982, Book II—July 3 To December 31, 1982*: "Remarks, Marking First Edition of *USA Today,* September 15, 1982," 1160–61; "Letter to Venezuelans on World Peace, Situation in Central America and Caribbean, November 5, 1982," 1433–35; "Responses to Questions, Latin American Newspapers, November 30, 1982," 1528–34; "Question-and-Answer, Reporters, President's Trip to Latin America, December 4, 1982," 1562–66.

1983

From *PPRR 1983, Book I—January 1 to July 1, 1983*: "Remarks, Honoring Senator Jesse Helms of North Carolina, June 16, 1983," 878–81; "Remarks, President Reagan and Provisional President Alvaro Alfredo Magana Borja of El Salvador, June 17, 1983," 882–85; "News Conference, June 28, 1983," 928–35; "Remarks, California Republican Party Fundraising Dinner, Long Beach, June 30, 1983," 955–60.

From *PPRR 1983, Book II—July 2, 1983 to December 31, 1983*: "Remarks, Ceremony Marking the Annual Observance of Captive Nations Week, July 19, 1983," 1052–54; "Remarks, Question-and-Answer Session, Reporters on Domestic and Foreign Policy Issues, July 21, 1983," 1066–69; "News Conference, July 26, 1983," 1082–90; "Remarks, Annual Convention of the United States Hispanic Chamber of Commerce in Tampa, Florida, August 12, 1983," 1150–55; "Radio Address, the Situation in Central America, August 13, 1983," 1156–57; "Remarks, Appointment of Donald Rumsfeld as the President's Personal Representative in the Middle East, November 3, 1983," 1533–36; "Question-and-Answer, with High School Students on Domestic and Foreign Policy Issues, December 2, 1983," 1642–47; "Interview, Marvin Stone and Joseph Fromm of *U.S. News & World Report,* December 15, 1983," 1717–20; "Interview, Reporters, Domestic and Foreign Policy Issues, December 23, 1983," 1741–46.

1984

From *PPRR 1984, Book I—January 1 to June 29, 1984*: "Remarks, Informal Exchange, Reporters on Foreign and Domestic Issues, January 6, 1984," 10–11; "Remarks, Young Leadership Conference of the United Jewish Appeal, March 13, 1984," 340–45; "Interview, Agence France Presse on Foreign and Domestic Issues, March 15, 1984," 361–63; "Written Responses to Questions, *Le Monde* of France, March 19, 1984," 382–85; "News Conference, April 4, 1984," 460–68; "Remarks, White House Luncheon, National Hispanic Leadership Conference, April 17, 1984," 547–49; "Question-and-Answer, Reporters, Trip to China, May 1, 1984," 610–13;

"Address to the Nation, United States Policy in Central America, May 9, 1984," 659–65; "Written Responses, Questions, Far Eastern Economic Review, May 9, 1984," 665–71; "Joint Communiqué, with President-Elect Jose Napoleon Duarte of El Salvador, May 21, 1984," 720–21; "Interview, Brian Farrell, RTE-Television, Dublin, Ireland, Foreign Issues, May 28, 1984," 750–56; "Interview, Foreign Journalists, May 31, 1984," 789–95; "Toasts, President and Prime Minister Garret FitzGerald of Ireland, June 3, 1984," 801–4; "News Conference, June 14, 1984," 851–59; "Remarks, Question-and-Answer, Elected Republican Women Officials, June 29, 1984," 927–31.

From *PPRR 1984, Book II—June 30 to December 31, 1984*: "Proclamation 5223—Captive Nations Week, 1984, July 16, 1984," 1049–50; "Remarks, Signing the Captive Nations Week Proclamation, July 16, 1984," 1046–48; "Remarks, Outreach Working Group, United States Policy in Central America, July 18, 1984," 1055–56; "Remarks, Summit Conference of Caribbean Heads of State, University of South Carolina in Columbia, July 19, 1984," 1059–61; "News Conference, July 24, 1984," 1076–83; "Telephone Interview, Forrest Sawyer, WAGA-TV, Atlanta, Georgia, July 27, 1984," 1115–17; "Remarks, International Convention of B'nai B'rith, September 6, 1984," 1242–46; "Remarks, Farm Credit Initiative Program, September 18, 1984," 1310–11; "Statement, Situation in El Salvador, October 10, 1984," 1492; "Remarks, Reagan-Bush Rally (hereafter RBR), Glen Ellyn, Illinois, October 16, 1984," 1556–60; "Debate, President and Former Vice President Walter F. Mondale, Kansas City, Missouri, October 21, 1984," 1589–608; "Remarks RBR, Medford, Oregon, October 22, 1984," 1618–22; "Remarks RBR, Portland, Oregon, October 23, 1984," 1622–26; "Remarks RBR, Seattle, Washington, October 23, 1984," 1626–31; "Remarks RBR, Columbus, Ohio, October 24, 1984," 1632–37; "Interview, Representatives of the Scripps-Howard News Service, October 25, 1984," 1645–52; "Remarks RBR, Hackensack, New Jersey, October 26, 1984," 1659–63; "Remarks RBR, Fairfield, Connecticut, October 26, 1984," 1655–59; "Remarks RBR, Media, Pennsylvania, October 29, 1984," 1669–73; "Remarks RBR, Millersville, Pennsylvania, October 29, 1984," 1664–69; "Remarks RBR, Parkersburg, West Virgina, October 29, 1984," 1674–79; "Informal Exchange, Reporters, Winterset, Iowa, November 3, 1984," 1750–56; "Question-and-Answer, Reporters, Foreign and Domestic Issues, November 7, 1984," 1802–6; "Statement, Signing the Intelligence Authorization Act for Fiscal Year 1985, November 9, 1984," 1815; "Interview, *Washington Times*, November 27, 1984," 1840–46; "Remarks, Welcoming Ceremony for President Jaime Lusinchi of Venezuela, December 4, 1984," 1859–61; "Interview, Tom Winter and Joseph Baldacchino, Jr., *Human Events*, December 6, 1984," 1891–96; "Remarks, Signing the International Human Rights Day Proclamation, December 10, 1984," 1880–83.

1985

From *PPRR 1985, Book I—January 1 to June 28, 1985*: "News Conference, January 9, 1985," 23–30; "Remarks, Western Hemisphere Legislative Leaders Forum, January 24, 1985," 66–68; "Interview, Representatives of Independent Radio Networks, January 26, 1985," 76–82; "Address, Joint Session of the Congress on the State of the Union, February 6, 1985," 130–36; "Interview, *Wall Street Journal*, February 7, 1985," 140–46; "Interview, Bernard Weinraub and Gerald Boyd, *New York Times*," February 11, 1985, 156–62; "Radio Address on Central America, February 16, 1985," 172–74; "News Conference, February 21, 1985," 197–204; "Remarks, Annual Dinner, Conservative Political Action Conference, March 1, 1985," 226–30; "Interview, Morton Kondracke and Richard H. Smith, *Newsweek* Magazine, March 4, 1985," 258–63; "Remarks, Question-and-Answer Session, Regional Editors and Broadcasters, March 11, 1985," 268–71; "Remarks, Question-and-Answer Session, White House Briefing for Members of the Magazine Publishers Association, March 14, 1985," 282–85; "Toast, Luncheon with Provincial and Community Leaders in Quebec City, Canada, March 18, 1985," 301–5; "Remarks, Welcoming Ceremony for President Raul Alfonsin of Argentina, March 19, 1985," 311–13; "News Conference, March 21, 1985," 326–34; "Remarks, White House Briefing for Central American Leaders, March 25, 1985," 341–43; "Written Responses, Questions Submitted by Il Resto Del Carlino of Italy, March 27, 1985," 371–74; "Radio Address, the Situation in Central America, March 30, 1985," 370–71; "Remarks, Discussions, President Belisario Betancur Cuartas of Colombia, April 4, 1985," 396–99; "Remarks, Central American Peace Proposal, Question-and-Answer Session, Reporters, April 4, 1985," 400–404; "Remarks, Interview, Nicholas Ashford and Charles Douglas-Home of the *Times of London*, April 4, 1985," 414–18; "Letter, Presidents of Colombia, Mexico, Panama, and Venezuela, the Central American Peace Proposal, April 4, 1985," 468–69; "Informal Exchange, Reporters, April 5, 1985," 407–9; "Radio Address, Federal Budget and the Central American Peace Proposal, April 6, 1985," 412–13; "Remarks, Fundraising Dinner, Nicaragua Refugee Fund, April 15, 1985," 427–31; "Remarks, White House Meeting, the Deficit Reduction Coalition, April 16, 1985," 440–43; "Remarks, Conference on Religious Liberty, April 16, 1985," 437–40; "Written Responses, ABC of Spain, April 18, 1985," 497–500; "Remarks, Question-and-Answer Session, Regional Editors and Broadcasters, April 18, 1985," 451–57; "Radio Address, the Central American Peace Proposal, April 20, 1985," 467–68; "Letter, Senate Majority Leader Dole, the Central American Peace Proposal and United States Assistance for the Nicaraguan Democratic Resistance, April 23, 1985," 489–90; "Statement, Senate Approval of United States Assistance for the Nicaraguan Democratic Resistance, April 23, 1985," 489; "Statement, House of Representatives Disapproval of United States Assistance for the Nicaraguan Democratic Resistance, April 24, 1985," 497; "Written Responses, to *La Vanguardia* of Spain, April 25, 1985," 516–18; "Written Responses, to *El Pais* of Spain, April 29, 1985," 558–59; "Statement, Principal Deputy Press Secretary Speakes on Economic Sanctions against Nicaragua, May 1, 1985," 549–50; "Radio Address, the Bonn Economic Summit, May 4, 1985," 556–57; "Remarks, Joint German-American Military Ceremony at Bitburg Air Base, Federal Republic of Germany, May 5, 1985," 565–68; "Remarks, Community Leaders in Madrid, Spain, May 7, 1985," 575–78; "Address, Special Session of the European Parliament in Strasbourg, France, May 8, 1985," 581–88; "News Conference, May 10, 1985," 597–602; "Remarks, Convention of the National Republican Heritage Groups Council, May 17, 1985," 624–27; "Radio Address, Armed Forces Day and Defense Spending, May 18, 1985," 633–34; "Informal Exchange, Reporters, prior to a Meeting between President Reagan and President Roberto Suazo Cordova of Honduras, May 21, 1985," 639–40; "Remarks, Annual Conference of the Council of the Americas, May 21, 1985," 646–48; "Remarks, Annual Meeting of the National Association of Manufacturers, May 24, 1985," 664–67; "Remarks, Fundraising Dinner for Senator Paula Hawkins in Miami, Florida, May 27, 1985," 673–76; "Remarks, Fundraising Dinner for Senator Mack Mattingly in Atlanta, Georgia, June 5, 1985," 720–23; "Remarks, Fundraising Luncheon for Senator Don Nickles in Oklahoma City, Oklahoma, June 5, 1985," 716–20; "Remarks, Fundraising Luncheon for Senator Jeremiah Denton in Birmingham, Alabama, June 6, 1985," 727–31; "Radio Address, United States Assistance for the Nicaraguan Democratic Resistance, June 8, 1985," 737–38; "Statement, House of Representatives Approval of United States Assistance for the Nicaraguan Democratic Resistance, June 12, 1985," 753; "News Conference, June 18, 1985," 778–85; "Statement, Actions against Terrorism, June 20, 1985," 800–801.

From *PPRR 1985, Book II—June 29, to December 31, 1985*: "Remarks, Annual Convention of the American Bar Association, July 8, 1985," 894–900; "Remarks, Question-and-Answer, Reporters, August 5, 1985," 971–76; "Statement, Signing the International Security and Development Cooperation Act of 1985, August 8, 1985," 983–84; "Telephone Interview, Tomas Regalado, WRHC Radio in Miami, Florida, August 24, 1985," 1013–14; "Statement, Establishment of the Nicaraguan Humanitarian Assistance Office, August 30, 1985," 1023–24; "Interview, Representatives of College Radio Stations, September 9, 1985," 1064–71; "Interview, Guillermo Descalzi of the Spanish International Network, September 13,

1985," 1090–93; "Remarks, Question-and-Answer, Regional Editors and Broadcasters, September 16, 1985," 1095–100; "Remarks, White House Meeting, Reagan-Bush Campaign Leadership Groups, October 7, 1985," 1199–202; "Radio Address, International Stability, October 26, 1985," 1294–95; "Informal Exchange, Reporters, prior to a Meeting with Soviet Foreign Minister Eduard Shevardnadze in New York, New York, October 24, 1985," 1290–91; "Address, Fortieth Session of the United Nations General Assembly in New York, New York, October 24, 1985," 1285–90; "Interview, Brian Widlake, British Broadcasting Corporation, October 29, 1985," 1310–16; "Message, Congress, Economic Sanctions against Nicaragua, October 31, 1985," 1327–28; "Interview, Representatives of the Wire Services, November 6, 1985," 1349–55; "Address, Nation, Upcoming Soviet–United States Summit Meeting in Geneva, November 14, 1985," 1388–91; "Letter, Congressional Leaders Transmitting a Report on the Central American Conflict, November 14, 1985," 1387–88; "Address, Joint Session of the Congress, Following Soviet–United States Summit Meeting in Geneva, November 21, 1985," 1411–15; "Question-and-Answer, Students at Fallston High School in Fallston, Maryland, December 4, 1985," 1434–40; "Letter, Accepting Resignation of Robert C. McFarlane, Assistant to the President, National Security Affairs, December 4, 1985," 1443–44; "Remarks, Announcing Resignation of Robert C. McFarlane, Assistant to the President for National Security Affairs and Appointment of John M. Poindexter, December 4, 1985," 1440–43; "Radio Address, Tax Reform and Situation in Nicaragua, December 14, 1985," 1476–77.

1986

From *PPRR 1986, Book I—January 1 to June 27, 1986*: "Written Responses, Questions, by Noticias de Mexico, January 2, 1986," 3–6; "Radio Address, Relations with Mexico and Canada, January 4, 1986," 9–10; "News Conference, January 7, 1986," 17–24; "Remarks, Annual Dinner of the Conservative Political Action Conference, January 30, 1986," 104–9; "Address, Joint Session of Congress, State of the Union, February 4, 1986," 125–30; "Message, Congress, America's Agenda for the Future, February 6, 1986," 146–49; "Remarks, 1986 Reagan Administration Executive Forum, February 6, 1986," 169–72; "Remarks, Annual National Prayer Breakfast, February 6, 1986," 144–46; "Remarks, Signing the Message on America's Agenda for the Future and the Annual Economic Report of the President, February 6, 1986," 146–49; "Remarks, Question-and-Answer Session, Regional Editors and Broadcasters, February 10, 1986," 185–90;

"Interview, Lou Cannon and David Hoffman, *Washington Post,* February 10, 1986," 193–97; "News Conference, February 11, 1986," 200–208; "Remarks, Informal Exchange with Reporters, United States Assistance for the Nicaraguan Democratic Resistance, February 18, 1986," 216–17; "Written Responses, Questions Submitted by Caribbean Journalists, February 18, 1986," 220–25; "Message, Congress, Transmitting the Annual Report of the National Endowment for Democracy, February 19, 1986," 227; "Remarks, Citizens in St. George's, Grenada, February 20, 1986," 237–40; "Radio Address, Grenada and Nicaragua, February 22, 1986," 245–46; "Message, Congress, Transmitting a Request for Assistance for the Nicaraguan Democratic Resistance, February 25, 1986," 253–59; "Address, Nation, National Security, February 26, 1986," 272–76; "Remarks, White House Meeting for Supporters of United States Assistance for the Nicaraguan Democratic Resistance, March 3, 1986," 284–85; "Statement, Principal Deputy Press Secretary Speakes on the Conflict in Central America, March 5, 1986," 294–95; "Remarks, Jewish Leaders, White House Briefing on United States Assistance for the Nicaraguan Democratic Resistance, March 5, 1986," 295–99; "Remarks, White House Meeting with the House Republican Whip Organization on United States Assistance for the Nicaraguan Democratic Resistance, March 6, 1986," 299; "Remarks, Question-and-Answer, Reporters, Announcing the Appointment of Philip C. Habib as Special Envoy for Central America, March 7, 1986," 300–305; "Radio Address, United States Assistance for the Nicaraguan Democratic Resistance, March 8, 1986," 308–9; "Remarks, White House Briefing for Supporters of United States Assistance for the Nicaraguan Democratic Resistance, March 10, 1986," 309–11; "Remarks, Question-and-Answer, Regional Editors and Broadcasters on United States Assistance for the Nicaraguan Democratic Resistance, March 11, 1986," 316–20; "Informal Exchange, Reporters, prior to Special Envoy Philip C. Habib's Departure for Central America, March 12, 1986," 323–25; "Interview, the *Baltimore Sun,* March 12, 1986," 327–33; "Remarks, Exhibit of Weapons Captured in Central America, March 13, 1986," 334–36; "Remarks, Elected Officials during a White House Briefing on United States Assistance for the Nicaraguan Democratic Resistance, March 14, 1986," 338–41; "Message, Congress, Freedom, Regional Security, and Global Peace, March 14, 1986," 341–49; "Radio Address, Situation in Nicaragua, March 15, 1986," 351–52; "Address, Nation, the Situation in Nicaragua, March 16, 1986," 352–56; "Informal Exchange, Reporters, prior to a Meeting with Ambassador Philip C. Habib, Special Envoy for Central America, March 17, 1986," 358–59; "Informal Exchange, Reporters, prior to a Meeting with Prime Minister Brian Mulroney of Canada, March 18, 1986," 367; "Message,

Congress on United States Assistance for the Nicaraguan Democratic Resistance, March 19, 1986," 374–77; "Statement, House of Representatives Disapproval of United States Assistance for the Nicaraguan Democratic Resistance, March 20, 1986," 380–81; "Remarks, White House Reception for Private Sector Supporters of United States Assistance for the Nicaraguan Democratic Resistance, March 21, 1986," 381–82; "Radio Address, United States Assistance for the Nicaraguan Democratic Resistance, March 22, 1986," 384–85; "Remarks, Senate Campaign Fundraiser for Representative W. Henson Moore in New Orleans, Louisiana, March 27, 1986," 409–12; "Statement, Senate Approval of United States Assistance for the Nicaraguan Democratic Resistance, March 27, 1986," 413; "Radio Address, Nation, International Violence and Democratic Values, March 29, 1986," 414–15; "News Conference, April 9, 1986," 438–46; "Statement, Principal Deputy Press Secretary Speakes, Negotiations between the Contadora Group and Nicaragua, April 8, 1986," 428; "Remarks, Question-and-Answer, the American Society of Newspaper Editors, April 9, 1986," 430–36; "Statement, Principal Deputy Press Secretary Speakes on United States Assistance for the Nicaraguan Democratic Resistance, April 10, 1986," 446; "Remarks, the Associated General Contractors of America, April 14, 1986," 466–67; "Remarks, Members of the American Business Conference, April 15, 1986," 472–74; "Statement, Principal Deputy Press Secretary Speakes Urging Congressional Approval of United States Assistance for the Nicaraguan Democratic Resistance, April 16, 1986," 478–79; "Remarks, Annual White House Correspondents Dinner, April 17, 1986," 483–85; "Remarks, Heritage Foundation Anniversary Dinner, April 22, 1986," 497–501; "Notice of the Continuation of the National Emergency with Respect to Nicaragua, April 22, 1986," 496; "Message, Congress, Continuation of the National Emergency with Respect to Nicaragua, April 22, 1986," 496; "Remarks, International Forum of the Chamber of Commerce of the United States, April 23, 1986," 508–13; "News Conference, May 7, 1986," 563–68; "Remarks, Annual Republican Senate/House Fundraising Dinner, May 21, 1986," 648–50; "Message, Congress Reporting on the National Emergency with Respect to Nicaragua, May 23, 1986," 660–61; "Message, Congress, Reporting on the National Emergency with Respect to Iran, May 23, 1986," 661–63; "Remarks, with President Jose Simeon Azcona Hoyo of Honduras, May 27, 1986," 676–77; "Statement, Principal Deputy Press Secretary Speakes on the Central American Summit Meeting, May 27, 1986," 675; "Written Responses, Questions on Central America Submitted by Radio Marti, June 9, 1986"; "Remarks, Georgetown University Center for Strategic and International Studies on United States Assistance for the Nicaraguan Democratic Resistance,

June 9, 1986," 737–39; "Letter, Congressional Leaders Transmitting a Report on the Situation in Central America, June 10, 1986," 742; "News Conference, June 11, 1986," 748–55; "Remarks, Question-and-Answer, White House Luncheon for Regional Editors and Broadcasters, June 13, 1986," 764–70; "Remarks, White House Briefing, Supporters of United States Assistance for the Nicaraguan Democratic Resistance, June 16, 1986," 772–74; "Statement, Principal Deputy Press Secretary Speakes on the President's Meeting with Nicaraguan Democratic Resistance Leaders, June 18, 1986," 794; "Interview, Eleanor Clift, Jack Nelson, and Joel Havemann, *Los Angeles Times,* June 23, 1986," 825–32; "Statement, Principal Deputy Press Secretary Speakes on United States Assistance for the Nicaraguan Democratic Resistance, June 23, 1986," 822; "Address, Nation, United States Assistance for the Nicaraguan Democratic Resistance, June 24, 1986," 833–38; "Statement, House of Representatives Approval of United States Assistance for the Nicaraguan Democratic Resistance, June 25, 1986," 840–41; "Remarks, Senate Campaign Fundraising Dinner for Jim Santini in Las Vegas, Nevada, June 25, 1986," 841–45.

From *PPRR 1986, Book II—June 28 to December 31, 1986*: "Radio Address, Independence Day and the Centennial of the Statue of Liberty, July 5, 1986," 924–26; "Interview, Bruce Drake, *New York Daily News,* July 8, 1986," 931–37; "Remarks, Signing the Captive Nations Week Proclamation, July 21, 1986," 975–77; "Remarks, Campaign Fundraiser for William Clements in Dallas, Texas, July 23, 1986," 989–93; "Remarks, Republican Party Rally in Miami, Florida, July 23, 1986," 993–96; "Remarks, Telephone to the Annual Convention of the Knights of Columbus in Chicago, Illinois, August 5, 1986," 1053–56; "News Conference, August 12, 1986," 1081–89; "Statement, Senate Approval of United States Assistance for the Nicaraguan Democratic Resistance and for Economic Development in Central America, August 13, 1986," 1098; "Remarks, Interview, Excelsior of Mexico, Written Responses to Questions, August 14, 1986," 1114-20; "Address, 41st Session of the United Nations General Assembly, New York, New York, September 22, 1986," 1227–33; "Remarks, Republican Governors Association Dinner, October 7, 1986," 1340–43; "Remarks, Campaign Rally for Senator Mack Mattingly in Atlanta, Georgia, October 8, 1986," 1349–53; "Informal Exchange, Reporters, Budget, October 8, 1986," 1343–44; "Address, Nation, Meetings with Soviet General Secretary Gorbachev in Iceland, October 13, 1986," 1367–71; "Remarks, White House Briefing, Senior Staff on the Congressional and Gubernatorial Election Results, November 5, 1986," 1517–19; "Letter, to Speaker of the House and the President of the Senate Reporting on the Nicaraguan Emergency, November 10, 1986," 1537–38.

1987

PPRR 1987, Book I—January 1 to July 3, 1987: "Statement, Principal Deputy Press Secretary Speakes, Iran Arms and Contra Aid Controversy, January 5, 1987," 13; "State of the Union Address, January 27, 1987," 56–61; "Statement, Special Counselor to the President Abshire on the Iran Arms and Contra Aid Controversy, January 29, 1987," 90; "Statement, Principal Deputy Press Secretary Speakes on the Iran Arms and Contra Aid Controversy: January 30, 1987," 92; "Announcement, Resignation of William J. Casey and Nomination of Robert M. Gates as Director of Central Intelligence, February 2, 1987," 99–100; "Letter, Accepting the Resignation of William J. Casey as Director of Central Intelligence, February 2, 1987," 100–101; "Statement, Assistant to the President for Press Relations Fitzwater on the Iran Arms and Contra Aid Controversy, February 2, 1987," 102; "Remarks, Annual Leadership Conference, American Legion, February 10, 1987," 122–25; "Statement, Assistant to the President for Press Relations Fitzwater, Iran Arms and Contra Aid Controversy, February 10, 1987," 125; "Remarks, Receiving the Final Report of the President's Special Review Board on the National Security Council, February 26, 1987," 181–82; "Statement, Resignation of Donald T. Regan and the Appointment of Howard H. Baker, Jr., as Chief of Staff, February 27, 1987," 185; "Letter, Accepting Resignation, Donald T. Regan, Assistant to the President and Chief of Staff, February 28, 1987," 186; "Message, Congress, Economic Assistance for Central America, March 3, 1987," 193–95; "Informal Exchange, Reporters, March 4, 1987," 206; "Address, Nation, Iran Arms and Contra Aid Controversy, March 4, 1987," 208–11; "Remarks, White House Briefing for Members of the National Newspaper Association, March 5, 1987," 212–15; "Presidential Determination No. 87-10—Assistance for the Nicaraguan Democratic Resistance, March 5, 1987," 217; "Proclamation 5617—Amending the Generalized System of Preferences, March 6, 1987," 219–20; "Radio Address, Regional Conflicts, March 7, 1987," 221–22; "News Conference, March 19, 1987," 258–66; "Informal Exchange, Reporters, March 25, 1987," 282; "Informal Exchange, Reporters, Columbia, Missouri, March 26, 1987," 282–83; "Remarks, Students at Fairview Elementary School, Columbia, Missouri, March 26, 1987," 284–86; "Remarks, Question-and-Answer, Reporters, on United States Embassy Security in Moscow, April 7, 1987," 345–47; "Statement, Assistant to the President for Press Relations Fitzwater, Iran Arms and Contra Aid Controversy Investigations, April 8, 1987," 353; "Remarks, Question-and-Answer, Los Angeles World Affairs Council Luncheon in California, April 10, 1987," 365–72; "Notice of the Continuation of the National Emergency with Respect to Nicaragua, April 21, 1987," 391; "Informal Exchange, Reporters, April 24,

1987," 410–11; "Interview, White House Newspaper Correspondents, April 28, 1987," 424–29; "Remarks, Annual Republican Congressional Fundraising Dinner, April 29, 1987," 434–38; "Message, Congress Reporting on the National Emergency with Respect to Nicaragua, May 1, 1987," 448–49; "Informal Exchange, Reporters, Iran Arms and Contra Aid Controversy, New York, New York, May 3, 1987," 451–52; "Remarks, 100th Annual Convention of the American Newspaper Publishers Association, New York, New York, May 3, 1987," 452–57; "Informal Exchange, Reporters, Iran Arms and Contra Aid Controversy, May 5, 1987," 470; "Remarks, Members, American Association of Editorial Cartoonists, May 7, 1987," 479–81; "Remarks, Reporters, Decline in the Unemployment Rate, May 8, 1987," 484; "Statement, Investigation of Attorney General Edwin Meese III, May 11, 1987," 498; "Informal Exchange, Reporters, May 11, 1987," 499; "Written Responses, Questions, Kuwaiti Newspaper *Al-Qabas,* May 12, 1987," 529–33; "Remarks, White House Briefing for Members of the Council of the Americas, May 12, 1987," 501–3; "Informal Exchange, Reporters, the Iran Arms and Contra Aid Controversy, May 13, 1987," 508; "Remarks, Question-and-Answer, Southeast Regional Editors and Broadcasters, May 15, 1987," 512–16; "Statement, Attack against the *U.S.S. Stark,* May 18, 1987," 524–25; "Statement, Assistant to the President for Press Relations Fitzwater on the Attack against the *U.S.S. Stark,* May 18, 1987," 525; "Question-and-Answer, Area Reporters, Chattanooga, Tennessee, May 19, 1987," 534–36; "Remarks, Memorial Service, Crewmembers of the *U.S.S. Stark* in Jacksonville, Florida, May 27, 1987," 553–55; "Interview, Foreign Journalists, prior to Venice Economic Summit, May 26, 1987," 563–68; "Interview, Foreign Television Journalists, prior to Venice Economic Summit, May 27, 1987," 568–73; "Remarks, United States Policy in the Persian Gulf, May 29, 1987," 581–82; "News Conference, June 11, 1987," 623–29; "Remarks, Question-and-Answer, Economic Reporters, June 16, 1987," 655–60; "Statement, Assistant to the President for Press Relations Fitzwater on the Meeting between President Reagan and President Oscar Arias Sanchez of Costa Rica, June 17, 1987," 669; "Remarks, Fundraising Reception for Senator Orrin G. Hatch of Utah, June 17, 1987," 678–80; *PPRR, 1987, Book II—July 4 To December 31, 1987* (Washington: United States Government Printing Office, 1988) "Remarks, White House Briefing for Right to Life Activists, July 30, 1987," 895–99; "Informal Exchange, Reporters, July 31, 1987," 904; "Remarks, Receiving the Report of the Presidential Task Force on Project Economic Justice, August 3, 1987," 910–13; "Remarks, Reporters, Announcing the Central American Peace Initiative, August 5, 1987," 916–17; "Remarks, Reporters, Covert Action Procedural Reforms, August 7, 1987," 925–26; "Statement, Central

American Peace Agreement, August 8, 1987," 930; "Interview, Hugh Sidey, *Time,* August 12, 1987," 961–67; "Address, Nation, Iran Arms and Contra Aid Controversy and Administration Goals, August 12, 1987," 942–45; "Remarks, Citizens in North Platte, Nebraska, August 13, 1987," 949–53; "Radio Address, Administration Goals, August 15, 1987," 959–60; "Address, People of Nicaragua on the Central American Peace Plan, August 22, 1987," 975–76; "Remarks, Soviet–United States Relations, Town Hall of California Meeting in Los Angeles, August 26, 1987," 977–82; "Remarks, Meeting with Nicaraguan Democratic Resistance Leaders in Los Angeles, California, August 27, 1987," 985; "Radio Address, Soviet–United States Relations, August 29, 1987," 987–88; "Radio Address, Situation in Nicaragua, September 12, 1987," 1024–25; "Address, 42nd Session of the United Nations General Assembly, New York, New York, September 21, 1987," 1058–63; "Remarks, Annual Convention of Concerned Women for America, September 25, 1987," 1079–82; "Address, Permanent Council, Organization of American States, October 7, 1987," 1141–46; "Remarks, Welcoming Ceremony, President Jose Napoleon Duarte Fuentes of El Salvador, October 14, 1987," 1175–77; "Toasts, State Dinner, President Jose Napoleon Duarte Fuentes of El Salvador, October 14, 1987," 1181–82; "Letter, Speaker of the House of Representatives and the President Pro Tempore of the Senate on the United States Reprisal against Iran, October 20, 1987," 1212; "News Conference, October 22, 1987," 1218–25; "Excerpts, Interview, European Journalists on Soviet–United States Relations, October 23, 1987," 1229; "Radio Address, Economy and Soviet–United States Relations, October 24, 1987," 1230–31; "Statement, Trade Sanctions against Iran, October 26, 1987," 1232; "Remarks, United States Military Academy, West Point, New York, October 28, 1987," 1238–42; "Executive Order 12613—Prohibiting Imports from Iran, October 29, 1987," 1244–45; "Remarks, Question-and-Answer Session, Reporters on the Soviet–United States Summit Meeting, October 30, 1987," 1256–58; "Message, Congress, Reporting on the National Emergency with Respect to Nicaragua, October 30, 1987," 1255–56; "Radio Address, Philippine–United States Relations and Situation in Central America, November 7, 1987," 1298–99; "Remarks, Representatives of the Organization of American States, November 9, 1987," 1303–6; "Notice of the Continuation of the National Emergency with Respect to Iran, November 10, 1987," 1318; "Message, Congress, Continuation of the National Emergency with Respect to Iran, November 10, 1987," 1318; "Statement, Assistant to the President for Press Relations Fitzwater on Discussions between the Speaker of the House of Representatives and President Daniel Ortega of Nicaragua, November 16, 1987," 1335; "Statement, Assistant to the President for Press Relations Fitzwater on the Report of the Congressional Committee Investigating the Iran Arms and Contra Aid Controversy, November 18, 1987," 1345–46; "Message, Congress Reporting on the Continuation of the National Emergency with Respect to Iran, November 20, 1987," 1361–63; "Remarks, Bipartisan Plan to Reduce the Federal Budget Deficit, Question-and-Answer Session with Reporters, November 20, 1987," 1365–68; "Remarks, Swearing-In Ceremony for Frank C. Carlucci, Secretary of Defense, November 23, 1987," 1371–73; "Remarks, Administration Supporters, White House Briefing on Arms Control, Central America, and the Supreme Court, November 23, 1987," 1374–76; "Remarks, Business Leaders, Deficit Reduction Plan, November 23, 1987," 1377–78; "Informal Exchange, Reporters, November 23, 1987," 1376–77; "Radio Address, Soviet–United States Relations, November 28, 1987," 1385–86; "Interview, Television Network Broadcasters, December 3, 1987," 1425–31; "Remarks, Question-and-Answer, with Area High School Seniors, Jacksonville, Florida, December 1, 1987," 1398–406; "Radio Address, Deficit Reduction and Soviet–United States Relations, December 5, 1987," 1442–43; "Excerpts, Interview with Conservative Columnists Following the Soviet–United States Summit Meeting, December 9, 1987," 1489–90; "Address, Nation, Soviet–United States Summit Meeting, December 10, 1987," 1501–4; "Remarks, Question-and-Answer, News Editors and Broadcasters, December 11, 1987," 1505–12; "Radio Address, Following the Soviet–United States Summit Meeting, December 12, 1987," 1515–16; "Remarks, Signing the Continuing Appropriations for Fiscal Year 1988 and the Omnibus Budget Reconciliation Act of 1987, December 22, 1987," 1540–41.

1988

From PPRR 1988, Book I—January 1 to July 1, 1988: "Remarks, Question-and-Answer Session, Members of the City Club of Cleveland, Ohio, January 11, 1988," 15–24; "Remarks, 1988 Reagan Administration Executive Forum, January 19, 1988," 48–51; "Statement, Assistant to the President for Press Relations Fitzwater, Central American Peace Process, January 19, 1988," 51–52; "Remarks, Civic Leaders, White House Briefing, Aid to the Nicaraguan Democratic Resistance, January 20, 1988," 62–66; "Remarks, Civic Leaders, White House Briefing on Aid to the Nicaraguan Democratic Resistance, January 22, 1988," 76–79; "Address, Joint Session of Congress, State of the Union, January 25, 1988," 84–90; "1988 Legislative and Administrative Message: A Union of Individuals, January 25, 1988," 91–121; "Informal Exchange, Reporters, January 26, 1988," 121–22;

"Remarks, Members, Reserve Officers Association, January 27, 1988," 125–30; "White House Statement, Aid to the Nicaraguan Democratic Resistance, January 27, 1988," 133–34; "Remarks, National Conference of State Legislators, January 29, 1988," 146–49; "Address, Nation, Aid to the Nicaraguan Democratic Resistance, February 2, 1988," 162–67; "Statement, Assistant to the President for Press Relations Fitzwater on the House of Representatives' Failure to Approve Aid for the Nicaraguan Democratic Resistance, February 3, 1988," 172; "Letter, Congressional Leadership on Aid to the Nicaraguan Democratic Resistance, February 3, 1988," 171–72; "Statement, House of Representatives' Failure to Approve Aid for the Nicaraguan Democratic Resistance, February 4, 1988," 174; "Remarks, Annual Conservative Political Action Conference Dinner, February 11, 1988," 193–98; "News Conference, February 24, 1988," 252–59; "Radio Address, Drug Abuse and Aid to the Nicaraguan Democratic Resistance, February 27, 1988," 265–66; "Statement, House of Representatives Disapproval of Aid to the Nicaraguan Democratic Resistance, March 3, 1988," 287; "Letter, Congressional Leaders on Aid to the Nicaraguan Democratic Resistance, March 3, 1988," 281–82; "Statement, House of Representatives Disapproval of Aid to the Nicaraguan Democratic Resistance, March 4, 1988," 287; "Remarks, Annual Conference of the Veterans of Foreign Wars, March 7, 1988," 296–99; "Interview, Alastair Burnet, ITN Television, United Kingdom, March 10, 1988," 316–18; "Remarks, Supporters, Israel, White House Briefing on United States Foreign Policy, March 15, 1988," 334–36; "Radio Address, Deployment of United States Forces to Honduras and the Strategic Defense Initiative, March 19, 1988," 356–57; "Remarks, State, Local Republican Officials on Federalism and Aid to the Nicaraguan Democratic Resistance, March 22, 1988," 363–66; "Remarks, Fundraising Reception for Senator Chic Hecht of Nevada, March 22, 1988," 366–68; "Remarks, Question-and-Answer, Members of the Center for the Study of the Presidency, March 25, 1988," 386–91; "Remarks, Interview, Gannett Foundation Fellows, March 29, 1988," 400–402; "Executive Order 12634—Delegating Authority to Provide Assistance and Support for Peace, Democracy, and Reconciliation in Central America, April 1, 1988," 418; "Remarks, Annual Convention of the National Association of Broadcasters, Las Vegas, Nevada, April 10, 1988," 429–34; "Remarks, Annual Convention of the American Society of Newspaper Editors, April 13, 1988," 449–56; "Remarks, World Affairs Council of Western Massachusetts, Springfield, April 21, 1988," 488–96; "Message, Congress, Continuation of the National Emergency with Respect to Nicaragua, April 25, 1988," 508; "Notice of the Continuation of the National Emergency with Respect to Nicaragua, April 25, 1988," 508–9; "Letter, Speaker of the

House of Representatives and the President of the Senate Reporting on the National Emergency with Respect to Nicaragua, April 29, 1988," 531–32; "Remarks, Question-and-Answer, Reporters, May 17, 1988," 602–6; "Interview, Foreign Television Journalists, May 19, 1988," 610–16; "Remarks, White House News Photographers Association Annual Dinner, May 19, 1988," 618–19; "Statement, Aid to the Nicaraguan Democratic Resistance, May 24, 1988," 638–39; "Remarks, World Gas Conference Participants, June 6, 1988," 727–30; "Letter, Resignation of Howard H. Baker, Jr., as Chief of Staff to the President, June 14, 1988," 771–72; "Statement, Assistant to the President for Press Relations Fitzwater on the Resignation of Howard H. Baker, Jr., as Chief of Staff to President, June 14, 1988," 769–70; "Statement, Appointment of Kenneth M. Duberstein as Chief of Staff to the President, June 14, 1988," 770; "Excerpts, Interview, International Newspaper Journalists, June 15, 1988," 778–79; "Radio Address, Nation, on Economic Growth and Situation in Nicaragua, June 18, 1988," 792–94; "News Conference, Toronto, Canada, June 21, 1988," 804–11; "Remarks, Presentation Ceremony, Prisoners of War Medal, June 24, 1988," 835–37; "Remarks, Campaign Fundraising Luncheon, Representative Connie Mack in Miami, Florida, June 29, 1988," 854–57.

From PPRR 1988, Book II—July 2, 1988 to January 19, 1989: "Radio Address, Resignation of Howard Baker as Chief of Staff to the President and the Administration's Agenda, July 2, 1988," 919–20; Statement, Assistant to the President for Press Relations Fitzwater on the Resignation of Attorney General Meese and President Reagan's Visit with President Duarte of El Salvador, July 5, 1988," 925; "Informal Exchange, Reporters, July 12, 1988," 942; "Statement, Assistant to the President for Press Relations Fitzwater on the Situation in Nicaragua, July 15, 1988," 967; "Remarks, Announcing the Nomination of Richard L. Thornburgh to Be Attorney General of the United States, July 12, 1988," 939–41; "Remarks, Signing the Captive Nations Week Proclamation, July 13, 1988," 946–48; "Radio Address, Aid to the Nicaraguan Democratic Resistance, July 30, 1988," 1002–3; "Remarks, Media Executives at a White House Briefing on Nicaragua, August 3, 1988," 1019–21; "Radio Address, Nation, Veto National Defense Authorization Act, Fiscal Year 1989, August 6, 1988," 1034–35; "Radio Address, Administration's Goals and Achievements, August 13, 1988," 1072–73; "Radio Address, Nation, on Foreign Policy Achievements, August 27, 1988," 1110–11; "Remarks, National Convention of the American Legion, Louisville, Kentucky, September 6, 1988," 1121–24; "Remarks, Republican Party Rally, Waco, Texas, September 22, 1988," 1194–99; "Remarks, Republican Party Fundraising Dinner, Houston, Texas, September 22, 1988," 1201–4; "Remarks, Republican Party Fundraising Brunch, Boca

Raton, Florida, September 23, 1988," 1205–9; "Address, 43rd Session of the United Nations General Assembly, New York, New York, September 26, 1988," 1219–26; "Remarks, Georgetown University's Bicentennial Convocation, October 1, 1988," 1263–66; "Remarks, National Defense University on Signing the Department of Veterans Affairs Act, October 25, 1988," 1381–84; "Remarks, Question-and-Answer, World Affairs Council Luncheon in Los Angeles, California, October 28, 1988," 1403–11; "Informal Exchange, Reporters, October 31, 1988," 1418–20; "Letter, Speaker of the House of Representatives and President of the Senate Reporting on the Economic Sanctions against Nicaragua, November 9, 1988," 1489–91; "Remarks, Question-and-Answer, with Area Junior High School Students, November 14, 1988," 1500–1507; "Informal Exchange, Reporters, Colonel Oliver North, December 1, 1988," 1579; "Remarks, American Enterprise Institute for Public Policy Research, December 7, 1988," 1594–98; "News Conference, December 8, 1988," 1605–12; "Remarks, Question-and-Answer Session, University of Virginia in Charlottesville, December 16, 1988," 1631–41.

Notes

Abbreviations Used in the Notes

PPRR   *Public Papers of the Presidents of the United States: Ronald Reagan* (14 vols.)

RRPLA   Ronald Reagan Presidential Library Archives, Simi Valley, California

RR 1980 Campaign   Ronald Reagan Personal Papers 1980 Campaign, RRPLA

USGPO   United States Government Printing Office

USNWR   U.S. News and World Report

VFW   Veterans of Foreign Wars

WHORM   White House Office of Records Management

Introduction

1. "Yankee Doodle Magic," *Time*, July 7, 1986.

2. Ibid. (emphasis added).

3. Reagan 2020, at http://reagan2020.us/speeches/RNC_Convention.asp (accessed February 24, 2010).

4. Robert Dallek, *Ronald Reagan: The Politics of Symbolism* (Cambridge: Harvard University Press, 1984); Michael Rogin, *Ronald Reagan: The Movie* (Berkeley and Los Angeles: University of California Press, 1987); Sidney Blumenthal, *Our Long National Daydream: A Political Pageant of the Reagan Era* (New York: Harper and Row, 1988); Robert E. Denton, Jr., *The Primetime Presidency of Ronald Reagan* (New York: Praeger, 1988); Larry Speakes, *Speaking Out: The Reagan Presidency from inside the White House* (New York: Charles Scribner's Sons, 1988); Bob Schieffer and Gary Paul Gates, *The Acting President* (New York: Dutton, 1989); Haynes Johnson, *Sleepwalking through History: America in the Reagan Years* (New York: W. W. Norton, 1991); Wilbur Edel, *The Reagan Presidency: An Actor's Greatest Performance* (New York: Hippocrene Books, 1992); Douglas Brinkley, *The Boys of Pointe du Hoc: Ronald Reagan, D-Day, and the U.S. Army 2nd Ranger Battalion* (New York: William Morrow, 2005).

5. Paul D. Erickson, *Reagan Speaks: The Making of an American Myth* (New York: Praeger, 1985); Stephen Ducat, *Taken In: American Gullibility and the Reagan Mythos* (Tacoma: Life Sciences Press, 1988); Mary Stuckey, *Getting into the Game: The Pre-presidential Rhetoric of Ronald Reagan* (New York: Praeger, 1989), and *Playing the Game: The Presidential Rhetoric of Ronald Reagan* (New York: Praeger, 1990); Amos

Kiewe and David W. Houck, *A Shining City on a Hill: Ronald Reagan's Economic Rhetoric, 1951–1989* (New York: Praeger, 1991); Michael Weiler and W. Barnett Pearce, ed., *Reagan and Public Discourse in America* (Tuscaloosa: University of Alabama Press, 1992); Mary Stuckey, *Slipping the Surly Bonds: Reagan's Challenger Address* (College Station: Texas A&M Press, 2006). Wake Forest University maintains a current website of scholarship regarding the rhetoric of Ronald Reagan: http://www.wfu.edu/~louden/Political%20Communication/Bibs/REAGAN.html.

6. Eric Hobsbawm and Terence Ranger, *The Invention of Tradition* (Cambridge: Cambridge University Press, 1983); David Lowenthal, *The Past Is a Foreign Country* (Cambridge: Cambridge University Press, 1985); Paul Connerton, *How Societies Remember* (Cambridge: Cambridge University Press, 1989); Pierre Nora, "Between Memory and History: *Les Lieux de Mémoire*," *Representations* 26 (Spring 1989), 3–24; David Thelen, "Introduction: Memory and American History," and Michael Frisch, "American History and the Structures of Collective Memory," *Journal of American History* 75, no. 4 (March 1989): 1117–55; Michael Kammen, *Mystic Chords of Memory: The Transformation of Tradition in American Culture* (New York: Knopf, 1991); Lewis A. Coser, *Maurice Halbwachs: On Collective Memory* (Chicago: University of Chicago Press, 1992); John R. Gillis, *Commemorations: The Politics of National Identity* (Princeton, NJ: Princeton University Press, 1994).

7. Nora, "Between Memory and History," 7–24.

8. Coser, *Halbwachs.*

9. Erickson, *Reagan Speaks*; Dallek, *Politics of Symbolism*; Rogin, *Reagan: The Movie*; Blumenthal, *Our Long National Daydream*; Ducat, *Taken In*; Johnson, *Sleepwalking through History*; Edel, *Reagan Presidency*; Dinesh D'Souza, *Ronald Reagan: How an Ordinary Man Became an Extraordinary Leader* (New York: Touchstone, 1997); Peggy Noonan, *When Character Was King* (New York: Viking, 2001); Peter Robinson, *How Ronald Reagan Changed My Life* (New York: Regan Books, 2003); Dick Wirthlin, *The Greatest Communicator: What Ronald Reagan Taught Me about Politics, Leadership, and Life* (Hoboken, NJ: John Wiley and Sons, 2004).

10. Reagan post-presidency *Time* covers are November 5, 1990, February 24, 1992, August 16, 1993, September 29, 2003, June 14, 2004, and March 26, 2007; Kennedy appeared on November 14, 1983, May 6, 1996, November 17, 1997, August 13, 2001, and July 2, 2007; Lincoln on September 28, 1959, May 10, 1963, July 4, 2005, and October 27, 2008; Roosevelt on February 1, 1982, May 19, 2003, and October 27, 2008.

11. David Corn, "Why Obama Should Channel the Gipper," *Mother Jones*, http://motherjones.com/politics/2009/01/why-obama-should-channel-gipper (accessed January 8, 2009); Patrick Buchanan, "Obama's Choice: FDR or Reagan," Real Clear Politics, http://www.realclearpolitics.com/articles/2009/01/obamas_choice_fdr_or_reagan.html (accessed January 9, 2009); Steve Kornack, "Barack Obama and the Path of Reagan," *New York Observer*, http://www.observer.com/2009/politics/barack-obama-and-path-reagan (accessed January 13, 2009); Ronald Brownstein, "Obama's Reagan Moment Is Now," *National Journal Magazine*, www.nationaljournal.com/njmagazine/nj_20090131_4685.php (accessed January 30, 2009); David Paul Kuhn, "Public Stands between Reagan and Obama," Real Clear Politics, www.realclearpolitics.com/articles/2009/03/on_big_gov_public_more_with_re.html (accessed March 5, 2009). The trend continued into 2010 with *New Republic*, "How to Stop the Bleeding: Obama Needs to Learn Reagan's Lessons from 1982," www.tnr.com/article/politics/how-stop-the-bleeding (accessed March 22, 2010).

12. Gary W. Gallagher, *Cause Won, Lost, and Forgotten: How Hollywood and*

Popular Art Shape What We Know about the American Civil War (Chapel Hill: University of North Carolina University Press, 2008), 4.

13. Answers.com, at http://www.answers.com/topic/u-s-news-world-report (accessed March 11, 2010); also see Funding Universe, at http://www.fundinguniverse.com/company-histories/US-News-and-World-Report-Inc-Company-History.html (accessed November 18, 2010), and A History of *Time, Newsweek*, and *U.S. News and World Report* at http://www.bsu.edu/web/dsumner/Professional/newsmagazinehistory.htm (accessed November 18, 2010).

14. Brinkley, *Boys of Pointe du Hoc*, 195.

15. "The Romney-Reagan remix," at http://www.boston.com/ae/media/articles/2010/03/09/the_romney_reagan_remix/ (accessed March 10, 2010).

16. "How Reagan Stays Out of Touch," *Time*, December 8, 1986, 34.

17. Kiron K. Skinner, Annelise Anderson, and Martin Anderson, eds., *Reagan in His Own Hand: The Writings of Ronald Reagan that Reveal His Revolutionary Vision for America* (New York: Free Press, 2001), *Reagan: A Life in Letters* (New York: Free Press, 2003), and *Reagan's Path to Victory*.

18. Robinson, *Changed My Life*, 121.

19. Presidential Speech Planning Schedule, Folder Anthony "Tony" Dolan, Box 74 1981–1989 Series III, Schedules, Ronald Reagan Presidential Library Archives, Simi Valley, California (hereafter RRPLA).

20. Erickson, *Reagan Speaks*, 8.

21. Speakes, *Speaking Out*; Peggy Noonan, *What I Saw at the Revolution: A Political Life in the Reagan Era* (New York: Random House, 1990); Noonan, *When Character Was King*; Michael Deaver, *Behind the Scenes: In Which the Author Talks about Ronald and Nancy Reagan . . . and Himself* (New York: William Morrow, 1987); Michael Deaver, *A Different Drummer: My Thirty Years with Ronald Reagan* (New York: HarperCollins, 2001); Robinson, *Changed My Life*; Wirthlin, *Greatest Communicator*; Ian Jackman, ed., *Ronald Reagan Remembered* (New York: Simon and Schuster, 2004), 58.

22. Robinson, *Changed My Life*, 3–4, 9, 61–62, 94–95, 105.

23. Noonan, *What I Saw*, 51, 59, 69, 124–25, 267.

24. Landon Parvin, telephone interview, May 29, 2007, August 16, 2010.

25. Wirthlin, *Greatest Communicator*, 3, 8, 52, 55. See also Martin J. Medhurst, ed., *Beyond the Rhetorical Presidency* (College Station: Texas A&M University Press, 1996), xvi, xvii.

26. Noonan, *What I Saw*, 51, 59, 69, 124, 125, 267.

27. "Farewell Address to the Nation, January 11, 1989," *Public Papers of the Presidents: Ronald Reagan* (Washington, DC: USGPO, 1982–1991; hereafter *PPRR*), *1988–1989*, 2:1718–23.

28. Stephen F. Hayward, *The Age of Reagan, 1964–1980: The Fall of the Old Liberal Order* (Roseville, CA: Prima Publishing, 2001), *The Age of Reagan: The Conservative Counterrevolution, 1980–1989* (New York: Crown Forum, 2009); Sean Wilentz, *The Age of Reagan: A History, 1974–2008* (New York: HarperCollins, 2008).

1—States' Rights

1. Epigraphs are from Nora, "Between Memory and History," 8; Florence Mars, Witness in Philadelphia (Baton Rouge: Louisiana State University Press, 1977), 1.

2. *Jackson (MS) Clarion-Ledger* (hereafter *Clarion-Ledger*), August 3, 1980. For

additional background on the fair, please see Robert Craycroft, *The Neshoba County Fair: Place and Paradox in Mississippi* (Jackson: Mississippi State University, 1989); and the official website of the Neshoba County Fair, at www.neshobacountyfair.org.

3. Kurt Ritter, "Ronald Reagan's 1960s Southern Rhetoric: Courting Conservatives for the GOP," *Southern Communication Journal* 64 (Summer 1999).

4. Ibid., 342.

5. "Reagan Speaks at Local Banquet," *Clarion-Ledger*, November 17, 1973; "Reagan Visit to State No Bloc-Buster," ibid., August 5, 1976; "Reagan Brings His Presidential Non-Campaign into Mississippi," ibid., October 19, 1978.

6. Barry Goldwater, *The Conscience of a Conservative* (New York: MacFadden Books, 1963), 26. Ironically Goldwater, in the text, criticizes the Republican Party for providing only lip service to the belief. The local newspaper was the *Clarion-Ledger*, August 4, 1980.

7. *States' rights* was a term and argument used by many to oppose the national civil rights legislation enacted during the 1950s and 1960s. Only a handful of the hundreds of books dealing with the presidency of Ronald Reagan mention the speech at the Neshoba County Fair. Most of the citations come from the collected works of Lou Cannon, *Reagan* (New York: G. P. Putnam's Sons, 1982), *President Reagan: The Role of a Lifetime* (New York: Simon and Schuster, 1991), *President Reagan: The Role of a Lifetime* (New York: Public Affairs, 2001). See also Lou Cannon, *Governor Reagan: His Rise to Power* (New York: Public Affairs, 2003), 478, which reflects contemporary political problems of Mississippi senator Trent Lott. Cannon changes the earlier text of his Neshoba narrative to suggest that Lott played a large role in Reagan's visit, an assertion not cited in Cannon's earlier works. Also see Michael Schaller, *Reckoning with Reagan: America and Its President in the 1980s* (New York: Oxford University Press, 1992), and Lyn Nofziger, *Nofziger* (Washington, DC: Regnery Gateway, 1992). Other key members of Reagan's 1980 campaign team do not mention the Neshoba, Mississippi, visit in their respective works and memoirs: Nancy Reagan, *My Turn: The Memoirs of Nancy Reagan* (New York: Random House, 1989); Deaver, *Behind the Scenes*; Deaver, *A Different Drummer*; Martin Anderson, *Revolution* (San Diego: Harcourt Brace Jovanovich, 1988); Ed Meese III, *With Reagan: The Inside Story* (Washington, DC: Regnery Gateway, 1992). A review of works published just after the 1980 election often does not find a single mention of the Neshoba County Fair. In 1981 Marlene Michels Pomper's *The Election of 1980: Reports and Interpretations* (Chatham, NJ: Chatham House, 1981), Elizabeth Drew's *Portrait of an Election: The 1980 Presidential Campaign* (New York: Simon and Schuster, 1981), and Thomas Ferguson and Joel Rogers's *The Hidden Election: Politics and Economics in the 1980 Presidential Campaign* (New York: Pantheon Books, 1981) did not discuss the issue. William C. Adams's 1983 work *Television Coverage of the 1980 Presidential Campaign* (Norwood: Ablex, 1983) also did not examine the Neshoba visit. Further complicating matters is the lack of any mention of Neshoba in recent scholarship concerning President Reagan and civil rights. Steven A. Shull's 1993 work *A Kinder, Gentler Racism? The Reagan-Bush Civil Rights Legacy* (Armonk: M. E. Sharpe, 1993); in 1994 Hanes Walton, Jr., *Black Politics and Black Political Behavior: A Linkage Analysis* (Westport, CT: Praeger, 1994); Samuel L. Myers's 1997 piece *Civil Rights and Race Relations in the Post Reagan-Bush Era* (Westport, CT: Praeger, 1997); and Nicholas Laham's 1998 scholarship *The Reagan Presidency and the Politics of Race: In Pursuit of Colorblind Justice and Limited Government* (Westport, CT: Praeger, 1998), all did not give the Neshoba County Fair a single citation.

8. Cannon, *Reagan*, 269; Cannon, *Governor Reagan*, 477.

9. Paul Abramson, John Aldrich, and David Rohde, *Change and Continuity in the 1980 Elections* (Washington, DC: Congressional Quarterly Press, 1982), 121.

10. Sandra Denson to Kay Odle, May 30, 1980, Box 271, Ronald Reagan (hereafter RR) Personal Papers 1980 Campaign, RRPLA. The same file has the June 1980 *National Geographic* story on the fair and includes also a booklet put out by the Neshoba Fair Association, which includes many pictures (only one of which contains a black; another shows a "typical view" of the cabins, and one proudly flies two Confederate flags). Letters from Charles Pickering, co-chairman of Reagan's campaign in Mississippi, Michael Retzer, chairman of the Mississippi Republican Party, and Senator Thad Cochran (MS) to RR, Advance Scheduling—Tyson—Schedule Request by State—Mississippi, 8/1980–10/1980, Box 271, RR Personal Papers 1980 Campaign, RRPLA (hereafter RR 1980 Campaign). Cochran would later recall that he wished to have Reagan visit Mississippi but not necessarily the Neshoba County Fair. J. Kenneth Klinge, phone interview, November 7, 2003; Senator Thad Cochran, phone interview, November 21, 2003.

11. Trent Lott, *Herding Cats: A Life in Politics* (New York: Regan Books, 2005), 75–76, 246, 253. Lott does not comment on any of the controversy surrounding Reagan's remarks. Later in this book, Lott tried to explain his controversial December 5, 2002, comments at the hundredth birthday celebration for Senator Strom Thurmond: "I revived a bit I'd done back in 1980 at a campaign rally for Ronald Reagan in Mississippi." Lott referred to a fall 1980 political rally in Jackson, Mississippi, in which Thurmond was the keynote speaker. Reagan did not attend. *Washington Post*, December 11, 2002.

12. *Washington Post*, August 4, 1980, *Chicago Tribune*, August 5, 1980.

13. Klinge interview.

14. *Washington Post*, August 4, *Chicago Tribune*, August 5, and *Clarion-Ledger*, August 4, 1980.

15. Advance Scheduling—Schedules—Block Schedules 1980, Folder 1 of 2, Sched. Box 261, RR 1980 Campaign. The same calendar page, without the blue magic marker, is located in Calendar Page, Ed Meese—Schedules—August 1980, Box 143, ibid.

16. *Washington Post*, August 4, and *Chicago Tribune*, August 5, 1980.

17. *Atlanta (GA) Journal-Constitution*, August 4, 1980.

18. Klinge interview.

19. Memo, Ken Klinge to Chuck Tyson, Bill Timmons, Advance Scheduling—Schedules—8/3/1980 Neshoba County Fair, Box 258, RR 1980 Campaign.

20. Wirthlin, *Greatest Communicator*, 68.

21. Cochran interview.

22. Cannon, *Reagan*, 269–70; Cannon, *Role of a Lifetime* (1991), 577; Cannon, *Role of a Lifetime* (2001), 510; Cannon, *Governor Reagan*, 477; Nofziger, *Nofziger*, 256; Harry S. Ashmore, *Civil Rights and Wrongs: A Memoir of Race and Politics, 1944–1994* (New York: Pantheon Books, 1994), 290, 291; Jeremy D. Mayer, *Running on Race: Racial Politics in Presidential Campaigns, 1960–2000* (New York: Random House, 2002), 168.

23. *Clarion-Ledger*, August 2, 1980.

24. Retzer was no mere local supporter for the Republican Party. A native of Greenville, Mississippi, he served as the chairman of the Mississippi Republican Party in 1980. After years of dedication to the Republican Party, including appointment as

treasurer of the national party in 2002, Retzer gained appointment to the ambassadorship to the United Republic of Tanzania in 2005.

25. Untitled and undated Mike Retzer document, RBD Files—Southern Region—Mississippi States, Box RBD Southern 7, 376, RR 1980 Campaign. It remains unclear who Reed actually is, although it could mean Clarke Reed, a prominent national Republican from Mississippi.

26. The inability of the author to gain a meeting with Lott hampers an investigation into the full meaning of the paper.

27. "Reagan for Real," *Time*, October 7, 1966, 33; Ronald Reagan, *The Creative Society: Some Comments on Problems Facing America* (New York: Devin-Adair, 1968), 81, 138, 142; Jo Ann Klein, "Reagan Brings His Presidential Non-Campaign into Mississippi," *Clarion-Ledger*, October 19, 1978. Unfortunately, the newspaper story does not contain a direct quote, and in correspondence with the author, the reporter responded that she no longer possessed notes of the visit. See also Skinner, Anderson, and Anderson, *Life in Letters*, 271.

28. Note, undated, Folder Political Ops—Timmons—Schedule Request by State—Mississippi, Box 248, RR 1980 Campaign.

29. *Clarion-Ledger*, *Jackson (MS) Daily News*, *Washington Post*, and *Atlanta (GA) Journal-Constitution*, all August 4, 1980. The *Jackson (MS) Daily News* was the evening paper for the city and ceased publication in 1989.

30. Kenneth O'Reilly, *Nixon's Piano: Presidents and Racial Politics from Washington to Clinton* (New York: Free Press, 1995), 351.

31. *New Orleans Times-Picayune* (hereafter *Times-Picayune*), August 4, 1980.

32. *New York Times*, *Commercial Appeal*, and *Atlanta (GA) Journal-Constitution*, all August 4, 1980.

33. *Washington Post* and *New York Times*, August 5, 1980. Neither newspaper mentioned Reagan's Neshoba visit in relation to his New York schedule. Itinerary of Governor Reagan's Campaign Travel Schedule, Advance Scheduling—Schedules—Block Schedules 1980, Folder 1 of 2, Sched. Box 261, RR 1980 Campaign.

34. *Washington Post*, August 6, 1980.

35. Carl T. Rowan, *Breaking Barriers: A Memoir* (Boston: Little Brown, 1991), 311; "Reagan Talks about Jobs to Blacks," *Jackson Daily News*, August 6, 1980, "Don't Pigeonhole Me, Reagan Asks Blacks," *Washington Post*, August 6, 1980.

36. *Jackson (MS) Daily News*, *Washington Post*, and *Atlanta (GA) Journal-Constitution*, all August 6, 1980. None of these papers mentioned the Neshoba County Fair speech.

37. *Clarion-Ledger* and *New York Times*, August 6, 1980.

38. *Chicago Tribune*, August 6, 1980.

39. *New York Times*, August 6, 1980.

40. *Washington Post*, August 6, 1980; Cannon, *Governor Reagan*, 478 (quote).

41. Jeff Greenfield, *The Real Campaign: How the Media Missed the Story of the 1980 Campaign* (New York: Summit Books, 1982), 266; Nofziger, *Nofziger*, 256, 257; Mayer, *Running on Race*, 164, 165; *Washington Post*, August 6, 1980.

42. August 1980 Calendar Schedule, July 29, 1980, Advance Scheduling—Schedules—Block Schedules 1980 Folder 1 of 2, Sched. box 261; United Press International Wire Stories, Ed Meese—Schedules—August 1980, Box 143; and Advance Scheduling—Index (to campaign travel. 7/19/1980—10/4/1980), Box 258, all in RR 1980 Campaign.

43. McClaughry memo to Meese, Nofziger, Brady, Anderson, and Deaver, Au-

gust 7, 1980, Advance Scheduling—Schedules—8/5/1980 Urban League, folder 1 of 2, Box 258, ibid.

44. United Press International Wire Stories, Advance Scheduling—Index (to campaign travel. 7/19/1980—10/4/1980), Box 258, ibid; *Chicago Tribune*, August 6, 1980. This author's attempts to contact Reverend Jesse Jackson were unsuccessful.

45. *Chicago Tribune*, August 8, 1980 (emphasis added).

46. *Chicago Defender*, August 16, 1980.

47. Memo, Richard Wirthlin to RR, August 9, 11, 1980, Advance Scheduling—Schedules—8/5/1980 Urban League, Folder 1 of 2, Box 258, RR 1980 Campaign; Drew, *Portrait of an Election*, 374.

48. Cochran interview.

49. Personal Correspondence, National Urban League to RR, August 29, 1980, 1980 A–J, Box 6, RR 1980 Campaign.

50. *Clarion-Ledger*, September 19, and *Tupelo Northeast Mississippi Journal*, September 17, 1980; Mayer, *Running on Race*, 170.

51. *New York Times*, September 17, 1980; Cannon, *Reagan*, 280.

52. *Newsweek*, September 29, 1980.

53. Jack W. Germond and Jules Witcover, *Blue Smoke and Mirrors: How Reagan Won and Why Carter Lost the Election of 1980* (New York: Viking Press, 1981), 256, 262.

54. *Clarion-Ledger*, September 18, 1980.

55. *New York Times*, September 19, 1980.

56. *Clarion-Ledger* and *New York Times*, both September 19, 1980.

57. Hamilton Jordan, *Crisis: The Last Year of the Carter Presidency* (New York: G. P. Putnam's Sons, 1982), 343.

58. Jordan, *Crisis*, 348; Cannon, *Reagan*, 284.

59. *Chicago Tribune* and *Times-Picayune*, both October 23, 1980.

60. O'Reilly, *Nixon's Piano*, 351.

61. *Newsweek*, September 29, 1980.

62. Drew, *Portrait of an Election*, 383.

63. *Chicago Tribune*, October 23, 1980; Greenfield, *The Real Campaign*, 293; Cannon, *Reagan*, 279.

64. Drew, *Portrait of an Election*, 383–84.

65. Garrick memo to Brady, Nofziger, Anderson, Deaver, and Khachigian, October 22, 1980, Speech File (Garrick)—Columbus, MS Ranch Bar-B-Q 10/22/80, Box Speech Files, Garrick # 424, RR 1980 Campaign.

66. *Jackson (MS) Daily News*, October 21, 1980.

67. *Clarion-Ledger*, October 22, 23, 1980.

68. *Chicago Tribune*, *Clarion-Ledger*, *Times-Picayune*, *Tupelo Northeast Mississippi Journal*, all October 23, 1980. The outspoken Evers also endorsed Bush over Dukakis eight years later. *Clarion- Ledger*, October 21, 1988.

69. *Newsweek*, October 27, 1980.

70. *Jackson (MS) Daily News*, October 23, 1980.

71. *Chicago Tribune*, *Times-Picayune*, *Washington Post*, *New York Times*, all October 23, 1980.

72. *Jackson (MS) Daily News*, *Tupelo Northeast Mississippi Journal*, *Commercial Appeal*, and *Clarion-Ledger*, all October 23, 1980.

73. *Washington Post*, October 23, 1980.

74. *New York Times*, October 23, 1980.

75. "Memorandum II Debate Strategy: Patrick H. Caddell, October 21, 1980," in Drew, *Portrait of an Election*, 424.

76. Dave Leip, *Atlas of Presidential Elections*, to be found at http://uselection-atlas.org/RESULTS/; Roland Perry, *Hidden Power: The Programming of the President* (New York: Beaufort Books, 1984), 162; Jere Nash and Andy Taggart, *Mississippi Politics: The Struggle for Power, 1976–2006* (Jackson: University Press of Mississippi, 2006), 121–22.

77. *Clarion-Ledger*, August 5, 1988; Stephen D. Staffer, "Mississippi: Electoral Conflict in a Nationalized State," in Lawrence W. Moreland, Robert P. Steed, and Tod A. Baker, *The 1988 Presidential Election in the South: Continuity amidst Change in Southern Party Politics* (New York: Praeger, 1991), 97, 98.

78. *Commercial Appeal*, August 5, 1988; David R. Runkel, "*Campaign for President*": *The Managers Look at '88* (New York: Auburn House, 1989), 178.

79. Susan Estrich, e-mail to the author, August 9, 2007.

80. *Tupelo Northeast Mississippi Journal*, August 5, 1988.

81. Susan Estrich, e-mail to the author, August 9, 2007.

82. Similar to the numbers discrepancy surrounding Reagan's visit, an exact count is also difficult to obtain concerning Dukakis's speech. On August 5, 1988, the *New York Times*, the *Commercial Appeal*, and the *Washington Post* counted two thousand, the *Chicago Tribune* suggested three thousand, the *Clarion-Ledger* and Staffer, in "Mississippi," suggest between three and five thousand. The *Tupelo Northeast Mississippi Journal* on August 5, 1988, exceeded all others combined with a count of twelve thousand in attendance.

83. Staffer, "Mississippi," 98.

84. *Washington Post* and *Tupelo Northeast Mississippi Journal*, both August 5, 1988. Christine M. Black and Thomas Oliphant, *All by Myself: The Unmaking of a Presidential Campaign* (Chester, CT: Globe Pequot Press, 1989), included information that campaign manager Susan Estrich also opposed any mention of the 1964 murders, but they provide no notes or references for support. In an e-mail to the author on August 9, 2007, Estrich disagrees with their claim.

85. Susan Estrich, e-mail to the author, August 9, 2007.

86. *Clarion-Ledger*, August 4, 1988; *Tupelo Northeast Mississippi Journal* and *New York Times*, both August 5, 1988; Black and Oliphant, *All by Myself*, 186.

87. *Los Angeles Times* (hereafter *LA Times*) and *Washington Post*, August 5, 1988.

88. O'Reilly, *Nixon's Piano*, 388.

89. *New York Times*, *Chicago Tribune*, *Washington Post*, and *Clarion-Ledger*, all August 5, 1988.

90. *New York Times*, August 5, 1980.

91. *Tupelo Northeast Mississippi Journal*, August 5, 1988.

92. *Commercial Appeal*, August 5, 1988.

93. Black and Oliphant, *All by Myself*, 186.

94. Dave Leip, *Atlas of U.S. Presidential Elections*, http://uselectionatlas.org/RESULTS/ (accessed June 29, 2010).

95. Seth Cagin and Philip Dray's 1988 work, *We Are Not Afraid* (New York: Macmillan, 1988), offered a new examination of the murders. *Mississippi Burning*, a film loosely based on the 1964 murders, gained nationwide release on the birthday of Martin Luther King, Jr., in January 1989. The motion picture earned seven Oscar nominations, including Best Picture and Best Director.

96. Press Release, Reagan and Bush, Advance Scheduling—Schedules—9/1/1980

Liberty State Park, Box 258, RR 1980 Campaign.

97. *Chicago Tribune*, August 19, 1980.

98. "On the Road with the President of Black America," *Washington Post Magazine*, January 25, 1987, 19; *Chicago Tribune*, August 5, 1988.

99. *Chicago Tribune*, August 6, 1980.

100. Briefing Document, undated, California Headquarters—Briefing Documents from Policy Coordinator Office, 8/17–20/80, Box 55, RR 1980 Campaign.

101. *Clarion-Ledger*, August 4, 1988, and *New York Times, LA Times, Chicago Tribune*, and *Washington Post*, August 5, 1988.

102. Rowan, *Breaking Barriers*, 327; O'Reilly, *Nixon's Piano*, 350; Mayer, *Running on Race*, 168; Nash and Taggart, *Mississippi Politics*, 167; Joseph Crespino, *In Search of Another Country: Mississippi and the Conservative Counterrevolution* (Princeton, NJ: Princeton University Press, 2007), 1; Craig Shirley, *Rendezvous with Destiny: Ronald Reagan and the Campaign that Changed America* (Wilmington, DE: Intercollegiate Studies Institute, 2009), 592.

103. Andrew E. Busch, *Reagan's Victory: The Presidential Election of 1980 and the Rise of the Right* (Lawrence: University Press of Kansas, 2005), 98; Germond and Witcover, *Blue Smoke and Mirrors*; Pomper, *Election of 1980*; Drew, *Portrait of an Election*; Ferguson and Rogers, *The Hidden Election*; Jonathan Moore, ed., *The Campaign for President: 1980 in Retrospect* (Cambridge: Ballinger, 1981); Greenfield, *The Real Campaign*; Paul A. Smith, *Electing a President: Information and Control* (New York: Praeger, 1982); Adams, *Television Coverage*; and Perry, *Hidden Power*.

104. *Chicago Tribune* and *Raleigh (NC) News and Observer*, both June 9, 2004; *Atlanta (GA) Journal-Constitution*, June 10, 2004; *Boston Globe*, June 10, 11, 2004; *Washington Post*, June 13, 14, 2004; *Albany (NY) Times-Union*, June 14, 2004; *Charleston (WV) Gazette*, June 14, 2004; *Newsweek*, June 14, 2004, 44; *USNWR*, June 21, 2004, 50 (hereafter *USNWR*); *Ronald Reagan Remembered*, a commemorative book with an accompanying DVD published by CBS News (which also included the claim by reprinting the June 14, 2004, *Newsweek* article); *New York Times*, July 18, 2005, November 9, 12, 13, 18, 19, 2007; *USA Today*, September 11, 2007; *Clarion-Ledger*, November 25, 2007.

105. "Reagan Speaks to Thousands on Gulf Coast," *Clarion-Ledger*, October 2, 1984.

2—"A Noble Cause"

1. Drew, *Portrait of an Election*, 376.

2. For an additional listing of Reagan pre-presidential rhetoric regarding Vietnam, see Appendix A.

3. Peter Schweizer, *Reagan's War: The Epic Story of His Forty-Year Struggle and Final Triumph over Communism* (New York: Doubleday, 2002), 47, 48, 65, 71, 65.

4. Ibid., 68, 87.

5. Skinner, Anderson, and Anderson, *In His Own Hand*, 481. This book contains a copy of Reagan's remarks to the VFW as well as personal additions and deletions made by the candidate. Also see Speech, Veterans of Foreign Wars, August 18, 1980, 1979–1980, Box 949, RR 1980 Campaign.

6. Schweizer, *Reagan's War*, 120.

7. "Reagan Vows Strong U.S.," *Chicago Tribune*, August 19, 1980.

8. "Reagan Calls Arms Race Essential to Avoid a 'Surrender' or 'Defeat,'" *New*

York Times, August 19, 1980; "Reagan: 'Peace through Strength,'" *Washington Post*, August 19, 1980.

9. "Reagan Calls Vietnam War a 'Noble Cause,'" *LA Times*, August 18, 1980; "Reagan to VFW: Viet War Was a 'Noble Cause,'" ibid., August 19, 1980; "Letters to the Times," ibid., August 25, 1980.

10. "Reagan: 'Peace through Strength,'" *Washington Post*, August 19, 1980.

11. Rowland Evans and Robert Novak, "Making Reagan 'Fail-Safe,'" ibid., August 22, 1980.

12. "In Vietnam, More than a War Was Lost," *LA Times*, August 22, 1980.

13. "Reagan's Combative Rhetoric Is Working against Him," *Washington Post*, August 24, 1980. Johnson would later write *Sleepwalking through History*.

14. "Reagan's View of Vietnam War," *LA Times*, August 25, 1980; Frank McAdams, "What Price Glory, Captain Reagan?" ibid., August 27, 1980.

15. Cannon, *Governor Reagan*, 479, 480. As detailed in Chapter One, Reagan's campaign suffered several public image problems during the month of August 1980. A week after the Chicago VFW speech, Reagan again encountered difficulty when his vice-presidential choice, George H. W. Bush, seemingly disagreed with him publicly on American policy in dealing with China and Taiwan.

16. Eric T. Dean, Jr., *Shook over Hell: Post-Traumatic Stress, Vietnam, and the Civil War* (Cambridge: Harvard University Press, 1997), 12, 19.

17. Interestingly, Dean's book argues that perhaps the problems of Vietnam veteran readjustment were overstated. A somewhat similar argument is made in Jerry Lembcke, *The Spitting Image: Myth, Memory, and the Legacy of Vietnam* (New York: New York University Press, 1998). Whether this is true is irrelevant for the purposes of the work here. The perception of the downtrodden Vietnam veteran lasted well into the 1980s, and this element of sympathy is what Reagan played off and used in his words.

18. National newspapers and magazines provide many examples. A small sampling of *New York Times* stories detail the direction of newspaper coverage: "Ex-Pilot in Drug Smuggling Trial Cites Stress of Vietnam Fighting; Basis of Defense Prepared," August 31, 1980; "Jailed Veterans Case Brings Post-Vietnam Problem into Focus," February 26, 1982; "TV: Vietnam Veterans, U.S. Crime, and Prison," July 15, 1982; "Vietnam Veterans Need More than a Salute," November 21, 1982. *Time* magazine featured numerous stories: "A War of Angry Cousins," March 5, 1979; "We Love You," June 11, 1979; "Where Is My Country?" February 25, 1980; "Pleading PTSD," May 26, 1980; "Who Pays for the Damage?" June 21, 1980; "The Toxicity Connection," September 22, 1980; "The War Came Home," April 6, 1981; "Still Living with the War," June 8, 1981; "The Forgotten Warriors," June 13, 1981; "A Homecoming at Last," November 22, 1982. Journal articles included Loch Johnson, "Political Alienation among Vietnam Veterans," *Western Political Quarterly* 29, no. 3 (September 1976): 398–409; Eugene H. Freund and Earl G. Stormo, "A Resocialization Strategy for Black Vietnam Veterans," *Journal of Negro Education* 48, no. 4 (autumn 1979): 500–512; Robert S. Laufer, M. S. Gallops, and Ellen Frey-Wouters, "War Stress and Trauma: The Vietnam Veteran Experience," *Journal of Health and Social Behavior* 25, no. 1 (March 1984): 65–85; Robert S. Laufer and M. S. Gallops, "Life-Course Effects of Vietnam Combat and Abusive Violence: Marital Patterns," *Journal of Marriage and the Family* 47, no. 4 (November 1985): 839–53; Constance L. Shehan, "Spouse Support and Vietnam Veterans' Adjustment to Post-Traumatic Stress Disorder," *Family Relations* 36, no. 1 (January 1987): 55–60; Lynn R. August and Barbara A. Gianola, "Symptoms of War

Trauma Induced Psychiatric Disorders: Southeast Asian Refugees and Vietnam Veterans," *International Migration Review* 21, no. 3 (autumn 1987): 820–32, special issue on migration and health. Finally, books detailed many of the problems encountered by Vietnam veterans: Scott Blakey, *Prisoner at War: The Survival of Commander Richard A. Stratton* (Garden City, NY: Anchor Press/Doubleday, 1978); Michael Uhl and Tod Ensign, *G.I. Guinea Pigs: How the Pentagon Exposed Our Troops to Dangers More Deadly than War: Agent Orange and Atomic Radiation* (New York: Playboy Press, 1980); Fred Wilcox, *Waiting for an Army to Die: The Tragedy of Agent Orange* (New York: Vintage Books, 1983); William E. Kelly, *Post-Traumatic Stress Disorder and the War Veteran Patient* (New York: Brunner-Mazell, 1985).

19. *PPRR 1981*, 1–4.

20. This work examines the Vietnam rhetoric of Ronald Reagan and the subsequent impact on the perceptions of Americans, not the actual veterans policies of his administration.

21. Skinner, Anderson, and Anderson, *Life in Letters*, 395. For additional examples of the presidential rhetoric equating the Vietnam War with less divisive American conflicts, see Appendix A.

22. Skinner, Anderson, and Anderson, *Life in Letters*, 395.

23. "Remarks and a Question-and-Answer Session at a Los Angeles World Affairs Council Luncheon in *LA*, California, April 10, 1987," *PPRR 1987*, 1:365–72. For additional examples of Reagan's assertion that the Vietnam War remained a small part of an international struggle versus communism, see Appendix A.

24. "Statement on Granting Pardons to W. Mark Felt and Edward S. Miller, April 15, 1981," *PPRR 1981*, 358–59; Skinner, Anderson, and Anderson, *Path to Victory—The Shaping of Ronald Reagan's Vision: Selected Writings* (New York: Free Press, 2004), 159.

25. The last laugh may have been on Reagan. In June 2005 Felt admitted to his identity of "Deep Throat," the clandestine figure who supplied so much information to *Washington Post* reporters Bob Woodward and Carl Bernstein during the Watergate scandal, which resulted in the resignation of Republican president Richard Nixon.

26. "Remarks at Dedication Ceremonies for the Vietnam Veterans Memorial Statue, November 11, 1984," *PPRR 1984*, 2:1820–22.

27. "Remarks at the Heritage Foundation Anniversary Dinner, April 22, 1986," *PPRR 1986*, 1:497–501.

28. For additional examples of the consistent Reagan rhetorical pattern concerning the Vietnam War protestor, see Appendix A.

29. Skinner, Anderson, and Anderson, *Life in Letters*, 489–90.

30. Ibid., 265.

31. "Remarks at the Conservative Political Action Conference Dinner, February 18, 1983," *PPRR 1983*, 1:249–56; "Remarks at Memorial Day Ceremonies Honoring an Unknown Serviceman of the Vietnam War, May 28, 1984," *PPRR 1984*, 1:748–50.

32. "Remarks at a Question-and-Answer Session with Regional Editors and Broadcasters, April 18, 1985," *PPRR 1985*, 1:451–57.

33. Skinner, Anderson, and Anderson, *Life in Letters*, 534–35. For additional examples of the betrayal argument in the presidential rhetoric of Reagan, see Appendix A.

34. "Remarks on Presenting the Medal of Honor to Master Sergeant Roy P. Benavidez, February 24, 1981," *PPRR 1981*, 155–58.

35. Ibid.

36. "Remarks at a White House Luncheon for Representatives of the Hispanic Community, September 16, 1981," *PPRR 1981*, 803–5; "Remarks at a White House Briefing for Hispanic Appointees and Members of the Hispanic Community, July 20, 1982," and "Remarks at a White House Ceremony Celebrating Hispanic Heritage Week, September 15, 1982," *PPRR 1982*, 2:945–47, 1157–59; "Remarks at Cinco de Mayo Ceremonies in San Antonio, Texas, May 5, 1983," *PPRR 1983*, 1:650–54; "Remarks at a White House Luncheon for the National Hispanic Leadership Conference, April 17, 1984," *PPRR 1984*, 1:547–49.

37. "Remarks at Memorial Day Ceremonies Honoring an Unknown Serviceman of the Vietnam Conflict, May 28, 1984," *PPRR 1984*, 1:748–50.

38. Ibid. On May 13, 1998, the remains were removed and identified as Air Force 1st Lt. Michael Blassie. As of this spring (2010), the Vietnam tomb is now empty with only an inscription, "Honoring and Keeping Faith with America's Missing Servicemen."

39. "Remarks on Presenting the Medal of Honor to Master Sergeant Roy P. Benavidez, February 24, 1981," *PPRR 1981*, 155–58; F. Andy Messing, Jr., telegram to RR, February 25, 1981, Veterans folder 4 (of 4), Box 30 of 43, Elizabeth Dole, RRPLA.

40. Jan C. Scruggs to RR, March 18, 1981, Vietnam Veteran, L-XYZ (2), Box 41, WHORM: Alpha File, RRPLA.

41. The National Sponsoring Committee hoped to solicit funds for the construction of the memorial. Other members included Gerald Ford, Rosalyn Carter, Jimmy Stewart, Bob Hope, and William Westmoreland. "Mrs. Reagan on Vietnam Panel," *New York Times*, February 18, 1981; Robert W. Spanogle to Elizabeth Dole, March 20, 1981, Veterans (4 of 4) OA4359, Box 30 of 43, Elizabeth Dole, RRPLA; Charlotte Landes to RR, April 1981, Vietnam Veteran, L-XYZ (2), and Jan Scruggs to Nancy Reagan, December 2, 1981, Vietnam Veterans Memorial Fund (2), both in U-VOK Box 41, WHORM: Alpha File, RRPLA.

42. Scruggs to RR, March 19, 1982, and John Manita to RR, June 4, 1982, U-VOK Box 41, WHORM: Alpha File, RRPLA.

43. Skinner, Anderson, and Anderson, *Life in Letters*, 390–91.

44. Jim Taylor to RR, May 3, 1983, and Jan Scruggs to RR, October 7, 1983, U-VOK Box 41, WHORM: Alpha File, RRPLA.

45. James C. Moody to RR, February 18, Robert F. MacDonald to RR, March 20, Scruggs to RR, April 27, Daniel P. O'Neill to RR, May 16, Ronald E. Burch to RR, June 9, Robert M. Schnell to RR, June 18, David D. Phillips to RR, July 7, Kay Stough to Frederick J. Ryan, Jr., August 1, 1984, all in ibid.

46. "Remarks at the Annual Convention of the American Legion in Salt Lake City, Utah, September 4, 1984," *PPRR 1984*, 2:1227–33.

47. "Proclamation 5336—Vietnam Veterans Recognition Day, 1985, May 7, 1985," *PPRR 1985*, 1:574.

48. Dean, *Shook over Hell*, 19, 20.

49. Letters to RR, June 26, 1985; RR to Danny E. Cotton, June 28, 1984; Joseph Curatolo to RR, August 23, 1985; Thomas H. Lipscomb to RR, September 3, 1985; Nick Pistone to RR, undated (but for an event on October 12, 1985); Dortch Oldham to RR, March 14, 1986, all in Vietnam Veteran, L-XYZ (1), U-VOK Box 41, WHORM: Alpha File, RRPLA.

50. Reagan, *Speaking My Mind*, 366–68. (Reagan as president repeated on numerous occasions his conviction that the Vietnam veteran deserved the title of hero and that the war remained a noble cause. For other instances, see Appendix A.)

51. Ibid.

52. Jack Wheeler to Fred Ryan and Sandra Warfield, June 9, 1988, and Jack Wheeler to Fred Ryan and Edmund Morris, July 6, 1988, Vietnam Veteran, L–XYZ (1), U-VOK Box 41, WHORM: Alpha File, RRPLA.

3—"Do We Get to Win This Time?"

1. In this chapter we concentrate on the *Rambo* films of the 1980s and do not include a detailed discussion of the 2008 film, *Rambo*.

2. Lembcke, *Spitting Image*, 176, 177.

3. For a detailed examination of the production of *First Blood*, see David Morrell, *Lessons from a Lifetime of Writing: A Novelist Looks at His Craft* (Cincinnati: Writer's Digest Books, 2002), 195–214.

4. Telephone interview with David Morrell, January 25, 2005; Morrell, *Lessons*, 4–5.

5. "Drawing First Blood," audio commentary, *First Blood*, Artisan DVD, 2002.

6. Ibid.

7. Morrell interview.

8. "David Morrell Audio Commentary," *First Blood*, Artisan DVD, 2002.

9. rogerebert.com,http://rogerebert.suntimes.com/apps/pbcs.dll/article?AID=/19820101/REVIEWS/201010324/1023 (accessed June 29, 2010).

10. "First Blood," *New York Times*, October 22, 1982.

11. "Rebels with a Cause," *Newsweek*, October 25, 1982, 119.

12. "Stallone on Patriotism and Rambo," *New York Times*, June 6, 1985.

13. Thomas Doherty, "First Blood Part II," *Film Quarterly* (Fall 1986); Jeffery Walsh, "First Blood to Rambo: A Textual Analysis," in Alf Louvre and Jeffrey Walsh, *Tell Me Lies about Vietnam: Cultural Battles for the Meaning of the War* (Philadelphia: Open University Press, 1988); Gaylyn Studlar and David Desser, "Never Having to Say You're Sorry: *Rambo's* Rewriting of the Vietnam War," *Film Quarterly* (Fall 1988); Linda Dittmar and Gene Michaud, eds., *From Hanoi to Hollywood: The Vietnam War in American Film* (New Brunswick: Rutgers University Press, 1990); Gregory A. Waller, "Rambo: Getting to Win This Time," in Dittmar and Michaud, *From Hanoi to Hollywood*, 113–38. Susan Jeffords, *Hard Bodies: Hollywood Masculinity in the Reagan Era* (New Brunswick: Rutgers University Press, 1993) comes the closest to detecting the Reagan rhetorical impact as she argues in her work that the release of the three Rambo films in the beginning, middle, and end of the Reagan presidency revealed the progress of a reconstructed American masculinity imagery that mirrored the symbolism of the fortieth president.

14. "Proclamation 5356—National POW/MIA Recognition Day, June 27, 1985," *PPRR 1985*, 1:831.

15. *Rambo: First Blood Part II*, directed by George P. Cosmatos, TriStar Pictures, 1985.

16. For a complete breakdown of all monies concerning the film see www.imdb.com/title/tt0089880/business.

17. "Stallone on Patriotism and Rambo," *New York Times*, June 6, 1985.

18. "How Real Is 'Rambo'?" *Washington Post*, July 8, 1985.

19. "The U.S. Has Surrendered—Now *Rambo* Is Taking the World by Storm," *Business Week*, August 26, 1985, 109.

20. Morrell interview; Morrell, *Lessons*, 213–14.

21. "Rambo to the Rescue," *Life*, August, 1985, 11.

22. "Remarks at the Annual Convention of the National Association of Evangelicals, March 8, 1983," *PPRR 1983*, 1:359–64.

23. "Next: Rambo Goes to Nicaragua?" *Washington Post*, June 4, 1985.

24. "Remarks during a White House Briefing on the Program for Economic Recovery, February 24, 1981," *PPRR 1981*, 152–53; "Excerpts from an Interview with Walter Cronkite of CBS News, March 3, 1981," ibid., 191–202; "The President's News Conference, March 6, 1981," ibid., 205–12; "Interview with *USA Today*, April 26, 1983," and "Question-and-Answer Session with Reporters on Domestic and Foreign Policy Issues, May 27, 1983," *PPRR 1983*, 1:587–93, 782–89.

25. "An Outbreak of Rambomania," *Time*, June 24, 1985, 73.

26. "Grossed Out on the Summer's Top-Grossing Film," *Ms.* (August 1985): 71.

27. David Morrell, *Rambo: First Blood Part II* (New York: A Jove Book, 1985), 235–36. The adaptation of the sequel stayed on the *New York Times* best-selling list for six weeks. Morrell, *Lessons*, 212–13.

28. Morrell interview.

29. "Screen: Sylvester Stallone Returns as Rambo," *New York Times*, May 22, 1985.

30. "Film View: 'Rambo' Delivers a Revenge Fantasy," *New York Times*, May 26, 1985. See also "Why a 'Rambo II'? For Muddiest of Reasons," *LA Times*, May 22, 1985.

31. "An Outbreak of Rambomania," *Time*, June 24, 1985, 72. See also "Coleco Smitten by 'Rambo,'" *New York Times*, August 1, 1985; "Rambomania, Action Dolls, Other Tie-Ins Spark Toy War," *Advertising Age*, August 5, 1985, 3, 63; "The U.S. Has Surrendered—Now *Rambo* Is Taking the World by Storm," *Business Week*, August 26, 1985, 109.

32. Morrell interview.

33. "Somewhere over the Rambo," *Rolling Stone Magazine*, December 19, 1985, 101, 102, 107, 173.

34. "Sylvester Stallone," ibid., December 19, 1985, 126, 166. Stallone did well in 1985. *Rambo: First Blood Part II* was released on May 22, 1985, and *Rocky IV* was released on November 27, 1985.

35. "Showing the Flag: Rocky, Rambo, and the Return of the American Hero," *Newsweek*, December 23, 1985, 58–62.

36. Cover, *USNWR*, November 18, 1985.

37. Morrell interview.

38. "We Get to Win This Time: The Rambo Phenomenon," documentary, *Rambo: First Blood Part II: Special Edition*, Lion's Gate Studios, 2003.

39. "Business Data for *Rambo III*," http://www.imdb.com/title/tt0095956/business.

40. "Awards for *Rambo III*," http://www.imdb.com/title/tt0095956/awards. Originating in 1980 the Razzies annually confer awards on the worst films and performances produced by Hollywood. The awards do not always reflect popular opinion, as *Rambo: First Blood Part II*, an explicit box office success, received the 1985 Razzie for Worst Film.

41. "Afghanistan: Land in Crisis: An In-Depth Look," documentary, *Rambo III: Special Edition*, Lion's Gate Studios, 2003.

42. Ibid.

43. "Good Chemistry," *Time*, June 13, 1988, 12, 14, 17, 18, 27.

44. Review of *Rambo III*, *Washington Post*, May 25, 1988.

45. Morrell interview.

46. Repeated efforts to contact Oliver Stone have proved unsuccessful. Sarah Gilbert in his office contacted the author and stated that Mr. Stone would be happy to answer submitted questions. The author sent the requested material and, as of spring 2010, has heard nothing. Other works have examined the realism of *Platoon*. Harry W. Haines, in "'They Were Called and They Went': The Political Rehabilitation of the Vietnam Veteran," praised the film's graphic portrayal of life in the jungle, combat, and graphic death; Kevin Bowen, in "'Strange Hells': Hollywood in Search of America's Lost War," responded negatively to an oft-repeated term in the Reagan rhetoric and stated that *Platoon* clearly revealed "Vietnam is not a noble mission." See Dittmar and Michaud, *From Hanoi to Hollywood*, 91–93 (Haines), 233–34 (Bowen). Antony Easthope, in "Realism and Its Subversion: Hollywood and Vietnam," argued in part that, by the late 1980s, the declining influence of Reagan helped Hollywood ease out Rambo for more realistic films such as *Platoon*. In what he called the "revised ideological situation of Reagan's declining years, post-Irangate," the author suggested that the "vet had become a cliché" and "the ground was thus prepared for Hollywood to move from manifest exaggeration back to its traditional claim to show the real." Louvre and Walsh, *Tell Me Lies*, 43.

47. Advertisement, *LA Times*, January 25, 1987; http://www.imdb.com/title/tt0091763/taglines.

48. Bob Martin, "Oliver Stone and *The Hand*," in *Oliver Stone: Interviews*, ed. Charles L. P. Silet (Jackson: University Press of Mississippi, 2001), 9.

49. "*Platoon*: Vietnam, the Way It Really Was, on Film," *Time*, January 26, 1987, 56-57; "'Platoon'—Hollywood Steps on a Gold Mine," *LA Times*, January 25, 1987; Norman Kagan, *The Cinema of Oliver Stone* (New York: Continuum, 2000), 111; www.imdb.com/title/tt0091763/business and www.imdb.com/title/tt0091763/awards; Judy Lee Kinney, "Gardens of Stone, Platoon, and Hamburger Hill: Ritual and Remembrance," in Michael Anderegg, ed., *Inventing Vietnam: The War in Film and Television* (Philadelphia: Temple University Press, 1991), 157.

50. Paul Attanasio, "Platoon," *Washington Post*, January 16, 1987; "'Platoon'—Hollywood Steps on a Gold Mine," *LA Times*, January 25, 1987; David Kishiyama, "A Reason to Reflect on War: Seeing *Platoon*'s Gory Violence Unleashes Some Memories," *LA Times*, January 25, 1987; Roger Ebert, "Platoon," *Chicago Sun-Times*, December 30, 1986.

51. "The Vietnam War in Stone's 'Platoon,'" *New York Times*, December 19, 1986; "'Platoon'—Hollywood Steps on a Gold Mine," *LA Times*, January 25, 1987.

52. "After Seeing *Platoon*, Fonda Wept," *LA Times*, January 25, 1987; "Has *Platoon* De-Escalated War Movies?" *LA Times*, January 25, 1987.

53. "*Platoon*: Vietnam, the Way It Really Was, on Film," *Time*, January 26, 1987, 56–57.

54. "Viet Refugees Give *Platoon* Good Reviews," *LA Times*, January 26, 1987.

55. "A Ferocious Vietnam Elegy: Oliver Stone Brings It Brutally Back Home," *Newsweek*, January 5, 1987, 57; "A Document Written in Blood," *Time*, December 15, 1986, 83; "*Platoon*: Vietnam, the Way It Really Was, on Film," *Time*, January 26, 1987, 55–56, 58.

56. "*Platoon*—Hollywood Steps on a Gold Mine," *LA Times*, January 25, 1987.

57. "Drawing Flack from Norris," ibid., January 25, 1987.

58. "*Platoon*—Hollywood Steps on a Gold Mine," ibid., January 25, 1987.

59. Ibid.

60. "*Platoon:* Vietnam, the Way It Really Was, on Film," *Time,* January 26, 1987, 57. Al Santoli's works included *Everything We Had: An Oral History of the Vietnam War as Told by 33 American Men Who Fought It* (New York: Random House, 1981) and *To Bear Any Burden: The Vietnam War and Its Aftermath in the Words of Americans and Southeast Asians* (New York: Dutton, 1985), original emphasis.

61. Pat McGilligan, "Point Man," in Silet, *Oliver Stone,* 35, 39. A 1986 blockbuster film starring Tom Cruise, *Top Gun,* glamorized the life of U.S. Navy fighter pilots.

62. Gary Crowdus, "Personal Struggles and Political Issues: An Interview with Oliver Stone," in Silet, *Oliver Stone,* 54; Marc Cooper, "*Playboy* Interview: Oliver Stone," ibid., 77.

63. Kagan, *Cinema of Oliver Stone,* 111.

64. Robert Toplin, ed., *Oliver Stone's USA: Film, History, Controversy* (Lawrence: University Press of Kansas, 2000), 228. Toplin's work contains fifteen essays that offer scholarly examination of the controversial filmmaker and nine of his works. A professor of history at the University of North Carolina–Wilmington, Toplin invited Stone to the 1997 AHA meeting to discuss his film *Nixon* with a large audience of professional historians. Toplin's book included reviews of nine Stone movies by individuals such as David Halberstam, Stephen Ambrose, George S. McGovern, and Arthur M. Schlesinger, Jr. Following the critiques, Stone offered responses.

4—Reagan, the Vietnam Veteran, 1980s Television, and Comics

1. Tim Brooks and Earle Marsh, *The Complete Directory to Prime Time Network TV Shows, 1946–Present,* 9th ed. (New York: Ballantine, 2007), 26, 646, 825–26, 835–36, 850, 889–90, 1156.

2. Suzy Kalter, *The Complete Book of M*A*S*H* (New York: Abradale Press, 1984).

3. *The A-Team,* NBC, episode 1, "Pilot, Mexican Slay Ride," January 23, 1983.

4. Ibid., episode 85, "The Sound of Thunder," May 13, 1986.

5. "The Best and Worst We Saw," *TV Guide,* July 2, 1983, 5, 6; "Six Days with *The A-Team?* Pity the Fool Who Tries It!" ibid., March 10, 1983, 8, 9, 15 (original emphasis).

6. "I Like Mr. T. because He Always Throws the Bad Guys out the Window," ibid., May 5, 1984, 43; "He's Made a Lot of Enemies," ibid., August 31, 1985, 29.

7. "I Like Mr. T.," ibid., May 5, 1984, 43–47.

8. "The A-Team," ibid., March 26, 1983, 48.

9. "All Our Fantasies," *New Statesman,* July 29, 1983, 30.

10. "Let's Not Use Vietnam Vets as an Excuse for TV Violence," *TV Guide,* August 23, 1986, 18–19.

11. For the 1982 season, *The A-Team* ranked number ten, in 1983 number four, and in 1985 number six. See Brooks and Marsh, *Complete Directory,* 1104–6; "Kicked Around: *The A-Team* Seeks Nielsen Revenge," *TV Guide,* November 29, 1985, 42.

12. Brooks and Marsh, *Complete Directory,* 915–16.

13. L. Travis Clark, telephone interview, January 12, 2005.

14. Brooks and Marsh, *Complete Directory,* 915–16; "CBS Announces Vietnam War Series for the Fall," *Jet,* August 24, 1987, 22; "Tour of Duty," *TV Guide,* September 12, 1987, 67.

15. "Tour of Duty," *TV Guide,* January 23, 1988, 40.

16. Interview, Clark, January 12, 2005. *The Cosby Show* starring Bill Cosby

ranked number one from 1985 to 1990.

17. Brooks and Marsh, *Complete Directory*, 1106–7.

18. "From the Halls of Montezuma to the Trials of *The Young and the Restless*," *TV Guide*, July 2, 1988, 39.

19. "Call It Neglect of Duty," ibid., March 12, 1988, 34–36.

20. Ibid. (original emphasis).

21. "*E.A.R.T.H. Force*," ibid., September 15, 1990, 12; Brooks and Marsh, *Complete Directory*, 260.

22. Clark interview.

23. Daniel Miller, "Primetime Television's Tour of Duty," in Anderegg, *Inventing Vietnam*, 166–171, 178, 180, 183, 187.

24. Clark interview.

25. Brooks and Marsh, *Complete Directory*, 165.

26. "Let's Not Use Vietnam Vets as an Excuse for TV Violence," *TV Guide*, August 23, 1986, 18–19; "China Beach," ibid., February 18, 1989, 56.

27. "'China Beach,' Women at War," *New York Times*, April 26, 1988.

28. "Women and War Hit the 'Beach,'" *USA Today*, April 26, 1988.

29. "Vietnam's Prime-Time Tour of Duty," *USA Today*, April 26, 1988.

30. Ibid.

31. "China Beach Salutes the Women of Vietnam," *Rolling Stone*, May 19, 1988, 75, 79.

32. "It's Back to the Beach for Dana Delaney," *TV Guide*, June 16, 1990, 11; Brooks and Marsh, *Complete Directory*, 1090–91.

33. "War as Family Entertainment: Two Vietnam Shows Tackle the Issues but Avoid the Politics," *Time*, February 20, 1989, 84.

34. John Carlos Rowe, "From Documentary to Docudrama: Vietnam on Television in the 1980s," *Genre* 21 (Winter 1988): 451–77; Deborah Ballard-Reisch, "*China Beach* and *Tour of Duty*: American Television and Revisionist History of the Vietnam War," *Journal of Popular Culture, Bowling Green, Ohio* (Winter 1991): 135–47; Carolyn Reed Vartanian, "Women Next Door to War: *China Beach*," in Anderegg, *Inventing Vietnam*, 193, 194, 202; Leah R. Vande Berg, "*China Beach*, Prime Time War in the Postfeminist Age: An Example of Patriarchy in a Different Voice," *Western Journal of Communication* 57 (Summer 1993).

35. David Huxley, "Naked Aggression: American Comic Books and the Vietnam War," in Louvre and Walsh, *Tell Me Lies*, 98–100.

36. Bradford W. Wright, *Comic Book Nation: The Transformation of Youth Culture in America* (Baltimore: Johns Hopkins University Press, 2001), 193.

37. Huxley, "Naked Aggression," 107.

38. Ibid., 96–97; Marvel Comics, *Sgt. Fury and His Howling Commandos*, no. 9 (New York: Marvel Comics Group); DC Comics, *Our Army at War Featuring Sgt. Rock*, no. 250, October (New York: DC Comics, 1972).

39. Wright, *Comic Book Nation*, 189, 193, 197, 199; Charlton Publications, *Fightin' Marines*, no. 77, November (New York: Charlton Publications, 1967); Huxley, "Naked Aggression," 104.

40. Wright, *Comic Book Nation*, 215, 222, 240–41, 243.

41. Annette Matton, "From Realism to Superheroes in Marvel's *The 'Nam*," in Matthew P. McAllister, Edward H. Sewell, Jr., and Ian Gordon, eds., *Comics and Ideology* (New York: Peter Lang, 2001), 157.

42. Wright, *Comic Book Nation*, 215, 222, 240–41, 243.

43. Huxley, "Naked Aggression," 108.

44. Les Daniels, *Marvel: Five Fabulous Decades of the World's Greatest Comics* (Japan: Harry N. Abrams, 1991), 204.

45. Doug Murray, "'Nam: First Patrol," *The 'Nam* 1 (December 1986).

46. Doug Murray, "Three-Day Pass," *The 'Nam* 3 (February 1987); "Humpin' the Boonies," 5 (April 1987); "Monsoon," 6 (May 1987); "Good Ole Days," 7 (June 1987); "In the Underground," 8 (July 1987); "Pride Goeth . . .," 9 (August 1987); "Guerrilla Action," 10 (September 1987); "From Cedar Falls with Love," 12 (November 1987); " . . . and a Wakeup," 13 (December 1987); "Notes from the World," 15 (February 1988).

47. "Doug Murray," *Comics Interview* 53 (1987): 15.

48. "Marvel Sees a Winner in 'Nam Comics," *LA Times*, May 12, 1987.

49. "Vietnam: The Comic Book War," *Washington Post*, September 10, 1986; "Doug Murray," *Comics Interview* 53 (1987): 15.

50. "Marvel Sees a Winner"; "Vietnam: The Comic Book War."

51. "Vietnam: The Comic Book War."

52. "Notes from the World," *The 'Nam* 15 (February 1988); "Good for the Goose" *The 'Nam* 16 (March 1988).

53. "Doug Murray," *Comics Interview* 53 (1987), 12.

54. Ibid., 12, 15 (original emphasis).

55. Ibid., 6, 19; "Marvel Sees a Winner."

56. "Doug Murray," *Comics Interview* 53 (1987), 6; "Marvel Sees a Winner."

57. "Doug Murray," *Comics Interview* 53 (1987), 9.

58. Ibid., 6–7.

59. Ibid., 10, 13, 19.

60. Ibid., 11.

61. Murray, "Three-Day Pass," *The 'Nam* 3 (February 1987); "Monsoon," *The 'Nam* 6 (May 1987). The references to *G.I. Joe* in *The 'Nam* letters derived from the national reemergence of the action figure in 1982. In 1969 Hassenfeld Brothers (later Hasbro), the company that had created *G.I. Joe* six years earlier, responded to the growing unpopularity of the Vietnam War. The corporation dropped any military imagery assigned to the toy and instead adopted a more universal "action" concept. Discontinued entirely in 1978 due to lack of interest in military toys, the product returned with a vengeance in 1982, restored and expanded its original military concept, and by the middle of the decade it had outsold all other children's toys.

62. Murray, "In the Underground," *The 'Nam* 8 (July 1987); "Pride Goeth . . .," *The 'Nam* 9 (August 1987); "Back in the Boonies," *The 'Nam* 17 (April 1988).

63. Matton, "From Realism to Superheroes," 151–52, 163, 165–66; Murray, "In the Underground," *The 'Nam* 8 (July 1987).

5—Falling from Grace

1. Speech, "Address to the Nation on the Iran Arms and Contra Aid Controversy, November 13, 1986," Folder 504 (11/13/86), Box 26, Presidential Handwriting File, RRPLA.

2. George Gallup, Jr., *The Gallup Poll: Public Opinion, 1986* (Wilmington: Scholarly Resources, 1987), 255 (hereafter *Gallup Poll*). See also *Time*, July 7, 1986, 12; "Assessing the Summit," *Time*, October 27, 1986, 27. An ABC News–*Washington Post* poll reported Reagan's approval/disapproval rating at 57%–40%. An NBC News–*Wall*

Street Journal poll surveyed identical numbers; "Opinion Roundup," *Public Opinion* (September/October 1987): 30–31. (After the recession of 1991–1992, President Bill Clinton would preside over the longest period of uninterrupted economic growth in American history.)

3. For a complete list of Reagan's presidential remarks regarding Nicaragua and the Contras, see Appendix B.

4. "Unraveling Fiasco," *Time*, November 24, 1986, 19.

5. "Remarks and an Informal Exchange with Reporters prior to a Meeting with David Jacobsen, November 7, 1986," *PPRR 1986*, 2:1533–34; "The U.S. and Iran," *Time*, November 17, 1986, 14; "Reagan's Backdoor Hostage Deal with Iran," *USNWR*, November 17, 1986, 8.

6. "Letter to the Speaker of the House and the President of the Senate Reporting on the Nicaraguan Emergency, November 10, 1986," and "Radio Address to the Nation on Administration and Congressional Goals, November 15, 1986," *PPRR 1986*, 2:1537–38, 1559–60.

7. Talking Points, November 12, 1986, Folder PRO16 Public Relations: Publicity (438001–450000), PR Public Relations PR 016 432001–486659 (1), WHORM: Subject File, RRPLA.

8. RR note to David L. Chew, November 13, 1986, Folder 504 (11/13/86), Presidential Handwriting File Presidential Speeches, Box 26, Presidential Handwriting File, Series III: Presidential Speeches 11/1/86–3/26/87, RRPLA (original emphasis).

9. Speech Draft, 12:45p.m., November 13, 1986, ibid.

10. Speech, "Address to the Nation on the Iran Arms and Contra Aid Controversy, November 13, 1986," ibid.; "Remarks at the Ethics and Public Policy Center Anniversary Dinner, November 18, 1986," *PPRR 1986*, 2:1563–67.

11. Johnathan S. Miller, memo to Donald T. Regan, November 17, 1986; Nicholas Platt, memo to John M. Poindexter, November 14, 1986; Carlos J. Garcia, telegram to RR, November 14, 1986; Donald T. Regan, letter, November 18, 1986; all in Folder SP1111 Begin–End, Speechwriting, Box 27, WHORM: Subject File, RRPLA.

12. "Unraveling Fiasco," *Time*, November 24, 1986, 19–20; "Who's in Charge Here?" *USNWR*, November 24, 1986, 18–19.

13. "Opinion Roundup," *Public Opinion* (September/October 1987): 24.

14. "The Presidential News Conference, November 19, 1986," *PPRR 1986*, 2:1567–75.

15. "The Tower of Babel," *Time*, December 1, 1986, 18, 21–22; "In Troubled Waters," *USNWR*, December 1, 1986, 12–13.

16. Deborah Hart Strober and Gerald Strober, eds., *Reagan: The Man and His Presidency* (Boston: Houghton Mifflin Company, 1998), 160.

17. *Report of the Congressional Committees Investigating the Iran-Contra Affair; with the Minority Views*, chairman, Daniel K. Inouye (New York: Random House, 1988), 344–45.

18. *Gallup Poll 1986*, 255; "Escalating the Contra Battle," *Time*, July 7, 1986, 26; *Report of the Congressional Committees*, 344; "Superpowers Gear It Up," *USNWR*, November 10, 1986, 8.

19. Skinner, Anderson, and Anderson, *Life in Letters*, 503–4, 637–41. For an extensive record of Reagan's rhetorical consistency regarding the Contras, see Appendix B.

20. Trends in public polling can be found in "Opinion Roundup," *Public Opinion* (September/October 1987): 21, 22, 24; *Gallup Poll 1985*, 70–72, 127.

21. "Remarks Announcing the Review of the National Security Council's Role in the Iran Arms and Contra Aid Controversy, November 25 1986," *PPRR 1986*, 2:1587–88.

22. Speech, "Remarks Announcing the Review of the National Security Council's Role in the Iran Arms and Contra Aid Controversy," November 25, 1987, Folder 507, Box 26, Presidential Handwriting File, Series III: Presidential Speeches 11/1/86–3/26/87, RRPLA.

23. "Remarks at a Meeting with the President's Special Review Board for the National Security Council," 1 December 1986, *PPRR 1986*, 2:1591; Report, "White House News Summary," December 2, 1986, Folder SP1114 Begin–End, WHORM: Subject File, RRPLA.

24. "Who Was Betrayed?" *Time*, 8 December 1986, 16–18.

25. "What Did They Know, and When?" *USNWR*, December 8, 1986, 16–17.

26. Ibid.

27. "Opinion Roundup," *Public Opinion* (September/October 1986): 30–31; Document, "Today's News Events, December 4, 1986," Folder PR016 Public Relations: Publicity (479001–482000), PR Public Relations PR 016 432001–486659 (1), WHORM: Subject File, RRPLA.

28. An NBC News–*Wall Street Journal* poll at the same time asked Americans, "Do you approve or disapprove of the Reagan administration's support of the rebels in Nicaragua?" The numbers returned 28% approved, 55% did not, and 17% had no opinion. "Opinion Roundup," *Public Opinion* (September/October 1987): 24.

29. "Address to the Nation on the Investigation of the Iran Arms and Contra Aid Controversy, December 2, 1986," *PPRR 1986*, 2:1594–95. As with earlier remarks, the White House closely monitored media reaction: Report, "White House News Summary, December 2, 1986," Folder SP1114 Begin–End, Box SP1111 to SP1127 485620 (2 of 3), WHORM: Subject File, RRPLA; "Under Heavy Fire," *Time*, December 15, 1986, 18–19.

30. *Gallup Poll 1986*, 255–67.

31. Radio Address, "Presidential Radio Talk, December 4, 1986," Folder 508 (11/30/86–12/6/86), Box 26, Presidential Handwriting File, RRPLA.

32. "Radio Address to the Nation on the Iran Arms and Contra Aid Controversy, December 6, 1986," *PPRR 1986*, 2:1607–8.

33. "Under Heavy Fire," *Time*, December 15, 1986, 18–21.

34. "Trying to Turn Back a Rising Tide," *USNWR*, December 15, 1986, 25.

35. Shirley Waldman to RR, December 1986; RR to Jimmy Carter, December 12, 1986, Folder CO O71 448022 (2 of 2); Patrick Buchanan, memo to Donald Regan, December 19, 1986, Folder COO62–COO74, WHORM: Subject File, RRPLA.

36. White House Talking Points, December 1986, Iran Briefing Material, December 1986, Folder CO O71 448022 (1 of 2), and Peter J. Wallison, memo to Thomas Gibson, December 8, 1986, Folder CO O71 448022 (2 of 2), WHORM: Subject File, RRPLA.

37. "What He Needs to Know," and "Is It Curtains?" *Time*, December 22, 1986, 14, 17–18, 38–40; "Now, Time to Connect the Dots," *USNWR*, December 22, 1986, 21.

38. "Statement on the Iran Arms and Contra Aid Controversy, December 16, 1986," *PPRR 1986*, 2:1631; "Not Much Wiser than Before," *Time*, December 29, 1986, 13–14.

39. "Statement on the Appointment of an Independent Counsel to Investigate the Iran Arms and Contra Aid Controversy, December 19, 1986," *PPRR 1986*, 2:1636.

40. "Opinion Roundup," *Public Opinion* (September/October 1987): 24, 30–31; *Gallup Poll 1987*, 9, 14–19; Research, West European Brief Office of Research, January 21, 1987, Folder CO O71 473288, Box COO62–COO74 (4725589) Loc: 027/09/1, WHORM: Subject File, RRPLA; "Iranscam's Grim Tidings," *Time*, January 5, 1987, 40, 45; "Mixed Blessings," *Time*, January 19, 1987, 16–17; "Reagan at Ground Zero," *USNWR*, January 12, 1987, 20, 22, 41.

41. "Sunset for a Presidency," *USNWR*, February 9, 1987, 23; "The State of Reagan," *Time*, February 9, 1987, 16.

42. "Remarks at the State of the Union Address, January 27, 1987," *PPRR 1987*, 1:56–61.

43. Editorials, January 1987, Folder PR016 Public Relations, Box PR Public Relations PR 016 432001–486659 (1), WHORM: Subject File, RRPLA.

44. TOW stands for Tube-launched, Optically tracked, Wire-guided missile. "Sunset for a Presidency," *USNWR*, February 9, 1987, 22.

45. "Opinion Roundup," *Public Opinion* (September/October 1987): 30–31; "Washington Whispers," *USNWR*, March 2, 1987, 17.

46. *The Tower Commission Report: The Full Text of the President's Special Review Board* (New York: Bantam Books, 1987), xii–xiv, xviii, 55, 61, 69, 79–80, 82.

47. "Remarks on Receiving the Final Report of the President's Special Review Board on the National Security Council, February 27, 1987," *PPRR 1987*, 1:181–82; *Gallup Poll 1987*, 41.

48. "Can He Recover?" and "Laying Out the Brutal Facts," *Time*, March 9, 1987, 20, 24, 32.

49. "Damning with Faint Praise," *USNWR*, March 9, 1987, 14.

6—Iran-Contra and Reagan's Return to Consistency

1. "Speech, Address to the Nation on the Iran Arms and Contra Aid Controversy, March 4, 1987," Folder 522, Box 26, Presidential Handwriting File Presidential Speeches, RRPLA.

2. Document, "Today's News Events, March 4, 1987," Folder PR016 Public Relations, Box PR Public Relations PR 016 432001–486659 (1), WHORM: Subject File, RRPLA.

3. Quotations in this and the following paragraphs are from "Speech, Address to the Nation on the Iran Arms and Contra Aid Controversy, March 4, 1987," Folder 522, Box 26, Presidential Handwriting File Presidential Speeches, RRPLA.

4. The speech did not provide an author's name but was located in the file of speechwriter Landon Parvin. The apologetic draft differed a great deal from known Parvin speeches on Iran-Contra. Speech Draft, NSC Draft, February 27, 1987, Folder Address to the Nation: Response to Tower Board Report, March 4, 1987 (Parvin) (No Researcher) (1 of 2), Box 29, Speechwriting, WHO Speech Drafts, RRPLA.

5. Speech Draft, Butler draft of President Reagan's Wednesday Night Speech, undated, Folder SP1120, Box 2 of 3, WHORM: Subject File, RRPLA.

6. Landon Parvin, telephone interviews, May 29, 2007, and August 16, 2010; Lou Cannon, *Ronald Reagan, the Presidential Portfolio: A History Illustrated from the Collection of the Ronald Reagan Library and Museum* (New York: Public Affairs, 2001), 230; Reagan, *My Turn*, 40.

7. Parvin interview, May 29, 2007. Reagan's diaries record that on Friday, February 27, 1987, Tower indeed stopped by "early evening" to discuss the "next week

speech about the Tower Commission Report etc." Reagan does not record that Parvin was present at the meeting. *The Reagan Diaries: Ronald Reagan*, ed. Douglas Brinkley (New York: HarperCollins, 2007), 479.

8. Cannon, *President Reagan*, 653; Ronald Reagan, *An American Life* (New York: Simon and Schuster, 1990), 540; Draft, Address to the Nation, January 1, 1987, Folder 522, Box 26, Presidential Handwriting File Presidential Speeches, RRPLA. A copy of one of the Parvin drafts is in Cannon, *Presidential Portfolio*, 232–33.

9. "Address to the Nation, January 1, 1987," and "Address to the Nation on the Iran Arms and Contra Aid Controversy, March 4, 1987," Folder 522, Box 26, Presidential Handwriting File Presidential Speeches, RRPLA.

10. "Remarks Announcing the Review of the National Security Council's Role in the Iran Arms and Contra Aid Controversy, November 25, 1986" and "Statement on the Special Review Board for the National Security Council, November 26, 1986," *PPRR 1986*, 2:1587–88.

11. "A Stunning Indictment," *Newsweek*, March 9, 1987, 25.

12. *Tower Commission Report*, 2.

13. "Remarks on Receiving the Final Report of the President's Special Review Board on the National Security Council, February 27, 1987," *PPRR 1987*, 1:181–82.

14. *Reagan Diaries*, 472, 473.

15. Ibid., 478–80. The answer was evidently no, since on March 3, Reagan announced the nomination of William H. Webster to be director of the CIA.

16. Cannon, *President Reagan*, 653.

17. David M. Abshire, memo to Donald Regan and Frank Carlucci, February 19, 1987; Speech, "Address to the Nation: Response to Tower Board Report, March 4, 1987," Folder Address to the Nation: Response to Tower Board Report, March 4, 1987 (Parvin) (No Researcher) (1 of 2), Box 29, WHO Speech Drafts, RRPLA.

18. Parvin interview, August 16, 2010.

19. Abshire, memo to Parvin, March 2, 1987, Master, March 3, 1987, Folder Address to the Nation: Response to Tower Board Report, March 4, 1987 (Parvin) (No Researcher) (1 of 2), Box 29, WHO Speech Drafts, RRPLA.

20. Cannon, *President Reagan*, 655.

21. The file contains hundreds of telegrams and approximately thirty letters that used very similar language. The telegrams are dated until March 6, the letters continue into April. No negative telegrams and letters are included in the collection. For brevity, three telegrams are cited here: Kay Bernhardt to RR, March 4, 1987; Doris and Merrill Green to RR, March 4, 1987; Sandra J. Fromm to RR, March 4, 1987, Folder SP1120, Box 2 of 3, WHORM: Subject File, RRPLA; Billy Graham to RR, March 6, 1987, ibid.; Richard Nixon to RR, March 5, 1987, ibid. See also Efrem Zimbalist, Jr., Charlton Heston, Al Davis, Ray Charles, Fess Parker, prime minister of Japan Yasu Nakasone, Congressman Jack Kemp, ibid.

22. Marlin Fitzwater, memo to RR, March 4, 1987; Johnathan S. Miller, memos to Howard H. Baker, March 5, 1987; Foreign Media Reaction, memo, March 6, 1987, ibid.; Parvin interview, August 16, 2010.

23. "Trying a Comeback," *Time*, March 16, 1987, 18; "The Hard Road Ahead on the Comeback Trail," *USNWR*, March 16, 1987, 16–17.

24. *Gallup Poll 1987*, 41.

25. "Radio Address to the Nation on Regional Conflicts, March 7, 1987," *PPRR 1987*, 1:221–22.

26. "Opinion Roundup," *Public Opinion* (September/October 1987): 24, 30–31;

"Opinion Roundup," *Public Opinion* (May/June 1988): 40; "Charging up Capitol Hill," *Time*, July 20, 1987, 15. Lt. Col. North held the nation spell-bound during his testimony. That a National Security Council aide could run such an operation puzzled and angered many Americans. Others saw a brave soldier of freedom committed to the fight against worldwide communist expansion.

27. "Remarks at a White House Briefing for Members of the National Newspaper Association, March 5, 1987," *PPRR 1987*, 1:212–15.

28. "The President's News Conference, March 19, 1987," *PPRR 1987*, 1:258–66.

29. "Well, He Survived," *Time*, March 30, 1987, 20–22.

30. "Remarks to Students at Fairview Elementary School in Columbia, Missouri, March 26, 1987," *PPRR 1987*, 1:287–88.

31. Ibid.; "A Trouper Plays America Again," *Time*, April 6, 1987, 22.

32. "Statement by Assistant to the President for Press Relations Fitzwater on the Iran Arms and Contra Aid Controversy Investigations, April 8, 1987," *PPRR 1987*, 1:353; "Remarks and a Question-and-Answer Session at a Los Angeles World Affairs Council Luncheon in California, April 10, 1987," ibid., 365–72; "Interview with White House Newspaper Correspondents, April 28, 1987," ibid., 424–29.

33. "Opinion Roundup," *Public Opinion* (September/October 1987): 30–31; *Gallup Poll 1988*, 213, 219.

34. "Informal Exchange with Reporters on the Iran Arms and Contra Aid Controversy in New York, New York, May 3, 1987," *PPRR 1987*, 1:451–52; "Remarks to the 100th Annual Convention of the American Newspaper Publishers Association in New York, New York, May 3, 1987," ibid., 452–57; "Remarks and a Question-and-Answer Session with Southeast Regional Editors and Broadcasters, May 15, 1987," ibid., 512–16.

35. "Opinion Roundup," *Public Opinion* (September/October 1987): 30–31; *Gallup Poll 1988*, 213, 219.

36. "I Am for Morality," *USNWR*, May 18, 1987, 25; "But What Laws Were Broken?" *USNWR*, June 1, 1987, 19; "Week 3: A Marine's Problems Multiply," *Time*, June 1, 1987, 24–26.

37. "The President's News Conference, June 11, 1987," *PPRR 1987*, 1:623–29; "Statement by Assistant to the President for Press Relations Fitzwater on the Meeting between President Reagan and President Oscar Arias Sanchez of Costa Rica, June 17, 1987," ibid., 669; "Remarks at a Fundraising Reception for Senator Orrin G. Hatch of Utah, June 17, 1987," ibid., 678–80; "Remarks at a White House Briefing for Right to Life Activists, July 30, 1987," and "Informal Exchange with Reporters, July 31, 1987," *PPRR 1987*, 2:895–99, 904.

38. "Shredded Policies, Arrogant Attitudes," *Time*, June 22, 1987, 21; "Charging up Capitol Hill," *Time*, July 20, 1987, 14–15. Lynch and Bogen, *The Spectacle of History*, and Thelen, *Becoming Citizens in the Age of Television*. Fried, *Muffled Echoes* (and specifically chapters 3 and 6), examines in great detail North's testimony and the subsequent impact on American culture.

39. "Opinion Roundup," *Public Opinion* (September/October 1987): 30–31; *Gallup Poll 1987*, 148–51, 213; "A Distinct Sense of Unease," *USNWR*, 13 July 1987, 22–23.

40. "Opinion Roundup," *Public Opinion* (September/October 1987): 30–31; *Gallup Poll 1987*, 172; "Opinion Roundup," *Public Opinion* (March/April 1988): 36–37.

41. "Passing the Buck," and "The Admiral Takes the Hit," *Time*, July 7, 1987, 8–13; "For Reagan, a Bit of Relief," *USNWR*, July 27, 1987, 14–17.

42. RR to Henry Salvatori, August 4, 1987, Folder CO 071 509131, WHORM: Subject File, RRPLA.

43. "How They See It in Arkansas," *Time*, August 3, 1987, 16–17.

44. *Reagan Diaries*, 524.

45. "Interview with Hugh Sidey of *Time* Magazine, August 12, 1987," *PPRR 1987*, 2:961–67.

46. Quotations in this and the following paragraphs are from "Address to the Nation on the Iran Arms and Contra Aid Controversy and Administration Goals, August 12, 1987," *PPRR 1987*, 2:942–45.

47. Speech rough draft, unnamed, August 12, Folder 572 (8/11/87 cont.–8/12/87), Box 28, Presidential Handwriting File Presidential Speeches, RRPLA.

48. Parvin interviews, May 29, 2007, and August 16, 2010.

49. "Never Give Up," *Time*, August 24, 1987, 14–15; "Trying to Put It All behind Him," *USNWR*, August 24, 1987, 20–21.

50. "Statement by Assistant to the President for Press Relations Fitzwater on the Report of the Congressional Committee Investigating the Iran Arms and Contra Aid Controversy, November 18, 1987," *PPRR 1987*, 2:1345–46.

51. "Where the Buck Finally Stops," *Time*, November 30, 1987, 19; "'Meese Messes' Galore," *USNWR*, November 30, 1987, 18.

52. "Opinion Roundup," *Public Opinion* (March/April 1988): 36–37.

53. "'I Had a Plan . . . to Deal from Strength,'" and "Iran Arms Deal Was More Serious than Watergate," *USNWR*, December 7, 1987, 30–33.

54. See "Remarks and a Question-and-Answer Session with Members of the City Club of Cleveland, Ohio, January 11, 1988," *PPRR 1988*, 1:15–24; "Remarks and a Question-and-Answer Session with the Members of the Center for the Study of the Presidency, March 25, 1988," ibid., 1:386–91; "Interview with Foreign Television Journalists, May 19, 1988," ibid., 1:610–16; "The President's News Conference in Toronto, Canada, June 21, 1988," ibid., 1:804–11; "Informal Exchange with Reporters, October 31, 1988," ibid., 2:1418–20; and "The President's News Conference, December 8, 1988," ibid., 2:1605–12.

55. For examples of Reagan's 1988 Nicaraguan citations from the Public Papers of Ronald Reagan (RRPL), see Appendix B.

56. *Gallup Poll 1988*, 22.

57. "The Contra Tangle," *Time*, March 28, 1988, 14–15.

58. "Bushwacked," *Time*, February 8, 1988, 16–20.

59. *Gallup Poll 1988*, 228.

60. "Informal Exchange with Reporters, October 31, 1988," *PPRR 1988*, 1:1418–20; "The President's News Conference, December 8, 1988," ibid., 2:1605–12.

61. *USNWR* did not cover the president's exit in detail, so *Newsweek* substituted for this portion of the chapter. "Conventional Wisdom Watch," and "You're Going to Miss Me," *Newsweek*, November 28, 1988, 18, 29; "Going Home a Winner," *Newsweek*, January 23, 1989, 14–18; "The Gipper Says Goodbye," *Time*, January 30, 1989, 29.

62. Bosch, *Reagan*, 332, 340.

7—Reagan's Death and the Enduring Power of Collective Memory

1. Cokie Roberts, American Broadcasting Company (ABC), "Special Report," aired June 9, 2004; Parvin interview, August 16, 2010; "Farewell to a President," *Ronald Reagan: An American Legend*, produced and directed by ABC News, 2004, DVD.

2. Cannon, *President Reagan*, xvii; Noonan, *When Character Was King*, 324; Michael Deaver, *Nancy: A Portrait of My Years with Nancy Reagan* (New York: HarperCollins, 2004), 174–75.

3. "Integration, a Dream Deferred: Fifty years after the Brown Decision, Americans Remain Separate and Unequal," *Raleigh (NC) News and Observer*, May 16, 2004.

4. "Some Find Little to Celebrate in Reagan's Policies, Legacy," *Chicago Tribune*, June 9, 2004; "With Power of Personality, He Made His Mark," *Boston Globe*, June 10, 2004; "South Helped Propel Initial Reagan Success: Theme Struck Chord with White Voters," *Atlanta (GA) Journal-Constitution*, June 10, 2004; Donna Britt, "Tears for Reagan Obscure His Complexities," *Washington Post,* June 13, 2004.

5. "Mississippi Officials React to Reagan's Death," The Associated Press State & Local Wire, June 6, 2004, Jackson, Mississippi. The *Commercial Appeal* only mentioned Reagan's visit and high attendance numbers. "Reagan's Visits Built Local Constituency," *Commercial Appeal*, June 6, 2004.

6. "Reagan in the Rough," *Raleigh (NC) News and Observer*, June 9, 2004; "Reagan, the South and Civil Rights," Juan Williams, NPR.org., June 10, 2004.

7. "He Brought Back Black and White," *Boston Globe*, June 11, 2004.

8. Quotes in this and the following paragraphs are from William Raspberry, "Reagan's Race Legacy," *Washington Post*, June 14, 2004.

9. Ibid., the following papers printed Raspberry's column: *Albany (NY) Times-Union* and on the same date *Charleston (WV) Gazette*.

10. "Grieve-a-thon Is Over: Reagan Presidential Legacy Doesn't Make U.S. Feel Good about Itself," *Charleston (WV) Gazette*, June 21, 2005.

11. "Believe It or Not, Things Have Been Worse," *New York Observer*, November 15, 2004.

12. "American Dreamer," *Newsweek*, June 14, 2004, 29; "'He Knew How to Lead People," *Newsweek*, June 14, 2004, 44; "Why Critics Are Still Mad as Hell," *USNWR*, June 21, 2004, 50.

13. *Ronald Reagan Remembered*, 117.

14. "Ronald Reagan Dies at 93; Fostered Cold War Might and Curbs on Government," *New York Times*, June 6, 2004, 1; "Ronald Reagan Dies; Fortieth President Reshaped American Politics," *Washington Post*, June 6, 2004.

15. "Through One Man's Strength, the World Is a Better Place," *Chicago Sun-Times*, June 6, 2004; "Ronald Reagan: Fortieth President Restored America's Faith in Itself," *Columbus (OH) Dispatch*, June 6, 2004.

16. "Ronald Reagan," *Richmond (VA) Times-Dispatch*, June 7, 2004; "Reagan Allowed America to Puff Out Its Chest Again," *Norfolk Virginian Pilot*, June 7, 2004; "Reagan Legacy a World Transformed," *Lancaster (PA) New Era*, June 7, 2004.

17. "Reagan's Defense Buildup Bridged Military Eras; Huge Budgets Brought Life back to Industry," *Washington Post*, June 9, 2004; "Reagan Leaves Big Shoes to Fill," *Boston Herald*, June 9, 2004.

18. Metro, "The Man Who Put Us Back in the Saddle," *Tampa (FL) Tribune*, June 11, 2004; "Winning the Cold War," *Washington Times*, June 11, 2004.

19. Metro, "President Bush Must Follow Reagan's Inspiring Example," *Augusta (GA) Chronicle*, June 12, 2004; "A Gifted President," *Lancaster (PA) Sunday News*, June 13, 2004.

20. "Reagan's Calming Confidence Makes a Welcomed Curtain Call," *Seattle Times*, June 10, 2004.

21. "Services to Honor Reagan on State Holiday," Associated Press Wire Story, June 11, 2004.

22. "American Dreamer," *Newsweek*, June 14, 2004, 28; "The Eyes of All People Are Upon Us," *Newsweek*, June 21, 2004, 28.

23. "How His Legacy Lives On," and "He Could See for Miles," *Time*, June 14, 2004, 51, 55, 94; "He Led a Revolution: Will It Survive?" *Economist*, June 12–18, 2004, 25.

24. Cable News Network (CNN), *Larry King Live*, aired June 5, 2004.

25. National Broadcasting Company (NBC), *Meet the Press with Tim Russert*, aired June 6, 2004.

26. CNN, *Larry King Live*, aired June 7, 2004.

27. ABC, "Special Report, 6:30 pm EST," aired June 11, 2004.

28. "We Were Soldiers," *Chicago Sun-Times*, March 1, 2002; "Do We Get to Win This Time?" *Manchester Guardian*, February 1, 2002; "We Were Soldiers," *Rolling Stone*, March 28, 2002; "Early in the Vietnam War, on an Ill-Defined Mission," *New York Times*, March 1, 2002.

29. "Ronald Reagan Dies at 93: Fostered Cold War Might and Curbs on Government," *New York Times*, June 6, 2004.

30. "Once Again, Reagan Lands the Big Television Moment," *New York Times*, June 7, 2004; "Legacy of Reagan Now Begins the Test of Time," ibid., June 11, 2004; "First Reagan, Now His Stunt Double," Arts and Leisure Desk, ibid., June 13, 2004.

31. "Former President Ronald Reagan Dies at 93," *Chicago Tribune*, June 6, 2004; "Nancy Reagan Noted for Style, Understated Influence," ibid., June 8, 2004; "Ronald Reagan Dies: Fortieth President Reshaped American Politics," "Ronald Wilson Reagan," and "Hastening an End to the Cold War," all in *Washington Post*, June 6, 2004; "Reagan Veterans Bring Back the '80s: Ex-Officials Are Embraced by Washington," *Washington Post*, June 11, 2004.

32. "Secret Arms Sale to Iran Put Presidency in Jeopardy," *Chicago Sun-Times*, June 6, 2004.

33. "The Reagan Presidency: Foreign Policy, Star Wars, 'Evil Empire' and Iran-Contra," *San Diego Union-Tribune*, June 6, 2004; "Iran-Contra Scandal Tarnished Credibility; But Americans Forgave President after He Admitted Judgment Errors," *San Francisco Chronicle*, June 6, 2004.

34. "Reagan Being Remembered by a New Generation of Republicans," *St. Paul (MN) Legal Ledger*, June 10, 2004; "With Power of Personality, He Made His Mark," *Boston Globe*, June 10, 2004.

35. "Reagan's Chance for Greatness Ended after Getting Duped on Iran-Contra," *Augusta (GA) Chronicle*, June 15, 2004; "Readers Take Sides on Reagan," *Springfield (IL) State Journal-Register*, June 17, 2004.

36. "The All-American President," *Time*, June 14, 2004, 44, 47; "American Dreamer," *Newsweek*, June 14, 2004, 29, 40.

37. "The Smashing Final Act of a Cold Warrior," "Snuffing the Evil Empire," and "A Man on a Mission," *USNWR*, commemorative edition, June 14, 2004, 58, 60, 67.

38. *Gallup Poll 1987*, 172, 213.

39. "An American Story," "The Reagan Legacy," "Why Critics Are Still Mad as Hell," and "Why He Meant So Much to Us," *USNWR*, June 21, 2004, 38, 49, 51, 80; "Journey's End," *People*, June 21, 2004, 99.

40. ABC, "Special Report," aired June 5, 2004.

41. NBC, *Dateline*, aired June 5, 2004; NBC, *Meet the Press with Tim Russert*, aired June 6, 2004.

42. CNN, *Larry King Live*, aired June 7, 2004.

43. NBC, "Special Report: Ronald Wilson Reagan, 1911–2004, 10:00 AM ET," and "Special Report: Ronald Wilson Reagan, 1911–2004, 9:00 PM ET," aired June 11, 2004.

44. "The Man Who Beat Communism," *Economist*, June 12–18, 2004, 13.

45. "The Nation Says Goodbye to Ronald Reagan," *Week*, June 18, 2004, 4.

46. "Reagan Critics Decry Glowing Tributes," *Washington Times*, June 8, 2004; "Reagan Was a Bit Player," *Madison Wisconsin State Journal*, June 11, 2004.

47. "Editorial," *Chicago Sun-Times*, June 13, 2004.

48. "Political Civility Would Be a Proper Tribute," *Saint Petersburg (FL) Times*, June 13, 2004.

49. "The Darker Side of the Legacy," *Saint Louis Post-Dispatch*, June 23, 2004; "Letters to the Editor," *Saint Louis Post-Dispatch*, June 25, 2004.

Conclusion

1. Peggy Noonan, "The Only Statue That Is Smiling, Ronald Reagan, Cast in Bronze, Arrives at the Rotunda," *Wall Street Journal*, June 5, 2009, at http://online.wsj.com/article/SB124414689022586385.html (accessed March 23, 2010).

Bibliography

Primary Sources

Ronald Reagan Presidential Library Archives, Simi Valley, California

Anthony "Tony" R. Dolan, speechwriting files
Elizabeth Dole, files
Presidential Handwriting file: Presidential speeches
Presidential speech planning schedule
Public Relations: Publicity, WHORM subject file
Ronald Reagan Personal Papers, 1980 Campaign
Speechwriting: Research Office Records
Speechwriting, White House Office (WHO) of Speech Drafts
Vietnam Veterans, WHORM Alpha File
Vietnam Veterans Memorial Fund, WHORM Alpha File

Interviews

L. Travis Clark, producer and writer, *Tour of Duty*. Phone interview, January 12, 2005.
Thad Cochran, Mississippi senator. Phone interview, November 21, 2003.
Susan Estrich, campaign manager, Michael Dukakis presidential campaign. E-mail interview, August 9, 2007.
J. Kenneth Klinge, southern field director of Ronald Reagan presidential campaign, 1980. Phone interview, November 7, 2003.
David Morrell, author of *First Blood*. Phone interview, January 25, 2005.
Landon Parvin, speechwriter for Ronald Reagan. Phone interviews, May 29, 2007, and August 16, 2010.

Published Works

Balitzer, Alfred, ed. *A Time for Choosing: The Speeches of Ronald Reagan, 1961–1982.* Chicago: Regnery Gateway, 1983.
Public Papers of the Presidents of the United States: Ronald Reagan, 1981–1989. Cited in notes as *PPRR*. 14 vols. Washington, DC: USGPO, 1982–1991.
Reagan, Ronald. *Speaking My Mind: Selected Speeches.* New York: Simon and Schuster, 1989.
Report of the Congressional Committees Investigating the "Iran-Contra Affair" with the Minority Views. Chairman, Daniel K. Inouye. New York: Random House, 1988.
The Tower Commission Report: The Full Text of the President's Special Review Board. New York: Bantam Books, 1987.

Newspapers

Albany (NY) Times-Union, June 2004
Atlanta (GA) Journal-Constitution, August 1980–June 2004
Augusta (GA) Chronicle, June 2004
Boston Globe, June 2004
Boston Herald, June 2004
Charleston (WV) Gazette, June 2004
Chicago Defender, August 1980–June 2004
Chicago Sun-Times, December 1986–March 2002
Chicago Tribune, August 1980–June 2004
Cincinnati (OH) Enquirer, January 1987
Cleveland (OH) Plain Dealer, January 1987
Columbus (OH) Dispatch, June 2004
Jackson (MS) Clarion-Ledger, November 1973–June 2004
Jackson (MS) Daily News, August 1980–June 2004
Lancaster (PA) New Era, June 2004
Lancaster (PA) Sunday News, June 2004
Los Angeles Times, August 1980–June 2004
Madison Wisconsin State Journal, June 2004
Manchester Guardian, February 2002
Memphis (TN) Commercial Appeal, August 1980–June 2004
National Journal Magazine, January 2009
Neshoba County (MS) Democrat, August 1980
New Orleans Times-Picayune, August 1980–June 2004
New York Observer, November 2004, January 2009
New York Times, August 1980–June 2004
Norfolk Virginian Pilot, June 2004
Oregonian, January 1987
Raleigh (NC) News and Observer, May 2004–June 2005
Reno Gazette-Journal, June 2008
Richmond (VA) Times-Dispatch, June 2004
Saint Louis Post-Dispatch, June 2004
Saint Paul (MN) Legal Ledger, June 2004
Saint Petersburg (FL) Times, June 2004
San Diego Union-Tribune, June 2004
San Francisco Chronicle, June 2004
Seattle Times, June 2004
Springfield (IL) State Journal-Register, June 2004
Tampa (FL) Tribune, June 2004
Tupelo Northeast Mississippi Journal, August 1980–June 2004
USA Today, April 1988–June 2004
Ventura (CA) County Star, June 2004
Wall Street Journal, June 2009
Washington Post, August 1980–June 2004
Washington Post Magazine, January 1987
Washington Times, June 2004

Periodicals

Advertising Age, August 1985
Business Week, August 1985
Comics Interview 53 (1987)
Economist, June 2004
Jet, August 1987
Life, August 1985
Ms., August 1985
The 'Nam, December 1986–April 1988
New Statesman, July 1983
Newsweek, September 1980–June 2004
People, June 2004
Public Opinion, September 1986–June 1988
Rolling Stone Magazine, December 1985–March 2002
Time, October 1966–October 2008
TV Guide, July 1983—September 1990
U.S. News and World Report, March 1982–June 2004
Vanity Fair, July–August 1998
Week, June 2004

Memoirs

Anderson, Martin. *Revolution*. San Diego: Harcourt Brace Jovanovich, 1988.
Deaver, Michael. *Behind the Scenes: In Which the Author Talks about Ronald and Nancy Reagan . . . and Himself.* New York: William Morrow, 1987.
———. *A Different Drummer: My Thirty Years with Ronald Reagan*. New York: Harper Collins, 2001.
———. *Nancy: A Portrait of My Years with Nancy Reagan*. New York: HarperCollins, 2004.
Lott, Trent. *Herding Cats: A Life in Politics*. New York: Regan Books, 2005.
Meese, Ed, III. *With Reagan: The Inside Story*. Washington, DC: Regnery Gateway, 1992.
Nofziger, Lyn. *Nofziger*. Washington, DC: Regnery Gateway, 1992.
Noonan, Peggy. *What I Saw at the Revolution: A Political Life in the Reagan Era*. New York: Random House, 1990.
———. *When Character Was King*. New York: Viking, 2001.
Reagan, Nancy. *My Turn: The Memoirs of Nancy Reagan*. New York: Random House, 1989.
Reagan, Ronald. *An American Life*. New York: Simon and Schuster, 1990.
———. *The Reagan Diaries: Ronald Reagan*. Edited by Douglas Brinkley. New York: HarperCollins, 2007.
Robinson, Peter. *How Ronald Reagan Changed My Life*. New York: Regan Books, 2003.
Speakes, Larry. *Speaking Out: The Reagan Presidency from inside the White House.* New York: Charles Scribner's Sons, 1988.
Wirthlin, Dick. *The Greatest Communicator: What Ronald Reagan Taught Me about Politics, Leadership, and Life*. Hoboken, NJ: John Wiley and Sons, 2004.

Polls

Gallup, George, Jr. *The Gallup Poll: Public Opinion, 1985–1988*. Wilmington: Scholarly Resources, 1986–1989.

Electronic Media

Television transcripts of ABC, CNN, and NBC television news programs obtained from Lexus Nexus and videotapes in possession of the author

American Broadcasting Company (ABC). "Special Report." June 5, 9, 2004.

———. "Special Report, 6:30 pm EST." June 11, 2004.

The A-Team. Stephen J. Cannell Productions. NBC Television, 1983–1987.

Cable News Network (CNN). "Larry King Live." June 5, 7, 2004.

China Beach. Warner Brothers Television, ABC Television, 1988–1991.

National Broadcasting Company (NBC). "Meet the Press with Tim Russert." June 6, 2004.

———. "Special Report: Ronald Wilson Reagan 1911–2004, 10:00 AM ET," and "9:00 PM ET." June 11, 2004.

Ronald Reagan: An American Legend. ABC News, 2004, DVD.

Tour of Duty. New World Television. CBS Television, 1987–1990.

Film

First Blood. Artisan DVD, 2002.

Platoon. Directed by Oliver Stone. Orion Pictures, 1986.

Rambo: First Blood Part II. Directed by George P. Cosmatos. TriStar Pictures, 1985.

Rambo: First Blood Part II: Special Edition. Lion's Gate Studios DVD, 2003.

Rambo III: Special Edition. Lion's Gate Studios DVD, 2003.

Secondary Sources

Books

Abramson, Paul, John Aldrich, and David Rohde. *Change and Continuity in the 1980 Elections.* Washington, DC: Congressional Quarterly Press, 1982.

Adams, William C. *Television Coverage of the 1980 Presidential Campaign.* Norwood, NJ: Ablex, 1983.

Anderegg, Michael, ed. *Inventing Vietnam: The War in Film and Television.* Philadelphia: Temple University Press, 1991.

Ashmore, Harry S. *Civil Rights and Wrongs: A Memoir of Race and Politics, 1944–1994.* New York: Pantheon Books, 1994.

Belfrage, Sally. *Freedom Summer.* New York: Viking Press, 1965.

Black, Christine M., and Thomas Oliphant. *All by Myself: The Unmaking of a Presidential Campaign.* Chester, CT: Globe Pequot Press, 1989.

Blakey, Scott. *Prisoner at War: The Survival of Commander Richard A. Stratton.* Garden City, NY: Anchor Press/Doubleday, 1978.

Blumenthal, Sidney. *Our Long National Daydream: A Political Pageant of the Reagan Era.* New York: Harper and Row, 1988.

———. *Pledging Allegiance: The Last Campaign of the Cold War.* New York: HarperCollins, 1990.

Bosch, Adriana. *Reagan: An American Story.* New York: WGBH Educational, 2000.

Brinkley, Douglas. *The Boys of Pointe du Hoc: Ronald Reagan, D-Day, and the U.S. Army 2nd Ranger Battalion.* New York: William Morrow, 2005.

Brooks, Tim, and Earle Marsh. *The Complete Directory to Prime Time Network TV Shows, 1946–Present.* 9th ed. New York: Ballantine, 2007.

Busby, Robert. *Reagan and the Iran-Contra Affair: The Politics of Presidential Recovery.* New York: St. Martin's Press, 1999.

Busch, Andrew E. *Reagan's Victory: The Presidential Election of 1980 and the Rise of the Right.* Lawrence: University Press of Kansas, 2005.

Cagin, Seth, and Philip Dray. *We Are Not Afraid.* New York: Macmillan, 1988.

Cannon, Lou. *Reagan.* New York: G. P. Putnam's Sons, 1982.

———. *President Reagan: The Role of a Lifetime.* New York: Simon and Schuster, 1991; Public Affairs, 2001.

———. *Ronald Reagan, the Presidential Portfolio: A History Illustrated from the Collection of the Ronald Reagan Library and Museum.* New York: Public Affairs, 2001.

———. *Governor Reagan: His Rise to Power.* New York: Public Affairs, 2003.

Connerton, Paul. *How Societies Remember.* Cambridge: Cambridge University Press, 1989.

Coser, Lewis A. *Maurice Halbwachs: On Collective Memory.* Chicago: University of Chicago Press, 1992.

Craycroft, Robert. *The Neshoba County Fair: Place and Paradox in Mississippi.* Jackson: Mississippi State University Press, 1989.

Crespino, Joseph. *In Search of Another Country: Mississippi and the Conservative Counterrevolution.* Princeton, NJ: Princeton University Press, 2007.

Dallek, Robert. *Ronald Reagan: The Politics of Symbolism.* Cambridge: Harvard University Press, 1984.

Daniels, Les. *Marvel: Five Fabulous Decades of the World's Greatest Comics.* Japan: Harry N. Abrams, 1991.

Dean, Eric T., Jr. *Shook over Hell: Post-Traumatic Stress, Vietnam, and the Civil War.* Cambridge: Harvard University Press, 1997.

Denton, Robert E., Jr. *The Primetime Presidency of Ronald Reagan.* New York: Praeger, 1988.

Dittmar, Linda, and Gene Michaud, eds. *From Hanoi to Hollywood: The Vietnam War in American Film.* New Brunswick: Rutgers University Press, 1990.

Drew, Elizabeth. *Portrait of an Election: The 1980 Presidential Campaign.* New York: Simon and Schuster, 1981.

D'Souza, Dinesh. *Ronald Reagan: How an Ordinary Man Became an Extraordinary Leader.* New York: Touchstone, 1997.

Ducat, Stephen. *Taken In: American Gullibility and the Reagan Mythos.* Tacoma: Life Sciences Press, 1988.

Edel, Wilbur. *The Reagan Presidency: An Actor's Greatest Performance.* New York: Hippocrene Books, 1992.

Erickson, Paul D. *Reagan Speaks: The Making of an American Myth.* New York: Praeger, 1985.

Fergerson, Thomas, and Joel Rogers. *The Hidden Election: Politics and Economics in the 1980 Presidential Campaign.* New York: Pantheon Books, 1981.

Gallagher, Gary W. *Cause Won, Lost, and Forgotten: How Hollywood and Popular Art Shape What We Know about the American Civil War.* Chapel Hill: University of North Carolina Press, 2008.

Germond, Jack W., and Jules Witcover. *Blue Smoke and Mirrors: How Reagan Won and Why Carter Lost the Election of 1980.* New York: Viking Press, 1981.

Gillis, John R. *Commemorations: The Politics of National Identity.* Princeton, NJ: Princeton University Press, 1994.

Goldwater, Barry. *The Conscience of a Conservative.* New York: MacFadden Books, 1963.

Greenfield, Jeff. *The Real Campaign: How the Media Missed the Story of the 1980 Campaign*. New York: Summit Books, 1982.

Hayward, Stephen F. *The Age of Reagan, 1964–1980: The Fall of the Old Liberal Order*. Roseville, CA: Prima Publishing, 2001.

———. *The Age of Reagan: The Conservative Counterrevolution, 1980–1989*. New York: Crown Forum, 2009.

Hobsbawm, Eric, and Terence Ranger. *The Invention of Tradition*. Cambridge: Cambridge University Press, 1983.

Jackman, Ian, ed. *Ronald Reagan Remembered*. New York: Simon and Schuster, 2004.

Jeffords, Susan. *Hard Bodies: Hollywood Masculinity in the Reagan Era*. New Brunswick: Rutgers University Press, 1993.

Johnson, Haynes. *Sleepwalking through History: America in the Reagan Years*. New York: W. W. Norton, 1991.

Jordan, Hamilton. *Crisis: The Last Year of the Carter Presidency*. New York: G. P. Putnam's Sons, 1982.

Kagan, Norman. *The Cinema of Oliver Stone*. New York: Continuum, 2000.

Kalter, Suzy. *The Complete Book of M*A*S*H*. New York: Abradale Press, 1984.

Kammen, Michael. *Mystic Chords of Memory: The Transformation of Tradition in American Culture*. New York: Knopf, 1991.

Kelly, William E. *Post-Traumatic Stress Disorder and the War Veteran Patient*. New York: Brunner-Mazell, 1985.

Kiewe, Amos, and David W. Houck. *A Shining City on a Hill: Ronald Reagan's Economic Rhetoric, 1951–1989*. New York: Praeger, 1991.

Laham, Nicholas. *The Reagan Presidency and the Politics of Race: In Pursuit of Colorblind Justice and Limited Government*. Westport, CT: Praeger, 1998.

Lembcke, Jerry. *The Spitting Image: Myth, Memory, and the Legacy of Vietnam*. New York: New York University Press, 1998.

Louvre, Alf, and Jeffrey Walsh. *Tell Me Lies about Vietnam: Cultural Battles for the Meaning of the War*. Philadelphia: Open University Press, 1988.

Lowenthal, David. *The Past Is a Foreign Country*. Cambridge: Cambridge University Press, 1985.

Mars, Florence. *Witness in Philadelphia*. Baton Rouge: Louisiana State University Press, 1977.

Mayer, Jeremy D. *Running on Race: Racial Politics in Presidential Campaigns, 1960–2000*. New York: Random House, 2002.

McAllister, Matthew P., Edward H. Sewell, Jr., and Ian Gordon, eds. *Comics and Ideology*. New York: Peter Lang, 2001.

Medhurst, Martin J., ed. *Beyond the Rhetorical Presidency*. College Station: Texas A&M University Press, 1996.

Moore, Jonathan, ed. *The Campaign for President: 1980 in Retrospect*. Cambridge: Ballinger, 1981.

Moreland, Lawrence W., Robert P. Steed, and Tod A. Baker. *The 1988 Presidential Election in the South: Continuity amidst Change in Southern Party Politics*. New York: Praeger, 1991.

Morrell, David. *Rambo: First Blood Part II*. New York: A Jove Book, 1985.

———. *Lessons from a Lifetime of Writing: A Novelist Looks at His Craft*. Cincinnati: Writer's Digest Books, 2002.

Myers, Samuel L. *Civil Rights and Race Relations in the Post Reagan-Bush Era*. Westport, CT: Praeger, 1997.

Nash, Jere, and Andy Taggart. *Mississippi Politics: The Struggle for Power, 1976–2006.* Jackson: University Press of Mississippi, 2006.

O'Reilly, Kenneth. *Nixon's Piano: Presidents and Racial Politics from Washington to Clinton.* New York: Free Press, 1995.

Perry, Roland. *Hidden Power: The Programming of the President.* New York: Beaufort Books, 1984.

Pomper, Marlene Michels. *The Election of 1980: Reports and Interpretations.* Chatham, NJ: Chatham House, 1981.

Reagan, Ronald. *The Creative Society: Some Comments on Problems Facing America.* New York: Devin-Adair, 1968.

Rogin, Michael. *Ronald Reagan: The Movie.* Berkeley and Los Angeles: University of California Press, 1987.

Rowan, Carl T. *Breaking Barriers: A Memoir.* Boston: Little Brown, 1991.

Runkel, David R. *"Campaign for President": The Managers Look at '88.* New York: Auburn House, 1989.

Santoli, Al. *Everything We Had: An Oral History of the Vietnam War as Told by 33 American Men Who Fought It.* New York: Random House, 1981.

———. *To Bear Any Burden: The Vietnam War and Its Aftermath in the Words of Americans and Southeast Asians.* New York: Dutton, 1985.

Schaller, Michael. *Reckoning with Reagan: America and Its President in the 1980s.* New York: Oxford University Press, 1992.

Schieffer, Bob, and Gary Paul Gates. *The Acting President.* New York: Dutton, 1989.

Schweizer, Peter. *Reagan's War: The Epic Story of His Forty-Year Struggle and Final Triumph over Communism.* New York: Doubleday, 2002.

Shirley, Craig. *Rendezvous with Destiny: Ronald Reagan and the Campaign that Changed America.* Wilmington, DE: Intercollegiate Studies Institute, 2009.

Shull, Steven A. *A Kinder, Gentler Racism? The Reagan-Bush Civil Rights Legacy.* Armonk, NY: M. E. Sharpe, 1993.

Silet, Charles L. P. *Oliver Stone: Interviews.* Jackson: University Press of Mississippi, 2001.

Skinner, Kiron K., Annelise Anderson, and Martin Anderson, ed. *Reagan in His Own Hand: The Writings of Ronald Reagan that Reveal His Revolutionary Vision for America.* New York: Free Press, 2001.

———. *Reagan: A Life in Letters.* New York: Free Press, 2003.

———. *Reagan's Path to Victory: The Shaping of Ronald Reagan's Vision—Selected Writings.* New York: Free Press, 2004.

Smith, Paul A. *Electing a President: Information and Control.* New York: Praeger, 1982.

Staffer, Stephen D. "Mississippi: Electoral Conflict in a Nationalized State." In Moreland, Steed, and Baker, *1988 Presidential Election.*

Strober, Deborah Hart, and Gerald Strober, eds. *Reagan: The Man and His Presidency.* Boston: Houghton Mifflin, 1998.

Stuckey, Mary. *Getting into the Game: The Pre-presidential Rhetoric of Ronald Reagan.* New York: Praeger, 1989.

———. *Playing the Game: The Presidential Rhetoric of Ronald Reagan.* New York: Praeger, 1990.

———. *Slipping the Surly Bonds: Reagan's Challenger Address.* College Station: Texas A&M Press, 2006.

Thelen, David. *Becoming Citizens in the Age of Television: How Americans Challenged the Media and Seized Political Initiative during the Iran-Contra Debate.* Chicago: University of Chicago Press, 1996.

Toplin, Robert, ed. *Oliver Stone's USA: Film, History, Controversy.* Lawrence: University Press of Kansas, 2000.

Uhl, Michael, and Tod Ensign. *G.I. Guinea Pigs: How the Pentagon Exposed Our Troops to Dangers More Deadly than War: Agent Orange and Atomic Radiation.* New York: Playboy Press, 1980.

Wallison, Peter J. *Ronald Reagan: The Power of Conviction and the Success of His Presidency.* Boulder, CO: Westview Press, 2003.

Walton, Hanes, Jr. *Black Politics and Black Political Behavior: A Linkage Analysis.* Westport, CT: Praeger, 1994.

Weiler, Michael, and W. Barnett Pearce, ed. *Reagan and Public Discourse in America.* Tuscaloosa: University Alabama Press, 1992.

Whitburn, Joel. *The Billboard Book of Top 40 Hits.* 8th ed. New York: Billboard Books, 2004.

Wilcox, Fred. *Waiting for an Army to Die: The Tragedy of Agent Orange.* New York: Vintage Books, 1983.

Wilentz, Sean. *The Age of Reagan: A History, 1974–2008.* New York: HarperCollins, 2008.

Wright, Bradford W. *Comic Book Nation: The Transformation of Youth Culture in America.* Baltimore: Johns Hopkins University Press, 2001.

Wroe, Ann. *Lives, Lies, and the Iran-Contra Affair.* London: I. B. Tauris, 1991.

Articles

August, Lynn R., and Barbara A. Gianola. "Symptoms of War Trauma Induced Psychiatric Disorders: Southeast Asian Refugees and Vietnam Veterans." *International Migration Review* 21, no. 3 (Autumn 1987): 820–32. Special issue on migration and health.

Ballard-Reisch, Deborah. "*China Beach* and *Tour of Duty*: American Television and Revisionist History of the Vietnam War." *Journal of Popular Culture* (Winter 1991), 135–49.

Doherty, Thomas. "First Blood Part II." *Film Quarterly* (Fall 1986).

Freund, Eugene H., and Earl G. Stormo. "A Resocialization Strategy for Black Vietnam Veterans." *Journal of Negro Education* 48, no. 4 (Autumn 1979): 500–512.

Frisch, Michael. "American History and the Structures of Collective Memory." *Journal of American History* 75, no. 4 (March 1989): 1130–55.

Huxley. David. "Naked Aggression: American Comic Books and the Vietnam War." In Louvre and Walsh, *Tell Me Lies*, 88–110.

Johnson, Loch. "Political Alienation among Vietnam Veterans." *Western Political Quarterly* 29, no. 3 (September 1976): 398–409.

Laufer, Robert S., and M. S. Gallops. "Life-Course Effects of Vietnam Combat and Abusive Violence: Marital Patterns." *Journal of Marriage and the Family* 47, no. 4 (November 1985): 839–53.

Laufer, Robert S., M. S. Gallops, and Ellen Frey-Wouters. "War Stress and Trauma: The Vietnam Veteran Experience." *Journal of Health and Social Behavior* 25, no. 1 (March 1984): 65–85.

"Marvel Sees a Winner in 'Nam Comics." *Los Angeles Times*, May 12, 1987.

Matton, Annette. "From Realism to Superheroes in Marvel's The 'Nam." In McAllister, Sewell, and Gordon, *Comics and Ideology.* 151–66.

Nora, Pierre. "Between Memory and History: Les Lieux de Mémoire." *Representations* 26 (Spring 1989): 3–24.

Ritter, Kurt. "Ronald Reagan's 1960s Southern Rhetoric: Courting Conservatives for the GOP." *Southern Communication Journal* 64 (Summer 1999), 333–45.

Rowe, John Carlos. "From Documentary to Docudrama: Vietnam on Television in the 1980s." *Genre* 21 (Winter 1988), 451–77.

Shehan, Constance L. "Spouse Support and Vietnam Veterans' Adjustment to Post-Traumatic Stress Disorder." *Family Relations* 36, no. 1 (January 1987): 55–60.

Studlar, Gaylyn, and David Desser. "Never Having to Say You're Sorry: *Rambo's* Rewriting of the Vietnam War." *Film Quarterly* (Fall 1988), 9–16.

Thelen, David. "Introduction: Memory and American History." *Journal of American History* 75, no. 4 (March 1989): 1117–29.

Vande Berg, Leah R. "*China Beach,* Prime Time War in the Postfeminist Age: An Example of Patriarchy in a Different Voice." *Western Journal of Communication* 57 (Summer 1993), 349–66.

"Vietnam: The Comic Book War." *Washington Post,* September 10, 1986.

Websites

Answers.com at http://www.answers.com/topic/u-s-news-world-report (accessed March 11, 2010).

Boston.com at http://www.boston.com/ae/media/articles/2010/03/09/the_romney_reagan_remix/ (accessed March 10, 2010).

Dave Leip's Atlas of U.S. Presidential Elections at http://uselectionatlas.org/RESULTS/ (accessed June 29, 2010).

Internet Movie Database at www.imdb.com

Mother Jones at http://motherjones.com/politics/2009/01/why-obama-should-channel-gipper (accessed January 8, 2009).

National Journal Magazine at www.nationaljournal.com/njmagazine/nj_20090131_4685.php (accessed January 30, 2009).

National Public Radio at NPR.org

Neshoba County Fair www.neshobacountyfair.org.

New Republic at www.tnr.com/article/politics/how-stop-the-bleeding (accessed March 22, 2010).

New York Observer at http://www.observer.com/2009/politics/barack-obama-and-path-reagan (accessed January 13, 2009).

Reagan 2020 at http://reagan2020.us/speeches/RNC_Convention.asp (accessed February 24, 2010).

Real Clear Politics at http://www.realclearpolitics.com/articles/2009/01/obamas_choice_fdr_or_reagan.html (accessed January 9, 2009).

Real Clear Politics at www.realclearpolitics.com/articles/2009/03/on_big_gov_public_more_with_re.html (accessed March 5, 2009).

Rogerebert.com at http://rogerebert.suntimes.com/apps/pbcs.dll/article?AID=/19820101/REVIEWS/201010324/1023 (accessed June 29, 2010).

Index